Unique
Value®

Unique Value®

THE SECRET OF ALL GREAT
BUSINESS STRATEGIES

ANDREA DUNHAM *and* BARRY MARCUS

with

MARK STEVENS and PATRICK BARWISE

———— ● ————

MACMILLAN PUBLISHING COMPANY
New York
Maxwell Macmillan Canada
Toronto
Maxwell Macmillan International
New York   Oxford   Singapore   Sydney

Macmillan Publishing Company
866 Third Avenue
New York, NY 10022

Maxwell Macmillan Canada,
Inc.
1200 Eglinton Avenue East
Suite 200
Don Mills, Ontario M3C 3N1

Macmillan Publishing Company is part of the Maxwell Communication Group of Companies.

Unique Value® and Unique Value = ROI® are registered trademarks of Dunham and Marcus International, Inc.

Library of Congress Cataloging-in-Publication Data

Unique value: the secret of all great business strategies/Andrea Dunham . . . [et al.].
    p.   cm.
    Includes bibliographical references and index.
    ISBN 0-02-614491-3
    1. Strategic planning. 2. Strategic planning—United States—Case studies.   3. Success in business—United States—Case studies.
I. Dunham, Andrea.
HD30.28.U54 1993   92-33543 CIP
658.4'012—dc20

Macmillan books are available at special discounts for bulk purchases for sales promotions, premiums, fund-raising, or educational use. For details, contact:

Special Sales Director
Macmillan Publishing Company
866 Third Avenue
New York, NY 10022

Designed by Michael Mendelsohn

10 9 8 7 6 5 4 3 2 1

Printed in the United States of America

The Five Fundamentals of a Unique Value Strategy

1. *Competitive Framework:* How you define and size your market. Definition of direct and indirect competitors. Who or what your product or service must displace.

2. *Market Target:* How you define the primary purchaser, or customer segment, for your product or service in terms of relevant demographics, purchase or consumption behavior, needs, attitudes and priorities.

3. *Basis for Perceived Competitive Superiority:* How your key customers define your product or service's superior value within a precisely defined competitive framework.

4. *Product Portfolio:* How your product line or service is configured to interrelate with Fundamentals 1, 2, 3 and 5.

5. *Key Profit Drivers:* What factors most affect the profitability of your product or service line.

The Four Building Blocks of
a Unique Value Strategy

1. What do you know about your customers—their needs, their priorities, their businesses? What are the key issues from their point of view? From your point of view? What understanding do you need to sustain success over the near term? Over the long term?

2. What do you know about your operational and organizational strengths—what do you have to build on? What are your operation's strengths and key skills from your customers' point of view?

3. What do you know about your products and technologies and their role in satisfying customers or developing a superior product or service? What are the strengths and weaknesses of your product or service line and technologies from your customers' point of view?

4. What do you know about your competitors' strengths and strategies? How are they evolving? How do your key customers perceive you and your products compared with your competitors and their products or services?

Contents

Acknowledgments

In the course of our professional careers, the authors have had the opportunity to meet and share ideas with some of the most talented and prominent business executives across an array of industries in Europe, Japan, North America and the United Kingdom. Many have allowed us to conduct extended personal interviews with them and their senior staffs. We would like to thank them for sharing their knowledge and experience with us. Our special thanks go to:

American Express Company	George Waters	Former Senior Advisor
	Roger Edgar	Senior VP of Information Systems, IDS Company
	Frank L. Skillern, Jr.	Executive VP, Optima Card and Consumer Lending; Former President, Acuma Ltd.
	Harvey Golub	President and CEO, American Express Company; Chairman and CEO, TRS Company
American Red Cross	Frederick W. Kyle	Senior VP of Biomedical Services, Former President of Commercial Operations, SmithKline Beecham Pharmaceuticals

AT&T Company	Robert E. Allen	Chairman and CEO
	John A. Hinds	Former President, AT&T International, Inc.
Avon Products, Inc.	Hicks Waldron	Former Chairman and CEO
Baker and McKenzie	Robert Cox	Chairman of Policy Committee, Former Chairman of Executive Committee
Bass PLC	Ian Prosser	Chairman and CEO
	Bryan D. Langton	Chairman and CEO, Holiday Inn Worldwide
Bristol-Myers Squibb Company	Stephen I. Sadove	President, Clairol, Inc.
British Airways	Sir Colin Marshall	Deputy Chairman and Chief Executive
BT PLC	Iain Vallance	Chairman and CEO
Campbell Soup Company	Frank E. Weise, III	CFO; Former CFO, P&G Food and Beverage
Channel Intl. Corp.	David A. Everett	Senior VP, Worldwide Sales, Wyse Technology, Inc.
Citicorp	Pei Chia	Senior EVP
	Walter Wriston	Former Chairman and CEO
	Pamela P. Flaherty	Vice President
	Steve H. Price	Vice President
Colgate-Palmolive Company	Lois D. Juliber	Chief Technological Officer
Collins & Aikman Group, Inc.	Robert Seelert	President and CEO, Kayser-Roth Hosiery, Inc.; Former President and CEO, Worldwide Coffee Intl., General Foods Corp.

Deutsche Bank GmbH	John A. Craven	Chairman, Morgan Grenfell Group plc
	Dr. Hans-Peter Ferslev	EVP, Strategic Planning
	Detlev Staecker	EVP and General Manager, Deutsche Bank North America Holding Corp.
E.I. Du Pont De Nemours and Company	Lee Tashjian	Vice President, External Affairs
Federal Express Corporation	Frederick W. Smith	Chairman, President and CEO
Fiat S.P.A.	Vittorio Vellano	President and CEO, Fiat USA
General Electric Company	Paul W. Van Orden	Former EVP, Strategic Planning
GTE Corporation	Joseph Citarella	Former Director of New Ventures
	John L. Segall	Vice Chairman, Corporate Planning and Development
Guinness PLC	R.T.S. Breene	Worldwide Marketing Director, United Distillers
Helene Curtis Industries, Inc.	Ronald J. Gidwitz	President and CEO
IBM Corporation	Richard Gerstner	Former VP, Special Assignments
	Dr. Lewis Branscomb	Former Chief Scientist
	Frank A. Metz, Jr.	Former Senior VP, Corporate Finance and Planning
J. Sainsbury PLC	David Sainsbury	Chairman and CFO
	David B. Jenkins	Chairman and CEO, Shaw's Supermarkets, Inc.

Joseph E. Seagram & Sons, Inc.	Edgar Bronfman, Jr.	President and COO
	C. Richard Coffey	Former President, Seagram Beverage Company
	Henry Hawley	VP and Director, Marketing, Seagram Beverage Company
	Mark Taxel	Executive VP, Marketing, Seagram Beverage Company
	John R. Preston	Treasurer
Konica Corporation	Sho Kamiiisaka	Chairman
LTU Group and Westdeutsche Landesbank	Christopher Rodrigues	CEO, The Thomas Cook Group, Ltd.
MacAndrews and Forbes	Jerry W. Levin	President and CEO, Revlon, Inc.
McGraw-Hill, Inc.	Joseph L. Dionne	Chairman, President and CEO
	Elisabeth K. Allison	Senior VP, Planning and Development
MCI Communications Corporation	H. Brian Thompson	Former Senior VP
	Jerry Taylor	Former President, MCI Airsignal
	Robert Harcharik	Former President, MCI Mail
Microsoft Corporation	William Gates	Chairman and CEO
Mitsubishi Motors Corporation	Richard D. Recchia	Executive VP and COO, Mitsubishi USA
Mitsui & Company, Ltd.	Naoyuki Kondo	Executive Managing Director
Motorola, Inc.	George Fisher	Chairman and CEO
Nintendo Company, Ltd.	Peter Main	Senior VP, Marketing, Nintendo of America
NYNEX Corporation	Frederic V. Salerno	Vice Chairman and President, Worldwide Services

Omnicom Group Inc.	Bruce Crawford	President and CEO
Paramount Communications Inc.	Martin S. Davis	Chairman and CEO
PepsiCo Inc.	Christopher Sinclair	President and COO, Pepsi-Cola International, Ltd.
	John G. Swanhaus	President, PepsiCo Wines & Spirits International
	Steve Reinemund	Chairman and CEO, Frito-Lay, Inc.
	Roger A. Enrico	Chairman and CEO, PepsiCo Worldwide Foods; Former Chairman and CEO, Frito-Lay, Inc.
Perdue Farms Inc.	Franklin P. Perdue	Chairman
Playboy Enterprises, Inc.	Christie Hefner	Chairman and CEO
RJR Nabisco Holdings, Inc.	Louis V. Gerstner Jr.	Chairman, President and CEO, Former CEO, American Express TRS
Robert Bosch GmbH	Marcus Bierich	Chairman
Sara Lee Corp.	John H. Bryan	Chairman and CEO
	Paul Fulton	President
	Gary M. Susnjara	VP, Marketing
SmithKline Beecham	Robert P. Bauman	CEO
Société Nationale Elf Aquitaine	Frederic Isoard	Executive President, Hydrocarbons, Elf Aquitaine, Inc., France
	Michel Schneider-Maunoury	Chairman, President and CEO, Elf Aquitaine, Inc.
	Dave Hurwitt	Former EVP, Sanofi Beauté (a division of Elf Sanofi)
Sony Corporation	Ken Iwaki	Deputy President

The Stanley Works	Donald W. Davis	Former Chairman
The Stride-Rite Corporation	Ervin Shames	CEO and President; Former President, Kraft USA
The Mead Corporation	Steven C. Mason	Vice-Chairman
	Burnell R. Roberts	Former Chairman and CEO
The Chase Manhattan Corp.	Jerry Weiss	Former Senior VP- Strategic Planning
Time Warner, Inc.	Robert W. Pittman	President and CEO, Time Warner Enterprises
Unilever PLC	Michael Perry	Chairman
	Sir Michael Angus	Former Chairman
	Robert Phillips	President and CEO, Elizabeth Arden Co.; Former CEO, Chese- brough-Ponds USA Inc.
Xerox Corporation	Yotaro Kobayashi	Chairman and CEO, Fuji-Xerox Co., Ltd. (Far East Affiliate)
	John Seely Brown	VP and Chief Scientist

Dunham & Marcus International would like to extend a special thank you to the many mentors, friends and clients who have shared their visions, frustrations, struggles and strategies with us along the way. Our thanks go particularly to Edgar Bronfman, Jr., and the Seagram Beverage Company management team for the privilege of being part of their initial success, and for their willingness to talk about how it happened in enough detail that others could learn from it; to the late Don Estridge, who was a maverick, a loyal IBMer, and an inspiration; and to the late Bill Bernbach, who revolutionized advertising creativity when he founded his agency, Doyle Dane Bernbach, and who gave us our early training in business philosophy, which was to get to the truth, and then make it motivating. Our thanks also go to John Naish, of the Hill

Samuel Bank in Tokyo, who worked with us on some of the Japanese interviews, to Eliza Collins, formerly a senior editor at the *Harvard Business Review* for her early encouragement, and to the Dunham & Marcus International research and project teams who have contributed their enthusiasm and professionalism, and without whom this project could not have been completed.

Andrea Dunham
Barry Marcus
New York

Preface

The study that led to this book started ten years ago, as a research project with the working title, "Creativity and Corporate Planning." As corporations and industries in transition struggled toward strategies that would accommodate all the new complexities generated by more sophisticated customers, consumers, technologies and competitors, the tension between the controls of central planning and the needs of line managers was becoming unbearable. Since the same symptoms were visible across an array of industries and markets as diverse as supercomputing and consumer package goods, we believed that our research results would be highly relevant to a wide audience.

In 1982, we were drawn into the preoccupations of IBM's new PC unit in Boca Raton, and the focus of our study evolved. It was not just a matter of central planners versus line managers, or the opportunities of the future versus the ways of the past—the problem appeared to be the absence of any framework for dialogue between planners and line managers. There could be no understanding between the parties when the questions being asked and answered had no shared frame of reference, and when the assumptions underlying the central planners' view of the world were regarded as so fundamental they would never be questioned.

The questions being asked by the IBM PC management team in Boca Raton, headed by Don Estridge, were very real. They were an attempt, by one single unit of IBM, to understand its role in the world of the future and the significance of its success. One of the questions asked was, "Is the new personal computer just a fad?" The internal discussions evolved into a 1983 address to the Harvard Business School Club of New York, titled "Computers and the home of the future."

Under Don Estridge, the Boca Raton unit was grappling with the difference between IBM's service- and sales-driven view of marketing and classic marketing skills as practiced by Procter & Gamble. In 1983 he was even considering a joint promotion with Procter & Gamble's Tide Laundry Detergent as a way of distributing coupons for IBM PCs, in an efort to acquire these new skills.

The difficulties involved in developing the required new skills, in the context of a lifetime of IBM training and protocol, led to the PC Jr. setback and a severely embarrassed corporate management.

IBM's history over the last ten years has been a slow and painful awakening to the marketplace realities that Don Estridge was dealing with ten years ago. Indeed, in the last ten years, there have been many painful lessons for corporate America.

Japanese corporations, until recently, have appeared to be riding an endless wave of success. But they, too, were making some conspicuous and costly errors.

Mistakes are part of learning, but do they have to be so expensive? Over the past ten years, we have revisited this question again and again in formal and informal interviews with business managers at every level of corporate life in America, Europe and Japan.

This book lays out the reasons for costly mistakes and the reasons for great successes, because they are two sides of the same coin. Ultimately, success is the reward for asking the right questions. Failure is the result of thinking you have all the answers.

But even the greatest successes cannot be sustained without constant vigilance and strategic learning. A precondition for strategic learning is knowing what questions to ask.

That is what this book is about. It is, therefore, about strategies that can be implemented, because they are firmly rooted in the fundamentals of good business; what great strategies have in common; and why they lead to the greatest success.

See Appendix A: Excerpts from "Computers and the Home of the Future" (address by Andrea Dunham, managing director, Dunham & Marcus International, Inc., delivered to the Harvard Business School Club of New York, November 12, 1983) for further information.

Introduction

Do the world's greatest businesses have something in common that sets them apart from lesser companies? If they do, do they fully understand it? If they fully understand it, are they more likely to be able to sustain their success, and avert the decline that seems to befall all great institutions in time? These are classic questions, but they are particularly relevant to a time of economic upheaval when the old ways no longer work and many of the new ways are still at the experimental stage.

Historically, what great businesses seem to have had in common was a set of fundamentals that came together at a moment in time in response to a market opportunity. The ability to exploit it, when a set of technologies and a competitive edge were all in alignment, was often guided by a visionary manager—Tom Watson of IBM, Alfred Sloan of GM, the Toyoda family of Toyota, Masura Ibuka and Akio Morita of Sony, Alfred Nixdorf of Nixdorf Computers, George Waters of American Express.

But what happened when the second and third generations took over? What happened when the founding vision was no longer in tune with the times?

If the original strategy was not clearly articulated in all its critical elements, if the components of its unique power in the marketplace were not explicitly understood, if the next generation was not equipped to build on it, then the decline of the institution followed.

But is this scenario inevitable?

Not if the concept of a Unique Value strategy is understood.

This concept is, at one level, a matter of common sense. A Unique Value strategy expresses a business' unique combination of capabilities in a way that fully integrates all functions and operations, to bring the maximum value to the marketplace.

But in a technologically complex world, managing or creating a Unique Value strategy requires sophistication as well as common sense.

Properly articulated, a Unique Value strategy makes the fundamentals explicit in such a way that they can be fully understood by every level and function in an organization. In time the entire organization develops a strategic sensibility and thus becomes both focused and flexible.

A Unique Value strategy leverages the special combination of assets, skills and strengths that reside in every enterprise in a way that is fully integrated to produce superior performance over the near and long term. It is thus the winning formula that builds the wealth of outstanding business enterprises. It is because such a strategy integrates all the internal and external drivers of success that it is so productive. It generates a superior return on investment which is sustainable and insulated from competitive attack.

Is a Unique Value strategy fortuitous, or can it be created? If it can be created, what is the right way?

The path to get there is one that the new business unit of a large established corporation took in the recent past. It created a significant new business that leveraged the tangible and intangible assets of the corporation to become the market leader in a fiercely competitive new category. It accomplished this feat in less than two years by building a strategy that was a unique fit between its capabilities and the requirements of the market, the competitive environment and its corporate parent.

In 1985, Joseph E. Seagram & Sons was a North American whiskey company trapped in a very profitable but narrow and declining core business. But its goal was to become transformed into a global company, positioned for long-term growth. It saw the creation of a new business as a first step to get there.

Following the creation of its nearly $500 million U.S. wine cooler business between 1986 and 1988, Joseph E. Seagram went on to acquire Tropicana for $1.2 billion and put plans in place to take that business global. Subsequently, reinvestments were made in the global spirits business, in which Seagram continues to be a leader.

As with all institutions, there are no guarantees that Seagram will continue to make the strategic integrations and investments required for continuing success. But in the United States, the new Seagram Beverage Company has held on to its leadership position in the nearly $1 billion wine cooler category, which it shares with Gallo's Bartles & Jaymes. As many previous competitors know to their cost, Ernest and Julio Gallo, a privately owned company that dominates the U.S. wine industry, has created one of the toughest competitive environments of any industry, anywhere in the world. While many new competitors have entered the broader "New Age" beverage category in which wine coolers now compete, Seagram has maintained its leadership position in the wine cooler segment and commands a price premium relative to Bartles & Jaymes.

The principles that Seagram applied to the development of a winning strategy to enter the wine cooler business were:

- Never stop analyzing the business.
- Never stop leveraging what you do uniquely well.
- Never stop learning.

These are all principles that successful businesses must implement if they want to survive. The purpose of this book is to show how a systematic approach to understanding the strategic drivers of a business can lead to continuously improving management over the near term, while laying the foundation of knowledge required to create the Unique Value strategies of the future.

CHAPTER 1

THE POWER OF A
UNIQUE VALUE STRATEGY

———— • ————

In the summer of 1981, Michael Crete and Stuart Bewley, a couple of laid-back former high school buddies turned fledgling entrepreneurs, sent the alcoholic beverage industry reeling by introducing an odd concoction called the "wine cooler." In short order, these unlikely industrialists would create a new category of alcoholic beverage so successful that they would retire as multimillionaires.

Their great American product—an easy-drinking mixture of chablis and fruit juices—started out as a homemade thirst quencher served up to Crete's volleyball buddies on the beach in Lodi, California. Soon demand for the product began to outstrip the limited supply whipped up each day in plastic tubs, and the twenty-eight-year-old inventor began to wonder if he could sell the lime-green liquid, and earn a living from his brainchild.

Crete teamed up with Bewley, who had been searching for a business of his own, and the partners contributed $5,000 to start up their lilliputian company, christened, appropriately enough, California Wine Coolers. Working out of an abandoned farm laborers' camp called Hog Hollow, the unlikely businessmen produced vats of wine cooler, poured their crude production into beer bottles (soaked in water to remove the original labels) and distributed samples to local bars and restaurants.

The response was staggering. As initial samples sold out, requests for even larger orders (this time, paid orders) flowed into the entrepreneurs' makeshift outpost at Hog Hollow. Learning of the quirky product's uncanny appeal, beer distributors (who at the time were eager for a low-alcohol beverage to take up the slack

1

created by a mature beer market) lined up—a ready-made channel of distribution. With teams of experienced salesmen muscling the product onto the shelves, the sales curve shot off the chart, soaring from 1,575 gallons (worth $12,000) in 1981 to 22 million gallons (worth $72 million) in 1984. Overnight, an offbeat drink had gone mainstream. America had a hot new product.

As with all success stories, this one attracted a pack of competitors. In short order, there were offerings from wine czars Ernest and Julio Gallo (Bartles & Jaymes), the spirits house of Joseph E. Seagram & Sons, New York's Canandaigua Winery (Sun Country) and a host of other local and regional competitors (figure 1.1). The category exploded, with retail sales skyrocketing from a pittance in 1982 to $500 million by 1984 (figure 1.2).[1]

Absent from the marketplace was the big Kentucky distiller Brown-Forman, owner of the venerable whiskey brands Jack Daniels and Canadian Mist. Fearing that they were watching the product of the future escape into the arms of competitors, the executives at Brown-Forman decided to make up for lost time by acquiring California Coolers in the fall of 1985. Price: a cool $63 million (plus cash bonuses tied to sales that could add another $83 million to the tab). Overnight Crete and Bewley (as well as their first worker, who was paid in stock rather than cash) became millionaires many times over.

After the purchase of California Coolers, Brown-Forman con-

FIGURE 1.1.   LIST OF COOLER BRANDS

	BRAND	MARKETER
NATIONAL:	Seagram Cooler	Seagram
	Bartles & Jaymes	E. J. Gallo Wines
	Sun Country	Canandaigua Valley
	California Coolers	Brown-Forman
REGIONAL:	Calvin Cooler	Hiram Walker
	Quinn's Cooler	Guild Wineries
	Wineberry	White Rock Products
	Harley-Davidson Cooler	Scooter Juice
	Steidl's Cooler	Paddington Corporation
	Dubonnet Splash	Schenley
	CalaBay Cooler	Thomas J. Lipton
	Red Lite Wine Cooler	Villa Bianchi

Source: New York magazine.

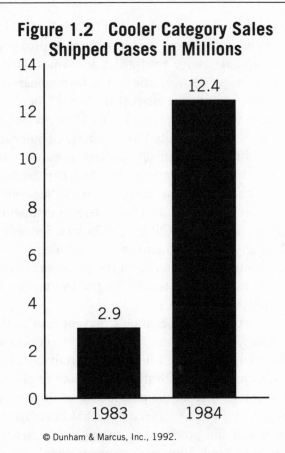

Figure 1.2 Cooler Category Sales Shipped Cases in Millions

© Dunham & Marcus, Inc., 1992.

trolled more than 50 percent of the cooler market. With cooler revenues projected to double in 1985, crossing the $1 billion threshold, Brown-Forman appeared to have climbed aboard a rocket ship. More importantly, it had diversified away from the declining spirits business, opening a promising new avenue for growth. As a sweetener, the acquisition propelled the Kentucky distiller past its arch rival, Seagram, whose entry languished near the bottom of the cooler market. For California Coolers, and in turn for Brown-Forman, the future looked bright.

But Brown-Forman failed to account for a critical factor: The success of smarter and savvier competitors, namely Gallo and subsequently Seagram. Trading on its enormous strength in the wine business (where it is the market leader), Gallo introduced its own entry, Bartles & Jaymes, in the spring of 1985, backed by an enormously appealing advertising campaign, which projected a more sophisticated upscale image for Bartles & Jaymes. Distributed by Gallo's powerful sales network, Bartles & Jaymes leapfrogged over the competition, claiming a market-leading 22 percent share in 1986, compared with 17.5 percent for California Coolers.

By contrast, Seagram's initial foray into the cooler market was less than successful. Its relatively sluggish sales were due to two basic problems. First, the company's product, christened Seagram's Wine Cooler, was a mediocre entry. With its "me-too" taste and lackluster flavoring, the product had little to distinguish it from the concoction marketed by California Coolers. Second, Seagram's cooler lacked any other distinctiveness and failed to leverage the premium credentials associated with the Seagram trademark. The product lacked cachet. As a result, Seagram's share of the market was only 13 percent in early 1986.

It was at this point that Seagram's present president and chief operating officer, Edgar Bronfman, Jr., had to decide whether to abandon the cooler business, which was unprofitable and was hurting Seagram's credentials with distributors and retailers. Seagram analyzed the category from the perspective of the consumers who were driving its growth to understand what beverages they were replacing and why the product was so appealing. Seagram recognized that its own credentials were more relevant and valuable to users than almost any name in America, and that the entire category represented an opportunity to take its name to a franchise of sociable, young adults who were not consumers of Seagram's traditional spirits products.

Seagram created a line of premium coolers, anchored by Seagram's Golden—a new product built on the premium credentials of the Seagram trademark. Seagram's Golden offered sophisticated packaging, premium taste and a distinctive marketing and advertising strategy. Complementing Seagram's Golden was a line of original flavors (led by Natural Peach) consistent with the sophisticated image. A highly focused effort by Seagram's internal departments and disciplines allowed the company to bring its new product line to market in May 1986 (the beginning of the cooler season), just five months after the commitment to a reentry strategy that would leverage Seagram's name and corporate capabilities with a completely reformulated product line.

Within a year, Seagram, which had carefully analyzed its competition and shrewdly targeted its product, had a hit on its hands. By the end of 1986, Seagram had doubled its share of the market and risen to second place (behind Bartles & Jaymes), outpacing California Coolers by 2.5 million cases. By July 1988, Seagram's wine coolers had assumed the number one spot, and its total sales of 18.5 million cases were triple the volume of a declining California Coolers (figure 1.3).

In sharp contrast, Brown-Forman's California Coolers suffered a severe reversal of fortune, with its market share dropping precipitously from 18 percent in 1986 to under 7 percent just two years later. As losses mounted, Brown-Forman transferred the rights to market and manufacture California Coolers to Stroh Breweries (January 1989) in exchange for a royalty agreement. That deal was terminated about a year later and ultimately Brown-Forman took a $93 million write-off on its $140 million California Coolers investment. All the excitement associated with the acquisition of California Coolers had turned into a costly disappointment for Brown-Forman's management and its shareholders.

FIGURE 1.3. COOLER SALES

BRAND COMPANY	CASES SOLD	
	JULY 1986–87	JULY 1987–88
	(In Millions)	
Seagram	14.5	18.5
Bartles & Jaymes (Gallo)	18.0	15.5
California Coolers (Brown-Forman)	12.0	6.7
Sun Country (Canandaigua)	7.2	4.3
Matilda Bay (Miller Brewing)	—*	3.5
Total Market:	61.0	51.7

*Not on market.
Source: Gomberg, Fredrickson & Associates; *Wall Street Journal*, October 1988.

*   *   *

The question is, why did Seagram succeed in the cooler business while Brown-Forman, a successful spirits producer and marketer, failed in the same arena? The answer is that Seagram made a commitment to understand the new category from both a business and a marketing perspective and to define precisely how the business was different from the spirits business it knew. Seagram systematically addressed the issues that would be critical to a successful plan. Who were the key competitors? Who was the key consumer? What could Seagram bring to the category? How could the product line deliver maximum value and be new and different? And what was the basis for long-term profitability? The key factors for marketing and business success in the cooler business were clearly different from the key factors for success in the spirits business in so many ways.

Brown-Forman apparently had not made the distinction between the rules of a market it knew intuitively (from generations of experience) and the new rules that were driving success in wine coolers.

Seagram, on the other hand, recognized that new thinking would be required to be successful in coolers. It had recently sold its wine business to concentrate on its core business, driven by five major spirits brands in the United States: Crown Royal Canadian Whiskey, Chivas Regal Scotch Whisky, Seagram's VO, Seagram's 7-Crown and Seagram's Extra Dry Gin. These "pillar brands" are all high-margin products. By comparison, tight deadlines, relentless cost cutting, mass merchandising and rapid changes in market conditions—all of which characterized the cooler business—were new to Seagram. To succeed in this market, management recognized from the start that the company would have to acquire new skills and new operating practices.

"Traditionally, ours was a hierarchical structure, with manufacturing talking to manufacturing and marketing talking to marketing" recalls Edgar Bronfman, Jr.

If we were going to be successful in a drastically different kind of business requiring quick and decisive action, that kind of rigid structure and departmental autonomy had to come to an end. And fortunately, we found that as we worked toward meeting our deadline for reentering the cooler business, the work flow and scheduling forced us out of the hierarchical structure and into a more fluid form of organization. Where in the past each department would hold its own meetings, make a decision and then pass its verdict onto another department, we now had to assemble everyone in joint meetings in order to compress the time.

Seagram had to be transformed from a hierarchical bureaucracy into a flexible, dynamic organization capable of managing tight timetables and rapid change. The Seagram Beverage Company's executive vice-president for marketing, Mark Taxel, explains that to make this happen, Seagram created multifunctional, multilevel teams to manage the cooler business:

> In the spirits business, there were Chinese walls between all of the critical functions: manufacturing, research & development, sales and marketing. The first time I went to a meeting with all of those people in the same room, I didn't know half of them because the various disciplines had never worked together before.
>
> To run the cooler business successfully and to integrate all functions effectively, we had to build teams of people who could move all dimensions of the business along at a relentless pace with a common set of goals, with each person understanding how those goals affected their individual tasks.

Beyond the organizational difficulties, Seagram was faced with the challenge of changing the attitudes of employees and managers who were comfortable with the stability and the consistent profitability of the spirits business.

"We faced an attitude that for generations the prestigious assignments at Seagram were in the spirits business," Taxel says.

We had to make our wine cooler people recognize that they would have a different but equal level of prestige. A prestige that would be drawn from having a personal impact on the product's success.

When we first started in the cooler business, we thought we were simply trying to build a business. But as we got further into it, we realized that we really had to change the corporate culture. We had to change our self-perception from that of managers continuing the traditional role of the company, to managers who were acting as agents of change.

I remember sitting in Edgar's office when he said something to me as we prepared to reenter the cooler business that no one in this company had ever said to me before. "People are going to have to learn to take risks and they can't be punished for taking those risks, even if they fail. In fact, sometimes they should be rewarded for taking risks and failing. We have to do everything possible to encourage innovation." We had to create an environment that enabled us to be entrepreneurial and take calculated risks—an environment where it was okay to make a mistake.

As Seagram developed its strategy for the cooler business, everyone involved in the effort had to learn a new skill that in most cases was the polar opposite of skills required for success in the spirits business.

Because we were going from a slow-moving, high-margin business to a fast-moving, low-margin business we had to learn to manage volatility. Just think of the challenges we were facing as our business doubled every year for three consecutive years: In 1985 we sold 4 million cases, in 1986 we did 8 million cases, in 1987 we sold 17 or 18 million cases.

We had to open up new channels of trade and get all the distributors to do things differently from the way they had done them before. We had to change the way we bought and distributed sales promotions, the way we shipped new products. We had to learn about "just-in-time" because our people had a habit of overinventorying.

For example, the margins of the spirits business provided little incentive for brand managers to invest time in finding ways to shave pennies from operating costs. But as Seagram Beverage Company president Dick Coffey pointed out, shaving pennies was crucial to making money in coolers: "As we entered the cooler business in earnest, we knew we had to learn to make the transition from double-digit margins to single-digit margins, and in some cases to decimal point margins. And we knew we had to do this while still remaining profitable. To make this happen, we had to focus on cutting costs to the bone in everything from glass to packaging to flavors—and that was something we weren't used to doing."

According to Seagram treasurer John Preston:

> Because of the tight margins, the financial controls on the coolers side had to be hawk eye, miserly and relentless, because if they were not, the profits would get away from us very, very fast. We had to watch our inventories closely because for the first time we would be dealing with a product with a limited shelf life. You can have cases of Seven Crown sitting around, but you can't do that with a wine cooler. We had to retrain our salespeople to make them understand this kind of basic difference between coolers and spirits.

Distribution was another challenge for Seagram. To make coolers succeed, Seagram had to ensure that the product was available at every potential purchase occasion or location. But Seagram's traditional distribution system was geared for spirits, and therefore was inadequate for a wine-based product like coolers.

"If we were going to succeed, it was imperative for us to open new channels of trade—channels like supermarkets and convenience stores—that we never needed access to in the spirits business," Dick Coffey remembers. "In effect, we had to adjust our distribution system to be driven by a very different market. We had to ask, Where is the consumer going to buy coolers? Who has the best access to these channels of trade and how do we get to them? As we developed our strategy for succeeding in the cooler market, these were examples of the factors we had to focus on. These were the questions we had to answer."

Also new to Seagram was the intensity of the competition in the cooler business. "In the cooler business we were up against a very competitive foe," John Preston says. "Gallo was going to be in our face every day. This translated into a constant pressure for price, for innovation, for cost reduction, for innovative advertising and promotion—most of which was new to us."

To succeed against a competitor as formidable as Gallo, the Seagram organization needed to be quicker, more agile and very willing to learn. In Mark Taxel's words:

> Everyone had to recognize that we were on a continuous learning curve, that our competition was relentless and that we couldn't afford to fall asleep at the wheel. This was a tremendous change for Seagram. In the spirits business, we didn't have to anticipate what the competition would do. No one would come up with a blockbuster advertising campaign that was going to knock the other guy out of place in the market share hierarchy. That we recognized this could happen in coolers, and that we went on the offensive—changing virtually all of our methods of operation—shows how extensive our cultural transformation had to be.

This transformation permeated every functional area of the organization. Seagram's management, from senior executives to line managers, needed to focus on identifying and understanding what factors propelled the cooler business, and then had to make sure that the entire business was geared to capitalize on those factors.

"In learning that we had to succeed in a business that was a departure from our core business, we challenged every single discipline in Seagram," recalls Dick Coffey. "We challenged our finance people, we challenged our manufacturing people, we challenged our R&D people, we challenged our distribution people. It was an all-out effort to identify and master the key drivers of a new business."

Seagram understood the need to determine issues such as how the Seagram name was to be leveraged for premium pricing and competitive advantage with consumers and distributors; how the distribution and bottling network would be strengthened; how the product line could change the rules against Gallo; and what it would take to establish Seagram as the gold standard in wine coolers compared with all potential competitors.

How did the team charged with realizing the wine cooler opportunity for Seagram achieve everything they set out to do—in a business that was completely new to them, in such a short time and against an entrenched competitor as formidable as Gallo? They succeeded by making strategic learning a priority for the organization, and by making everything they did strategic in its focus.

CHAPTER 2

THE NEW IMPORTANCE OF STRATEGY

———— • ————

The Fortune 500 is a listing of the largest American industrial corporations. Because of their size and apparent financial strength, they are perceived as the pillars of U.S. industrial strength. The top hundred of the first Fortune 500, published in 1956, are shown in figure 2.1. The top hundred companies of the Fortune 500 in 1991 are shown in figure 2.2. Since then, the hierarchy has already changed significantly, with Microsoft displacing IBM in size of market capitalization. When the New York Stock Exchange closed on January 22, 1993, Microsoft's 299 million fully diluted shares had a market value of $26.8 billion, whereas IBM's 571 million shares were valued at $26.5 billion.[1]

Some of the giants of 1955—like Cudahy Packing, Anaconda Copper Mining and American Radiator & Standard Sanitary—have disappeared, giving way to such relative upstarts as Whirlpool, Apple Computer and Xerox. But many of the giants of the fifties are still in the top echelon of U.S. industry. They have survived this century's technological change and the fierce competition from both Europe and Asia. Infrastructure and momentum have played a critical role in keeping many of the survivors at the top of the rankings. The awesome size and scope of General Motors or Exxon, and their enormous reach in the marketplace, may ensure that they will remain giants of their industries for some time to come regardless of their current strategies.

But the business community and the world in which it functions is being reshaped. Just a decade ago, IBM virtually monopolized the computer industry, PCs were a novelty and the Berlin Wall divided the communist and capitalist nations.

Today two overriding trends are redefining the prerequisites for success in a broad cross-section of markets and industries:

- Accelerating globalization.
- Rapidly advancing technology.

With these trends, many of the assumptions and instincts that have guided corporations for generations are no longer valid. There is, therefore, a heightened need for a comprehensive approach to strategy to guide businesses in monitoring and responding to change.

Accelerating Globalization

Until the twentieth century, global trade consisted predominantly of individual enterprises around the world conducting business with other companies in other countries. Only recently have businesses become transnational organizations, which span borders and continents.

The emergence of multinational corporations has accelerated since World War II, and continues to do so as new technologies make global communications almost instant. As companies expand internationally, they face the challenge of trying to appeal to people with increasingly diverse functional and emotional needs. In the view of Michael Perry, chairman of Unilever:

> The move toward increasing globalism means that consumers are being exposed to things coming from a much broader series of sources. Localization has disappeared. Businesses have to generate concepts which will work on the human condition in a lot of places. Corporations who understand that will move much faster. Those who don't and are too locally focused will find themselves at a very serious competitive disadvantage.

FIGURE 2.1. 1955 FORTUNE 500 (TOP 100)

RANK	COMPANY	SALES ($000)	RANK	COMPANY	SALES ($000)
1	General Motors	9,823,526	51	American Metal Products	519,743
2	Standard Oil (N.J.)	5,661,382	52	American Tobacco	509,457
3	U.S. Steel	3,250,369	53	Continental Oil	500,125
4	General Electric	2,959,078	54	Allis-Chalmers	492,949
5	Swift	2,510,805	55	Jones & Laughlin Steel	492,941
6	Chrysler	2,071,598	56	General Mills	487,587
7	Armour	2,056,149	57	National Steel Corp.	484,058
8	Gulf Oil	1,705,329	58	Curtiss-Wright	475,084
9	Socony-Vacuum Oil	1,703,575	59	Olin Mathieson Chemical	470,108
10	Du Pont (E. I.) de Nemours	1,687,650	60	American Smelting & Refining	466,775
11	Bethlehem Steel	1,667,377	61	International Business Machines	461,350
12	Standard Oil (Ind.)	1,660,343	62	Anaconda Copper Mining	461,067
13	Westinghouse Electric	1,631,045	63	Tide Water Associated Oil	459,030
14	Texas Co.	1,574,370	64	Cudahy Packing	454,794
15	Western Electric	1,526,231	65	Briggs Manufacturing	440,934
16	Shell Oil	1,312,060	66	Sperry	440,906
17	National Dairy Products	1,210,329	67	Reynolds (R. J.) Tobacco	438,274
18	Standard Oil of California	1,113,343	68	Pittsburgh Plate Glass	431,016
19	Goodyear Tire & Rubber	1,090,094	69	Dow Chemical	428,255
20	Boeing Airplane	1,033,176	70	Youngstown Sheet & Tube	428,180
21	Sinclair Oil	1,021,461	71	Kennecott Copper	423,642
22	International Harvester	994,074	72	National Lead	419,334
23	Radio Corp. of America	940,950	73	Standard Brands	415,855
24	Union Carbide & Carbon	923,693	74	Grace (W. R.)	413,402
25	Firestone Tire & Rubber	916,047	75	Caterpillar Tractor	401,041
26	Douglas Aircraft	915,217	76	American Motors	400,344
27	Procter & Gamble	911,050	77	Ralston Purina	399,558
28	Republic Steel	846,311	78	American Cyanamid	397,592

29	Cities Service	813,174	79	Pullman	391,023
30	Phillips Petroleum	794,559	80	Pure Oil	388,278
31	General Foods	783,008	81	Borg-Warner	380,317
32	U.S. Rubber	782,571	82	National Biscuit	376,392
33	Borden	776,839	83	Avco Manufacturing	375,406
34	Lockheed Aircraft	732,872	84	Union Oil	349,667
35	Aluminum Co. of America	708,344	85	Philco	349,277
36	International Paper	681,171	86	Burlington Mills	347,494
37	Wilson & Co.	680,466	87	Monsanto Chemical	341,823
38	Sun Oil	659,532	88	Campbell Soup	338,668
39	United Aircraft Corp.	654,240	89	Owens-Illinois Glass	336,709
40	American Can	652,391	90	Pillsbury Mills	335,955
41	General Dynamics	648,611	91	Singer Manufacturing	333,900
42	North American Aviation	645,821	92	Hormel (George A.)	331,822
43	Eastman Kodak	633,458	93	Hygrade Food Products	324,195
44	Goodrich (B. F.)	630,671	94	Republic Aviation	323,457
45	Continental Can	616,164	95	Carnation	310,038
46	Bendix Aviation	607,712	96	American Sugar Refining	308,837
47	Atlantic Refining	596,168	97	Reynolds Metals	306,779
48	Inland Steel	533,113	98	Morrell (John)	306,465
49	Armco Steel	532,045	99	Standard Oil (Ohio)	304,372
50	Allied Chemical & Dye	530,777	100	Am. Radiator & Std. Sanitary	303,386

FIGURE 2.2 1991 FORTUNE 500 (TOP 100)

RANK	COMPANY	SALES ($millions)	RANK	COMPANY	SALES ($millions)
1	General Motors	123,780	51	Raytheon	9,356
2	Exxon	103,242	52	Ashland Oil	9,322
3	Ford Motor	88,963	53	Monsanto	8,929
4	Int'l Business Machines	64,792	54	Citgo Petroleum	8,922
5	General Electric	60,236	55	Baxter International	8,921
6	Mobil	56,910	56	Unilever U.S.	8,855
7	Philip Morris	48,109	57	Weyerhaeuser	8,702
8	E. I. Du Pont De Nemours	38,031	58	Unisys	8,696
9	Texaco	37,551	59	Merck	8,603
10	Chevron	36,795	60	Archer-Daniels-Midland	8,568
11	Chrysler	29,370	61	American Brands	8,379
12	Boeing	29,314	62	TRW	7,913
13	Procter & Gamble	27,406	63	Textron	7,840
14	Amoco	25,604	64	Emerson Electric	7,427
15	Shell Oil	22,201	65	Ralston Purina	7,394
16	United Technologies	21,262	66	Union Carbide	7,346
17	Pepsico	19,771	67	Borden	7,235
18	Eastman Kodak	19,649	68	General Mills	7,153
19	Conagra	19,505	69	Pfizer	7,144
20	Dow Chemical	19,305	70	Hanson Industries NA	7,104
21	McDonnell-Douglas	18,718	71	American Home Products	7,103
22	Xerox	17,830	72	Deere	7,055
23	Atlantic Richfield	17,683	73	W. R. Grace	6,949
24	USX	17,163	74	Abbott Laboratories	6,922
25	RJR Nabisco Holdings	14,989	75	Hoechst Celanese	6,856
26	Hewlett-Packard	14,541	76	Kimberly-Clark	6,830
27	Tenneco	14,035	77	Texas Instruments	6,812
28	Digital Equipment	14,024	78	Whirlpool	6,770

29	Minnesota Mining & Mfg.	13,340
30	Westinghouse Electric	12,794
31	International Paper	12,703
32	Phillips Petroleum	12,604
33	Sara Lee	12,456
34	Johnson & Johnson	12,447
35	Rockwell International	12,028
36	Allied-Signal	11,882
37	Coca-Cola	11,572
38	Georgia-Pacific	11,524
39	Motorola	11,341
40	Bristol-Myers Squibb	11,298
41	Goodyear Tire & Rubber	11,046
42	Anheuser-Busch	10,996
43	Occidental Petroleum	10,305
44	Sun	10,246
45	Caterpillar	10,182
46	Aluminum Co. of America	9,981
47	Lockheed	9,809
48	Unocal	9,780
49	Coastal	9,603
50	General Dynamics	9,548
79	H.J. Heinz	6,682
80	Amerada Hess	6,416
81	Apple Computer	6,309
82	Campbell Soup	6,230
83	Honeywell	6,221
84	CPC International	6,200
85	Miles	6,197
86	Cooper Industries	6,163
87	LTV	6,117
88	Martin Marietta	6,107
89	Quaker Oats	6,101
90	Colgate-Palmolive	6,094
91	North American Philips	6,065
92	Kellogg	5,787
93	Reynolds Metals	5,785
94	Lyondell Petrochemical	5,757
95	Eli Lilly	5,726
96	PPG Industries	5,725
97	Northrop	5,706
98	Stone Container	5,399
99	Litton Industries	5,313
100	Warner-Lambert	5,167

©Dunham & Marcus International, Inc., 1992.

To compete successfully on an international scale, firms also require manufacturing and distribution systems that can respond to changes in regional and global demand and can take into account unpredictable variables, such as trade barriers (both official and unofficial); national and geographical factors (for example, raw materials cost and availability, wages, transportation, accessibility); and foreign exchange fluctuations.

Given these complexities, corporations are trying to manage joint ventures or acquisitions to minimize risk and cost-optimize global expansion. Pepsi-Cola International, for example, has entered strategic alliances in critical new markets that are not accessible to their key competitor, Coca-Cola, such as the landmark joint venture with the state of Punjab, in which Pepsi gained the local production facilities and distribution networks necessary to make inroads in the Indian soft drink market.

In the global marketplace, companies must deal with political and economic forces that continually change the rules under which businesses must compete.

Iain Vallance, chairman and CEO of BT PLC, emphasizes how difficult it was for BT to react to economic and regulatory changes in the United Kingdom. "The last ten years, beginning with the liberalization of the market in 1981 and privatization in 1984, have been a real organizational challenge for us. We believed that the combination of the two external forces—liberalization and privatization—would almost of themselves bring about significant change. But I don't think we realized the full measure of what was required and how radically it would have to be internalized to affect the old customs and systems. We probably underestimated the resistance of the organization to change."

Globalization has also resulted in an intensified and increasingly complex and demanding competitive environment. Through expansion and acquisition, many firms that, in the past, competed on a local or regional level are now developing into global players. Companies that fail to function on a global scale will find themselves at an increasing disadvantage as larger competitors leverage their greater resources and economies of scale to gain market share.

Even the strongest companies are facing formidable global competitors in every industry and market. Unilever's foods and personal products businesses, for example, did not, until recently, have to compete around the world with such powerful, global corporations as Procter & Gamble, Kao, Philip Morris and Nestlé to the same degree that they do today and will have to in the future.

Clearly, in high-tech businesses, the Japanese have eroded Western technological and share leadership. For example, America's share of the worldwide semiconductor market fell from 57 percent to 30 percent in ten years.[2]

In labor-intensive industries, such as textiles and apparel, countries with lower wages, such as Thailand and Malaysia, have taken the lead. And in the auto industry, Japanese brands' share of the U.S. car market has increased from 15 percent to 26 percent in the last decade. Every major Japanese auto manufacturer is also building or planning European production facilities to boost their quota-restricted share of the European market above the current 10.8 percent level (figure 2.3).[2]

Another emerging trend, evident in the automobile industry, is that of global partnerships, particularly in the areas of R&D and manufacturing. Ford's relationship with Mazda is one of the more prominent examples of companies collaborating in the develop-

FIGURE 2.3. JAPANESE TRANSPLANT PRODUCTION CAPACITY

JAPANESE COMPANY	NORTH AMERICAN PRODUCTION CAPACITY (1989)	PLANNED EUROPEAN PRODUCTION CAPACITY (MID-1990s)
Toyota	630,000[1]	215,000
Honda	610,000	180,000[2]
Nissan	480,000	350,000
Mazda	240,000	100,000[3]
Mitsubishi	240,000[4]	100,000[3]
Suzuki	200,000[5]	100,000
Isuzu	120,000[6]	80,000[5]
Subaru		

Notes
1) Includes NUMMI joint venture with General Motors
2) Production for Honda by Rover
3) Plants under discussion
4) Joint venture with Chrysler
5) Joint venture with General Motors
6) Isuzu/Subaru joint venture
Source: The Machine That Changed the World

ment and marketing of products to share technology and reduce engineering costs. In 1991, two of every five Mazdas sold in the United States benefited from some degree of Ford involvement, while one of every four Ford cars received input from Mazda.[4]

Of course joint ventures are not new. Thirty years ago, Fuji Film and Xerox Corporation entered into a landmark alliance in which Xerox would share certain xerography technology with Fuji in exchange for access to Far Eastern markets. But the alliance soon outgrew its initial objectives. "In the last ten years, Fuji-Xerox has become an inseparable part of Xerox," says Yotaro Kobayashi, chairman and CEO of Fuji-Xerox. "For example, we provide all of the facsimile products for Xerox worldwide. We provide nearly 100 percent of the special purpose drawing reproduction equipment. We provide most of their low-end copiers, which are those with thirty to forty copies per minute. About ten or fifteen years ago, we mostly just modified U.S. designs, but in the last decade, most of these products are our original designs."

Alliances of this type are appearing in an increasing number of industries. Apple, which traditionally had developed and manufactured all of its own products, had Sony produce its PowerBook laptop computer because it lacked the expertise needed to miniaturize its Macintosh hardware to the specifications it was targeting. The success of the venture has led Apple and Sony executives to consider a broad range of similar projects for the future.

The aviation industry, long dominated by American firms, is also seeing an increase in global technology sharing. "The aircraft business is quite a typical example of how the world has changed," says Naoyuki Kondo, executive managing director of Mitsui. "Neither Boeing nor McDonnell-Douglas planes are exclusively made in the United States anymore. We are sharing in the research and development cost for new airplanes, which are made out of thousands of parts manufactured worldwide by companies including Japanese. Many industries have become global rather than the exclusive domain of one particular country."

Rapidly Advancing Technology

Traditionally, only companies in "high-tech" industries have made innovation a key component of their long-term strategies. But in an increasing number of industries, products are being revolutionized by advancing technology, which is dramatically shortening product lifecycles. What does that mean? According to Christoph von Braun, head of technology strategy at Siemens, the German electronics and computer manufacturer, "The period between the introduction of a new product on the market and the time when it can no longer be successfully sold because of technological obsolescence is getting shorter and shorter." Von Braun, who has researched the impact of diminishing product lifecycles, adds that the phenomenon is "by no means restricted to technology-intensive branches of industry such as aerospace or pharmaceuticals; it also affects fields such as foods, which we do not normally associate with a high degree of technology content or technological change"[5] (figure 2.4). This trend is also evidenced by an overall decline in the average age of products on the market (figure 2.5).

As the development of superior products becomes increasingly dependent on new technology, firms that fail to innovate—and more importantly, that fail to bring innovation to market strategically —will be at the mercy of those with more marketable products.

To innovate successfully consistently, companies must make R&D an integral part of long-term corporate and business-unit strategy. One aspect of Toshiba's corporate strategy is continuously to develop and commercialize new technologies that management knows will make successful, existing products obsolete. Discussing Toshiba's development of dynamic random access memory (DRAM) chips, Tsuyoshi Kawanishi, the firm's senior managing director, notes that while "4M DRAMs are in the mass production stage, 16M DRAMs are under technological improvement, and 64M DRAMs are in the research and development stage. We make it a policy to handle three generations of our products simultaneously."[6]

In the successful, future-focused corporations, R&D must be closely linked to strategy formulation and implementation at the

Figure 2.4 Diminishing Product Lifecycles

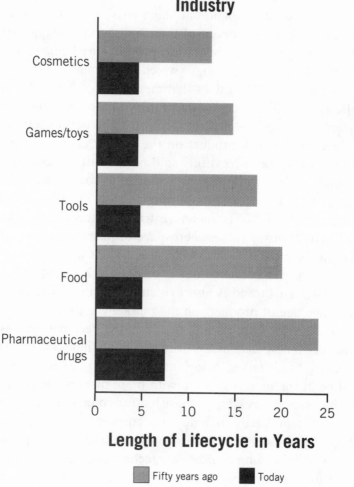

Industry

Cosmetics

Games/toys

Tools

Food

Pharmaceutical
drugs

Length of Lifecycle in Years

Fifty years ago ■ Today

Source: Christoph von Braun, "The Acceleration Trap," *Sloan Management Review,* Fall 1990, vol. 32, no. 1, p. 49.

business-unit level. For example, when G. D. Searle commercialized aspartame (an artificial sweetener marketed under the NutraSweet® brand name), the company needed a well-planned strategy to coordinate product development with its marketing effort. By managing the development of the NutraSweet brand,

Figure 2.5   Decline in Average Age of Products on the Market

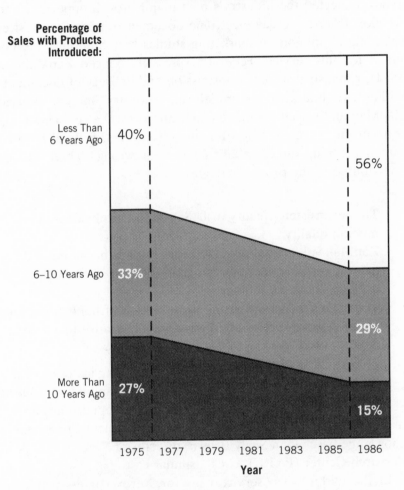

Percentage of Sales with Products Introduced:

Less Than 6 Years Ago — 40% ... 56%

6–10 Years Ago — 33% ... 29%

More Than 10 Years Ago — 27% ... 15%

Year: 1975 1977 1979 1981 1983 1985 1986

Source: Christoph von Braun, "The Acceleration Trap," *Sloan Management Review,* Fall 1990, vol. 32, no. 1, p. 49.

Searle built a competitive advantage, enhancing the product's long-term income potential.[7]

When innovation and product development are not strategically managed, the results are disastrous for near-term financial results and for long-term focus. Consider Federal Express's star-crossed experience with ZapMail. The package delivery firm, which set the standard for overnight shipping in the late 1970s and early 1980s, expected the industry's next major growth opportunity to develop from same-day electronic document transmission. After spending $2 million on marketing studies that confirmed the demand for this service, Federal Express introduced ZapMail (in 1984), promising pickup, transmission and delivery of documents within two hours of the initial call. Industry analysts praised ZapMail and voiced favorable expectations for the venture's long-term profit potential. But after just three years, Federal Express pulled the plug on ZapMail. What went wrong? Three factors contributed to the product's demise:

- The inconsistent quality of U.S. phone lines hampered transmission quality.
- ZapMail volume did not fulfill expectations because it did not meet a customer need better than or more cheaply than the evolving facsimile market.
- The reduced cost led to the proliferation of home and office facsimile machines as an inexpensive alternative to ZapMail.

As a result, Federal Express suffered operating losses of nearly $350 million plus an additional $400 million in capital investment.[8]

In the case of Federal Express, the technology opportunity analysis was not tied to the existing technology infrastructure or available knowledge base. John Seely Brown, director of Xerox's Palo Alto Research Center (PARC), cites a similar case.

In the early 1980s, service calls for Xerox copiers increased dramatically. The problem was not one of poor reliability; rather, Xerox's machines were so difficult to use that correcting even simple malfunctions, like a paper jam or insufficient toner, involved a complex, time-consuming process. Many users simply gave up and called for service. Says Brown:

We had to make radical changes in copier design, but it was difficult to sell that message within the company. The idea that there might be serious usability problems with our machines met with resistance in the Xerox development organization that designs our copiers. After all, they had tested their designs against all the traditional "human factors" criteria. There was a tendency to assume that any problems with the machines must be the users' fault.

When researchers from PARC began to study the problem, we discovered that the human-factors tests used by the development group didn't accurately reflect how people actually used the machines. A PARC anthropologist set up a video camera overlooking one of our new copiers in use at PARC, then had pairs of researchers (including some leading computer scientists) use the machine to do their own copying. The result was dramatic footage of very smart people, anything but idiots, becoming increasingly frustrated and angry as they tried and failed to figure out how to get the machine to do what they wanted it to do.

Xerox's researchers gradually came to realize that making it simple to *correct trouble* was just as important as minimizing the frequence of malfunctions. So Xerox designed their new 10 and 50 series copiers with the objective of "making it easy for the user to find out what is going on and to discover immediately what to do when something goes wrong," says Brown. "The results of these changes have been dramatic. Where it once took 28 minutes on average to clear a paper jam, it takes 20 seconds with the new design. And because such breakdowns are easier to fix, customers are more tolerant of them when they occur."[9]

The Xerox case illustrates that as products become increasingly complex, they cannot be designed without detailed consideration for the users' needs and usage patterns. Related examples involving the development of two Du Pont products drive this point home. Du Pont's expertise is in "materials replacement," developing artificial, laboratory-created replacements for natural materials used in consumer and commercial products. So the firm continually reinvests in the core petrochemical and fiber technologies that drive its ability to produce marketable synthetic replacements for natural materials.

Before introducing its successful line of Stainmaster carpets, Du Pont determined, through extensive consumer research, that a stain-resistant carpet would be desirable to its target consumers, who were middle-income household decisionmakers (primarily women) aged twenty-five to fifty-four. But consumers also were telling Du Pont that they would not be willing to sacrifice other factors, such as attractiveness or durability, to get this important new benefit. So Du Pont made sure that Stainmaster was available in a broad selection of stylish colors and patterns and would retain its good looks over time.

The Stainmaster case provides a strategic comparison with Du Pont's introduction of Corfam, a synthetic leather for shoes. Du Pont is the corporation that invented, patented and registered "Nylon" as the replacement for silk stockings. In the case of Corfam, the same corporation was studying leather shoes. "Wouldn't it be better if they were a lot more durable and didn't scuff?" Du Pont researchers asked. Predictably, consumers agreed. "The soles and heels wear out and have to be replaced. The tops scuff and have to be shined again and again, but eventually they don't look as good as they used to, and you have to buy a new pair of shoes." However, Du Pont's analysis looked at what consumers perceived to be wrong with leather, ignoring what was right. People wear leather shoes not just for the way they look, but for the way they feel on their feet. While Corfam could improve shoes' looks and durability, it was far inferior to leather in terms of breathability, comfort and wearability (the way that shoes crease to adjust to the shape of individual feet). Wearing Corfam was like putting on a new pair of shoes every single day.

Corfam was introduced in 1964. Over the next five years, shoe retailers sold 75 million pairs of Corfam shoes. But the new product failed to generate a profit in any year, and venture losses piled up until they reached about $70 million. These losses were much larger than the venture analysts had predicted because technical and marketing expenses turned out to be twice what had been assumed. Corfam encountered more retailer and consumer resistance than had been expected. This latter problem centered on foot comfort—about fifteen percent of Corfam shoe wearers complained of having hot feet. Du Pont researchers could prove scientifically that Corfam breathed better than leather under laboratory conditions, but this did not persuade skeptical consumers. Some at Du Pont linked the problem to bad fitting by retail shoe clerks. Corfam shoes did not stretch, so proper fit was essential, which usually meant buying a larger size shoe than usual, something that many consumers refused to do. By 1969, a substantial fraction of both retailers and consumers had turned against Corfam.[10]

An aspect of technology that dramatically affects strategy today is information technology. For example, McKesson Drug Company's Economost system, introduced in 1975, revolutionized the pharmaceutical industry by automating the order entry process and by better linking the firm with its customers (pharmacies). The immediate benefits to McKesson's customers were reduced product transaction and inventory costs, but the long-term impact on the industry was more significant, as the system has enabled independent pharmacies to effectively compete with larger, vertically integrated chains.

Across the board, information technology creates new opportunities to gain competitive advantage through more efficient manufacturing, distribution and inventory management. In the case of manufacturing, automation and robotization have diminished the contribution of labor to total manufacturing costs, allowing highly automated production facilities to compete with lower-wage workforces.

After World War II, Toyota combined automation and information technologies with other state-of-the-art techniques to develop "lean" production, which set new standards for manufacturing efficiency, product quality and inventory management in manufacturing industries. Lean production incorporates flexible manufacturing techniques, which cost-optimize usage of personnel and production facilities to meet rapid changes in consumer demand; just-in-time (JIT) production, which substantially reduces inventory demand by coordinating the supply and usage of manufacturing components; and vertical integration, which provides firms with a continuous source of customized low-cost supplies.

With the two dominant trends of accelerating globalization and rapidly advancing technology affecting every aspect of today's external business environment, the internal environment of the corporate entity must change in response. There is an urgent need to reshape organizational structures and ideas around the most productive business strategies—those that can leverage assets, skills and resources for sustainable growth, and can interact effectively with the rapidly evolving world outside.

CHAPTER 3

BENCHMARKING STRATEGY: THE NEED FOR A STANDARD

———— • ————

In the struggle to create and sustain a viable business strategy and to forge an organization that is strategically focused and therefore both efficient and effective, there are three key questions to be resolved.

Question one is: How rigorous should the process, the articulation and the implementation of strategy be? Question two is: Can and should the definition of strategy be different depending on a corporation's competitive environment, industry, world view or corporate leadership? Question three is: How many different kinds of strategy can there be?

Business writers' and managers' views on all three questions have varied widely over the years. For example, in his classic work *Strategy and Structure,* Alfred Chandler argued that it is the role of strategy to provide business with the longer-term focus so often lacking in the entrepreneurially driven American economy.

Just because the entrepreneurs make some of the most significant decisions in the American economy, they are not all necessarily imbued with a long-term strategic outlook. In many enterprises the executives responsible for resource allocation may very well concentrate on day-to-day operational affairs, giving little or no attention to changing markets, technology, sources of supply, and other factors affecting the long-term health of their company. Their decisions may be made without forward planning or analysis but rather by meeting, in an ad hoc way, every new situation, problem, or crisis as it arises. The entrepreneurs accept the goals of their enterprise as given or inherited. Clearly wherever they act like managers, wherever they concentrate on short-term activities to the exclusion or to the detriment of long-range planning, appraisal, and coordination, they have failed to carry out effectively their role in the economy as well as in their enterprise.[1]

Other definitions of business strategy vary broadly, from relatively precise to intentionally imprecise. For example, David Aaker, professor of marketing at Berkeley, defines business strategy quite precisely:

> A business strategy has two core elements. The first is the product-market investment decision which includes the product-market scope of the business strategy, its investment intensity and the resource allocation in a multiple business context. The alternatives range from a withdrawal from a business area to a milking strategy to various growth strategies such as market share growth, or expansion of the product line or served market. The second core element is the development of a sustainable competitive advantage which encompasses underlying competencies or assets, appropriate objectives, functional area policies, and the creation of synergy.[2]

In contrast, James Brian Quinn, professor of management at Dartmouth's Amos Tuck School of Business, theorizes that organizations develop strategy gradually through a process, which he terms "logical incrementalism," that does not require well-defined procedures and structure:

> Strategies in [large] institutions tend to emerge in ways that differ quite markedly from the usually prescribed textbook methodologies. The full strategy is rarely written down in any one place. The processes used to arrive at the total strategy are typically fragmented, evolutionary, and largely intuitive. Although one can frequently find embedded in these fragments some very refined pieces of formal strategic analysis, the real strategy tends to evolve as internal decisions and external events flow together to create a new, widely shared

consensus for action among key members of the top management team. In well-run organizations, managers proactively guide these streams of actions and events incrementally.[3]

Quinn's view is shared by Professor Henry Mintzberg of McGill University in Montreal, who maintains that "strategies can form as well as be formulated." According to Mintzberg, strategies "can emerge in response to an evolving situation" or be "brought about deliberately, through a process of formulation followed by implementation." He argues that the distinction that many business writers make between the development and implementation of strategy is misleading:

I believe that the problem often lies in the distinction we make between (strategy) formulation and implementation, the common assumption that thought must be independent of (and precede) action. . . . The notion that strategy is something that should happen way up there, far removed from the details of running an organization on a daily basis, is one of the great fallacies of conventional management. And it explains a good many of the most dramatic failures in business and public policy today.[4]

Most writers on business strategy reflect Western schools of thought. By contrast, Richard T. Pascale, a professor at Stanford's Graduate School of Business, dimensionalizes the differences between the Western and Japanese perspectives on strategy:

The Japanese don't use the term *strategy* to describe a crisp business definition or competitive master plan. They think more in terms of *strategic accommodation,* or *adaptive persistence,* underscoring their belief that corporate direction evolves more from an incremental adjustment to unfolding events. Rarely, in their view, does one leader (or a strategic planning group) produce a bold strategy that guides a firm unerringly. Far more frequently, the input is from below. It is this ability of an organization to move information and ideas from the bottom to the top and back again in continuous

dialogue that the Japanese value above all things. As this
dialogue is pursued, what in hindsight may be *strategy* evolves.
In sum, *strategy* is defined as *all things necessary for the
successful functioning of an organization as an adaptive
mechanism.*[5]

The distinction between strategy formulation and implementation tends to become increasingly blurred as strategy emerges more
and more from projects generated and largely appraised by the
people who are going to implement them, and as corporations
become decentralized so that business managers can be closer to
their respective markets. In this regard, business strategies may not
be formally planned or clearly articulated in many companies today.
But whether articulated or not, highly successful and profitable
businesses, both Western and Asian, are operating on the basis of
a strategy, much of which is intentionally hidden from the outside
world.

Historically, few businesses have shared with competitors the
tricks of the trade they have learned from years of experience, their
understanding of what factors to focus on, the way decisions are
made within the organization and the culture's system of rewards
and values, or how all these, in a successful business, work together
in a fully integrated way.

A business strategy works within a broadly defined concept of
corporate strategy, for the most part. And corporate strategy bears
little relationship to the requirements of strategy at the business-
unit level. Sir Michael Angus, former chairman of Unilever, defines
his approach by describing strategy as "forward thinking." From
his corporate perspective, "It is the direction of a business toward
whatever vision you have for the future. A strategy must define
the essential resources you have and how they will be allocated,
and is the basis for long-term planning."

Yotaro Kobayashi, chairman and CEO of Fuji-Xerox, in accordance with a Japanese corporate viewpoint, says that "for any
company, a strategy must be a very general statement, which, for
it to be meaningful, must be such that it would enable the company

to chart a course for a minimum of about five years, and hopefully beyond that."

Marcus Bierich, chairman of German auto parts manufacturer Robert Bosch, articulates the corporate perspective in terms of business-unit needs. Bierich views strategy "in terms of product-market combination: the definition of a product, the definition of a market segment. These are the key elements of our definition. But the overriding principle when we talk about strategy is that we try to be driven by the customer, competition and technology. What does the customer want? What is the competition doing? What does technology allow? These are the three critical issues we look for in developing strategies for our business units."

Discussing business-unit strategy, Iain Vallance, chairman and CEO of BT PLC, breaks down a series of components. He then elaborates on how each component relates to BT's business:

> The essence of our strategy is speed of reaction. Involved in this are four basic things we have to do. The first one is to understand our customers' needs better than anyone else. Second, we have to develop an organization which is able to move very quickly in those areas where movement is needed and yet has strength and stability where that characteristic is essential. Third, we have to master the technology—ours is a technology-driven industry. Fourth, and most important, we have to have the people in the organization with the skills and enthusiasm to do battle. That is the framework I use to define strategy.

In the relationship between corporate and business-unit strategy, "The challenge is to take the cosmic notion of strategy and translate it into specific instructions for the operating units. This is critical because for strategy to be effective, it must be internalized by the managers. So we develop it with them, unit by unit, country by country, looking at the local business environment, its place in the global picture, where we are and where we want to be. In addition, we develop a personnel strategy for the corporation, a manufacturing strategy and a financial strategy that are congruent with and serve those business strategies," according to Fred Kyle, president of commercial operations at SmithKline-Beecham Pharmaceuticals in the period following the merger between Beecham PLC and SmithKline Beckman Corp.

But in the varying descriptions of strategy formulation, what is seldom addressed is the struggle to get to strategy. Bruce Crawford, president and CEO of the Omnicom Group, the global advertising agency conglomerate whose clients include Apple Computer, Chrysler Corporation and General Electric, comments, for example, on the discrepancy between the vision and the implementable strategic plan:

> Quite often, the managers who bring their vision to a business are totally unrealistic, as is the strategy that emanates from that vision. In the advertising business, it is clear that the Saatchi brothers had a vision, and that vision was to be the biggest, and they would say, to be also the best. Their plan was to be the first truly global agency. They had a lot of vision.
>
> As events have proved, much of it was unrealistic. And some of it wasn't executed as well as it should have been. There is no doubt that in a business such as ours, one needs to be large, with an extensive geographic presence, excellence in services offered and the ability to service clients worldwide. All of these are components of a strategy that makes all the sense in the world. It is, however, very important to be realistic about this, and not simply decide that one wants to conquer the world. The Saatchis' fatal flaw was in executing their strategy on the basis of poorly conceived acquisitions that were virtually doomed to failure.

In a related industry, magazine publishing, Christie Hefner, CEO of Playboy Enterprises, Inc., comments on the challenge she faces:

> Playboy is an example of a company that had a strong sense of mission, and an undeveloped sense of strategy . . . where the kind of water in which everybody swims is creativity. One

of the things that's difficult when you go through a cycle where everything was nonrisk-taking, noninvestment, and then, in that sense, noncreative, is to bring back the kind of risk-taking, it's-ok-to-fail energy and to bring it back in a much more widespread way. Now what you want to say to people who have been there a long time is, we want your creativity. You're trying to democratize the notion that you have creativity and instill it in an environment where you deliberately put in more checks and balances and more financial controls and more requirement for analysis before investments are made and actions are taken and decisions are made.

As today's corporate and business-unit managers struggle to identify the basis for a sustainable competitive advantage in an overwhelmingly complex and demanding global marketplace, the answer to question one (How rigorous should the process, the articulation and the implementation of strategy be?) must be that, whether expressly articulated or not, successful business strategies require discipline, rigor and reality.

The answer to question two (Can and should the definition of strategy be different depending on a corporation's competitive environment, industry, world view or corporate leadership?) is that the structure and the fundamentals of a business unit's strategy are universal. Whether its strategy is explicit or implicit, formally stated or informally understood, every successful business must know its competitors and key competitive factors; its customer franchise and customer needs; its basis for business superiority and differentiating benefits; its optimal product portfolio; and the key factors that drive profitability. These are the fundamentals of strategy and should be incorporated into every definition of strategy at the business-unit level.

While the fundamentals of strategy do not change, the need for strategic rigor has been heightened by the increased competition and complexity of today's business environment. How can corporations introduce strategic discipline and a deep enough understanding of the fundamentals to drive strategic thinking through every business of the corporation? Since business-unit strategy drives the efficient use of corporate resources, corporate management should prioritize investments on the basis of relative strategic attractiveness. For that evaluation to be made, clear criteria must exist.

The quality of business-unit management can then be judged not just by performance, but by whether the business has a viable strategy and is acting on it. This determination can be made by formalizing the answers to a single set of questions that define the fundamentals of business strategy:

(1) What is the business's *Competitive Framework?* What is the scale of the business as it is currently defined and as it potentially might be? What is the industry structure and global competitive environment? With whom does the business directly or indirectly compete? At which competitors' expense does the business source sales and profits?

(2) What is the *Market Target* for the business's product or service? Within the global market structure, what are the consumer and customer segments that drive current sales? Which strategic segments will drive future sales and profit growth? What are the needs of these consumers and customers?

(3) What is the product or service's basis for *Perceived Competitive Superiority?* From the perspective of key consumer and customer segments, what benefits must be delivered to build and sustain competitive advantage? What differentiating benefits does the business bring to the marketplace? How are business skills and capabilities currently leveraged to enhance the portfolio of products or services?

(4) What is the optimal *Product Portfolio Configuration?* What is the competitive positioning of the business's products or services? How can the line of products or services be structured to ensure the highest return on technology and other investments over the near and long term?

(5) What are the business's *Key Profit Drivers?* Which aspects of the business have the greatest impact on income? How must the business be managed to maintain operating margins and profitability?

These are the five fundamentals of a business strategy. A strategy should articulate and address each of the fundamentals, and interrelate them in a way that can form the basis for a coherent, implementable plan.

Most businesses are able to answer some of these questions with some measure of precision. But a strategically focused business entity can answer these questions precisely, in both qualitative and quantitative terms. Strategy thus defines the cutting edge, the critical factors for success and the basis for sustainable profitability and competitive insulation.

Because no two businesses are exactly alike in their experience, skills, assets or other resources, a *superior* strategy integrates the fundamentals in a way that builds on the unique strengths of the organization and the enterprise. Thus, the answer to question three is that the most productive strategies fully leverage a unique set of capabilities in a way that is highly responsive to the business realities of the times. This is the essence of the Unique Value strategies that formed the world's great business institutions. In every age the challenge of the times is to create the Unique Value strategies of tomorrow.

CHAPTER 4

STRATEGY IN ACTION

——— • ———

In classic business literature, writers have tended to group and label business strategies according to their objectives and characteristics, classifying strategic options as, for example, "differentiation," "segmentation" or "low-cost producer." But a differentiation strategy is simply an approach to establishing Perceived Competitive Superiority by distinguishing the product or service from competitors. A segmentation strategy begins by defining the Market Target and subdividing it into segments according to customer needs. A low-cost strategy depends on being able to identify and exploit a business's Key Profit Drivers.

For any of these "strategies" to be successful in delivering a superior return on investment over the long term, they cannot be independent entities; they must take into account all of the fundamentals. An industry's low-cost producer is not guaranteed success if, say, consumer demand for its product is declining.

By contrast, a Unique Value strategy is a comprehensive approach to the management of a business, which, because it is cohesive, focuses the resources of the enterprise in the direction that can provide the highest possible return on all investments, in talent, time, technology and capital. A Unique Value strategy is defined by all of the five fundamentals in a fully integrated way.

Nintendo: Redefining an Industry

A real-world case that illustrates the importance of the five fundamentals of strategy, and the critical interrelationship between them, is that of Nintendo, the electronics giant based in Kyoto, Japan, whose performance in America has been remarkable. First invading the U.S. market in 1980 with its successful Donkey Kong arcade game, the century-old company viewed this early coup as the opening salvo in a master plan to blanket the nation with video games. With this in mind, its secret weapon—the Nintendo Entertainment System—was unveiled five years later in the fall of 1985.

But after experiencing lightning-fast growth in the early 1980s, the video game business had imploded, with sales collapsing from a 1983 high of $3 billion to less than $100 million by 1985. To the chain store merchants who had sold millions of Atari, Coleco and Mattel home video systems (and to the trade press that had chronicled the industry's roller-coaster ride), video games were just another fad that had come and gone.

However, from Nintendo's perspective, the only thing wrong with the video game business was the fast-buck, milk-it-and-ditch-it mentality of the companies marketing the first generation of games. As far as the Japanese were concerned, video games were hardly a fad. From their perspective, they were a revolutionary form of entertainment that, if managed carefully and strategically, could be as much a fixture in the American home as color television.

To make this happen, Nintendo developed a detailed and well-focused business strategy. Convinced that the early video boom went bust primarily because of poorly conceived, second-rate software that failed to challenge players once the novelty wore off, they set out to create an increasingly sophisticated line of games that would lure players into the Nintendo web and, once there, would hook them for years. For decades. Perhaps for life.

Nintendo's strategy scored a perfect bull's-eye. By 1991, Nintendo had sold more than 30 million units of video-game hardware and in excess of 175 million software cassettes, producing aggregate revenues of more than $10 billion (figure 4.1). So widespread is the Nintendo phenomenon that one of every three American homes is now equipped with NES hardware.

The mastermind behind the company's U.S. strategy is marketing vice-president Peter Main. A native of Kitchener, Ontario, Main earned his stripes in the corporate sector through a series of senior

Figure 4.1 Nintendo Drove Segment Growth and Sustained Sales/Share at the Expense of Competition.

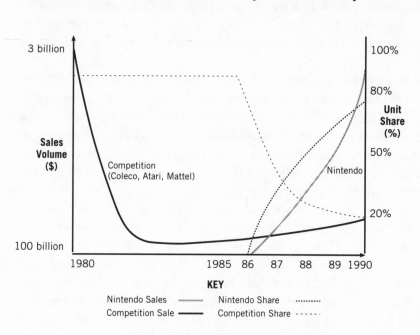

© Dunham & Marcus International, Inc., 1991.

marketing positions with Colgate Palmolive and General Foods, before assuming the presidency of White Spot Ltd., a diversified food service company based in British Columbia. Joining Nintendo in April 1987, the executive put his thoughtful, methodical style to work for the company, building bridges to the retail community and in the process boosting Nintendo's sales by about $3 billion in three years. Named *Adweek*'s Marketer of the Year in 1989, Main is given much of the credit for establishing a loyal consumer franchise on a scale never dreamed of by the pioneers of the video game phenomenon.

Nintendo's success demonstrates the power of a Unique Value strategy in terms of its five precisely defined and interrelated fundamentals.

(1) Competitive Framework

Before reentering the home video game market, Nintendo identified the companies that had pioneered the business (and that were still fighting it out for the remnants of consumer demand) and precisely what they had done wrong. In the course of their research, the marketers from Kyoto discovered that their predecessors made the fatal mistake of viewing video games as a short-term phenomenon, a toy, that would reach a quick sales peak and then die on the shelves in a year or two. Applying the traditional toy business mentality to video games—that is, any toy that lasts longer than three years is either Barbie or an aberration—they failed to develop games that would continue to challenge players and would bring new segments of consumers into the business. According to Main:

> Instead, they put good titles on their games, hyped the products with little regard for how they performed and then shipped, shipped, shipped. Their myopic approach was to extract a windfall and then move to the next fad.
>
> The E.T. video game is a perfect example of a creative idea that was turned into a phenomenal movie but was never translated into a quality video game. It sold hundreds of thousands of cartridges, only to be greeted with incredible disappointment once players put the cartridges into their machines. Why? Because the E.T. game didn't meet their expectations. It had no real substance.
>
> The early video game companies didn't understand that there is a world of difference between liking something in an arcade—where you pay a quarter and spend ten minutes with a game—and buying something for the home, where you spend forty dollars for it and hope to enjoy it for many hours. When you find you can master that forty-dollar game in sixty seconds, you are deeply dissatisfied.
>
> We recognized that it was erroneous to think that the original video game market collapsed because consumers walked away from it. The real reason it died was that the manufacturers, with their short-term perspective, killed it. The con-

sumers said "We enjoy this medium of play. This is a bona fide entertainment. But please give us games that will challenge us for more than a few hours."

Building on this understanding, Nintendo was confident it could drive segment growth and take the market well beyond the competition.

(2) Market Target

As Nintendo prepared to introduce a more sophisticated and higher-quality line of games to the United States, it set its sights on three distinct consumer segments—young children, adolescents and adults—each of which had different needs and would be targeted with different types of games. Says Main:

> We include Duck Hunt with every NES Action Set we sell. It's an instant gratification game that doesn't require a hundred-page manual to understand. Kids have fun with it and then quickly graduate to more complex games such as Super Mario Brothers and Zelda. That's when their older brothers and sisters, as well as their parents, are drawn into the excitement.
>
> The principle is that good software built around the critical triumvirate of fun, excitement and challenge attracts people and gets them to come back again and again knowing that they can gain gratification beating a set of hurdles they couldn't beat yesterday.

While Nintendo carefully identified and targeted key consumer segments, it also needed support from a key customer segment—retailers. Nintendo needed to overcome the outright skepticism of the retail community, which had witnessed the rise and fall of the video game business and which had lost millions of dollars on the unsold inventories of the Coleco and Atari systems. As Main explained:

> Our first job was to convince the trade to carry our product, because without that we couldn't hope to reach the consumer.

With this in mind, we decided to forgo the usual test markets in the Midwest and to launch our product (fall 1985) in the biggest test market of all: New York City. The idea was that if we could make it in New York, we could make it anywhere.

To counter the fears and the skepticism of the retail community, we offered the product on a guaranteed basis. We said "Don't pay for it until you sell it. We'll put it on your shelves, we'll advertise it and we'll promote it." Because we assumed all the risk, the stores were willing to give video games another try. And Eureka! by Christmas, the product had sold out. We moved almost one hundred thousand pieces of hardware. That's when the trade said, "Wow, we didn't believe those customers were still out there."

Not that all the skeptics were convinced. The diehards said New York was a fluke and that we'd be unable to duplicate our success elsewhere. That's when we went to Los Angeles, sold out there in the first half of 1986, and then followed up with a national rollout later that year.

(3) Basis for Perceived Competitive Superiority

To revitalize interest in a slumping category, Nintendo had to establish a strong reason for consumers and retail customers to believe in its superiority over the early video games and over newcomers likely to challenge it as the market soared again.

The company was convinced that its improved components produced superior audio and graphics, but its executives also knew that these technological refinements were inadequate to win back those customers who had been turned off by the first wave of video games. There could be no shortcuts here. Nintendo needed more than bells and whistles to establish its superiority. Says Main:

Unlike our predecessors in the industry, we knew video games weren't the toy business. We knew they were the "game" business.

Because producing quality games was Nintendo's forte, we said we're going to succeed in the video game business even though everyone else said it was dead and buried. Even though our president, Minoru Arakawa, was an abused Willy

Loman—even though he was ejected bodily from the buying offices of the retail chains, all of whom had given last rites to video games—we remained convinced that we could bring the industry back. Yes, the first chapter was over—we knew that—but we also believed that the consumer hadn't been given the chance to play good games. Were that to change, we knew he would return to the stores.

In three words—fun, excitement, challenge—Main crystallized the factors that would serve as the foundation for Nintendo's competitive superiority. But as Main points out, just delivering a superior product was not enough:

From the beginning, we knew we needed a device that would convince consumers that our video games were truly different. So we came up with a funny little robot called ROB, that was sold as part of the hardware system. ROB was used for playing some of the games. But even more important, he made a critical statement: "Here is a new generation of video games. One that is very different from the Coleco or the Atari 2600 that you were playing with before."

ROB would get people to buy the product and once they brought it home they would see the substantive differences in Nintendo compared with the earlier games. They would see that the graphics were indeed better and that the sound was better and most important they would see that the game play was better.

In getting people back into the market, we needed some sizzle and ROB represented that sizzle. People would say "Wow, that system has a robot and that's truly different from anything we've seen before." So from our perspective, ROB was an innovative marketing device designed to prompt trial use of the product. Needless to say, we would have bombed out quickly if we had relied totally on ROB. To succeed over the long term, which was at the core of our strategy, we knew the software had to deliver.

To make sure that it does, we listen carefully to the marketplace. Our game counselors are on the phones with consumers twenty hours a day, fielding more than 150,000 calls a week from our players. We offer guidance in playing the games, both in the fundamentals and in overcoming technical hurdles. We listen to what the players have to say about game ideas as well as their complaints about our products and we use this feedback to improve our product line, keeping it fresh and challenging (and, in turn, keeping players from getting bored). From our perspective, that's one of the best ways to protect against a deterioration in player interest and, ultimately, in product sales."

(4) Product Portfolio

As Nintendo strove to develop and maintain a product line that appealed to each of its target consumer segments, it eschewed the singular focus on hit games that preoccupied its predecessors in favor of a richer and broader range. Says Main:

> Our goal is to be an entertainment company that appeals to all segments of society. That means offering games like Duck Hunt for the youngest children and brainteasers like Tetris and Zelda for teenagers. But it also means selling Wheel of Fortune and Jeopardy, which don't sell anywhere near as well as the others. Why? Because Wheel of Fortune and Jeopardy are the entry point games for females aged twenty-five to forty-five and we want them to be Nintendo players.
>
> We've developed a full line of products for children and adults and our strategy requires that we stay at the leading edge in terms of product appeal. Sometimes, that means killing old titles before they go over the top of the bell curve.
>
> For example, our Ice Hockey game was a runaway success in 1987. But when Blades of Steel came out in 1988, it became the only game for all of those players attracted to that sport. We examined sales trends under a microscope and the information we got led us to kill Ice Hockey because it was on the way down. This kind of weeding out of the line can create anxiety among those retailers who haven't made their last sales of the product being replaced. They say "You're killing a product that's as strong as ever." But we know that's not true. Our research tells us that the retailers who say a declining

product is "as strong as ever" are acting on yesterday's news. We won't let that kind of stale data determine Nintendo's product portfolio. Our job is to show the retailers that optimizing the sale of each individual game is not as important as optimizing the sale of the Nintendo line of games.

By managing its product line strategically, Nintendo has also been able to extend the product lifecycle well beyond the industry average (figure 4.2). Why? Because carefully timed new game introductions, along with precisely planned phase-outs of older cartridges, help to sustain consumer interest and loyalty.

(5) Key Profit Drivers

A key to Nintendo's profitability is its success in helping retailers balance inventory and product demand by monitoring hardware

Figure 4.2   Nintendo Expanded the Product Lifecycle, Which Enhanced the Economics of the Business

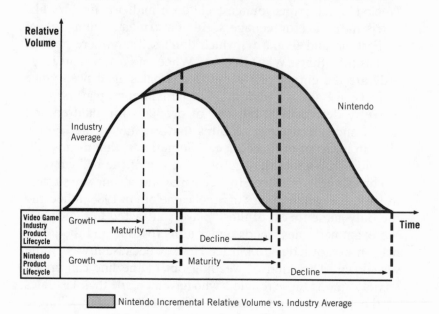

Nintendo Incremental Relative Volume vs. Industry Average

© Dunham & Marcus International, Inc., 1991.

and software sales with an eye toward stocking the shelves with the products consumers are demanding. As in the case of Ice Hockey, when the appeal of a game begins to decline and as others begin to soar in popularity, Nintendo identifies these trends and responds accordingly. Main states:

There's a science to this. At the beginning of every week, we examine the previous week's sell-through, which is the data showing precisely what the retailers sold by title during that seven-day period. By examining the sales trends of about 120 titles, we can see which products are strong and which are peaking. We can also gauge the impact of new titles on existing games. This gives us the input for making informed decisions on product supply.

Our goal in all of this is to see to it that the retailers have the appropriate amount of software to meet consumer demand. That doesn't mean stocking only the hottest-selling games. It means maintaining the ideal range of games to foster growth of the entire line.

Expense management is another of the company's profit drivers. To reduce the enormous expense of software development and thus to improve profit margins, Nintendo contracts with independent designers around the world to augment its internal development process. According to Main:

We use the services of sixty independent software licensees based in Canada, Australia, France, the United Kingdom, Russia, and the United States. One of our best-selling games, Tetris, was developed by a Russian, Alexy Pazhitov.

The designers bring us concepts for new games. At the earliest stages, these can range from the germ of an idea to a more elaborate storyboard treatment. We evaluate these proposals on a forty-point scale. If we like what we see, and if we are convinced that the creator has the financial ability to complete the project and bring it to market, we'll enter into a licensing agreement with him. Under this agreement, we manufacture the software in Kyoto and then sell it back to the developer for a predetermined price based on the cost of the memory chips in the cassette. He then undertakes full responsibility for marketing the game.

From concept to packaging, the upfront costs range from $150,000 to $300,000, all of which are borne by the independent producers. If a game is a total dud in the marketplace, Nintendo is spared the loss. When games succeed, an unusually high percentage of the revenues go directly to the bottom line.

In the case of Nintendo, the five fully integrated fundamentals of strategy are reflected in the day-to-day management of the business. For example, the robot ROB, used to establish the company's perceived competitive superiority, was also used as a critical device to attract its entry-level target segment, young children, who needed a tangible reason to return to video games. The daily monitoring of sell-through data (vital for managing the product portfolio configuration) is also a key profit driver. Throughout the worldwide Nintendo organization, there is a clear understanding of what the fundamentals of its Unique Value strategy are, and how they must be executed over the near and long term.

These five fundamentals of a Unique Value strategy were equally well defined and interrelated in the case of Seagram's cooler business, used throughout for consistency of illustration.

Seagram: A U.S. Leadership Strategy

Unlike Nintendo, Seagram was operating in what appeared to be a rapidly growing category with a number of apparently strong competitors. Seagram's goal in applying the five fundamentals was to build a superior business strategy that would cut through the clutter in the marketplace and would establish category leadership.

(1) Competitive Framework

When Seagram initiated a systematic analysis of the cooler market, the company identified a bewildering array of dynamic and well-financed competitors at the national level, as well as a number of regional players. Only California Coolers, Bartles & Jaymes, Sun Country and White Mountain had established a substantial market share on a national level. But regionally, a number of smaller brands, such as Steidl's and 20/20, were popular in local markets. California Coolers (the brand acquired from its entrepreneurial founders by Brown-Forman) and Bartles & Jaymes (the entry from the always formidable house of Gallo) were of the most concern to Seagram, with good reason. California Coolers, which pioneered the category, dominated nationwide sales and, as all signs indicated at the time, would only grow stronger backed by Brown-Forman's financial and marketing support.

Mark Taxel, executive vice-president of marketing for Seagram Beverage Company, remembers: "California Coolers took the beach heritage of the sixties as their theme. It was supposed to be the kind of product you mix up on the beach when the surf comes— a simple mix of fruit juice and wine."

As imposing as California Coolers appeared to be, rapidly growing Bartles & Jaymes represented an even greater threat. Gallo's superb wine distribution network and the efficiencies of its vertically integrated manufacturing system gave it the distribution and economic power to deliver Bartles & Jaymes cost efficiently to consumers across the country. Perhaps more ominously, Bartles & Jaymes had recognized the weakness of California Coolers' unsophisticated imagery and established a new price tier, with more attractive margins, which they called "premium coolers."

Recalls Taxel: "Bartles & Jaymes was a more sophisticated product than California Coolers. It had a unique flavor and relied on a sense of heritage as its theme. Bartles & Jaymes also had a famous, award-winning ad campaign with Frank and Ed, the two guys supposed to be a representative characterization of the American myth—garage to riches. It was very tongue in cheek."

(2) Market Target:

As Seagram assessed the competitive framework, it built on this knowledge to identify its target market.

Seagram's research segmented consumers into three distinct groups distinguished by behavioral and attitudinal characteristics (Figure 4.3).

1. *Contemporary segment:* Defined as young social drinkers (under thirty) who enjoyed and accepted coolers. From 1981 to 1985, this group drove cooler volume growth by responding to the beach party image projected by California Coolers.
2. *Transitional segment:* The next age bracket of consumers (thirty to forty-five) viewed coolers as a frivolous drink ac-

FIGURE 4.3 Wine Cooler Segmentation

1985 Behavioral Profile in Relation to Attitudinal Segmentation for Wine Cooler Users

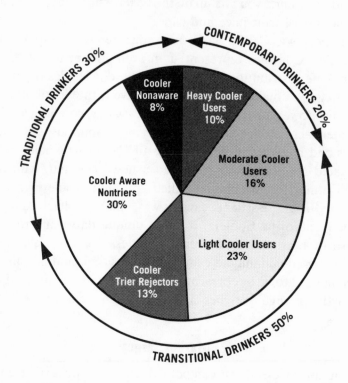

Source: Dunham & Marcus International, Inc., and Seagram Beverage Company Databases

ceptable for occasional use but regarded the beverage as unsophisticated and therefore unacceptable for most social occasions.
3. *Traditional segment:* Older consumers (over forty-five) who considered coolers socially unacceptable and therefore rejected them.

Seagram spent an intensive four months defining and understanding the segments it wanted to target, making sure that the product line, packaging, pricing and advertising appealed to the specific needs of those consumers and were perceived as uniquely superior to the competition. Through this analysis, Seagram identified a further benefit to entering the cooler category. Mark Taxel explains:

> The Seagram spirits customer is almost exclusively over thirty-five years old. The cooler customer is predominantly under thirty-five. So we had an opportunity to make the Seagram name relevant to participants in a dynamic new category, who ultimately might become consumers of our spirits brands. But we realized that this would only work if our coolers line was as premium as the image that our spirits maintained, which meant ensuring that we became not just a successful player in the cooler category—but the category leader.

(3) Basis for Perceived Competitive Superiority

Precisely because Seagram understood the competitive framework in which it was operating, and because it integrated this knowledge in identifying its target market, it was in a position to develop a product with specific features that would support premium pricing in the same tier as Gallo, but perceived by the targeted consumer segment as different and better. Research indicated that a sweeter taste and pulpy consistency were viewed by consumers as attributes of an unsophisticated drink. In response to this, Seagram's Golden was developed with a distinctive, less-sweet flavor and a clear, nonpulpy consistency to project a sophisticated, upscale image. To the trade and consumers at large, the Seagram name was already associated with a popular but premium-quality mixed drink—Seagram's 7&7. Says Taxel:

> We knew from our spirits business that beverage alcohol products with the greatest life span had the most relative sophistication in their respective categories. We determined that the competitions' products were perceived as "fun" only, which we believed was too similar to beer to provide a really new experience. Our fun-plus-sophistication strategy was the new twist, sufficient to carry margin, over time, which would give us the revenue to properly market the brand and deliver an attractive profit. The product, we felt, had to be seen not as a fad, but as a "real drink." To give it real drink credentials, we developed a product that had a complex, interesting taste. A bartender could not duplicate our formula by mixing wine and fruit.

While Seagram R&D was working to formulate a product and product line that were on strategy, Edgar Bronfman, Jr., was working with the advertising agency to execute a copy strategy that required a tone and manner of contemporary sophistication. Bronfman says:

> From the start, I thought Bruce Willis would be the ideal personality to launch the brand. But with that I ran into stiff resistance from our advertising agency account people, who believed strongly that a celebrity would deflect attention from the brand and for that reason we should go with an unknown actor. Well, we never had to split hairs over an advertising spokesperson before—that wasn't a critical factor for selling our spirits—so I deferred to their greater experience in these matters.
> Just weeks before our national sales meeting, when we would introduce our marketing strategy, including the ad campaign, I screened more than one hundred actors the agency had lined up to be our spokesperson—and I rejected them all. No question about it. From my perspective, they were all wrong.

With the deadline for the sales meeting approaching, I was in a state of near despair. That's when I told the agency, "Stop this nonsense. Get me Bruce Willis."

To which they replied, "Look, Edgar, we've been in contact with his agent and he won't do it. His acting career is just beginning to blossom and he doesn't want to jeopardize it by doing a commercial. It's not the money. He won't do it for a billion dollars."

I'd worked in Hollywood and I'd heard all of that before. So I said, "Call Willis's agent. Make him an offer he can't refuse and guarantee it for the next three years. And tell him he has until Monday at ten A.M. to get back to us." Well, we didn't have to wait that long because the deal was closed on Sunday.

It was a costly investment, but when we showed the first Willis tape to the salespeople and they went wild with enthusiasm, I knew the investment would pay off.

(4) Product Portfolio

Seagram's reentry strategy was tied to the premium image and specific appeal of its name. But the long-term health of the business required constant attention to related strategies and issues that would build the business and make it profitable after it had established its success with consumers. Initially, Seagram's Golden Wine Cooler, the most sophisticated product in the new line, was designed to establish the cooler category as a more sophisticated, adult experience, with Seagram at the top end.

"Originally, we wanted something that would be sophisticated and would appeal to upper-tier people who might drink a cooler carrying a name denoting a higher level of quality—a gold standard, if you will," says John Preston.

"Our initial market research indicated that we would achieve that upscale mystique by avoiding the use of specific product flavors. Which is why we developed Seagram's Golden."

But Seagram management came to realize that a sophisticated image alone would not be enough to build sales volume. So Seagram developed a unique product line that "changed the rules" of competition in the cooler category.

The original California Coolers had been conceived as a recipe of cheap wine and citrus flavoring. So competitors—including Seagram's original entry—also introduced citrus blends. Seagram came to recognize that to be distinct from less premium cooler brands, it needed to market flavors that complemented and reinforced its sophisticated credentials.

In its search for a better reformulated wine-and-fruit combination, Seagram's technical development department experimented with a high quality natural peach flavor, which the supplier, International Flavors and Fragrances, had developed for other successful alcoholic beverages. Peach Schnapps and the Fuzzy Navel (a trendy, sweet, mixed drink) had been recent big successes. The natural peach flavor was perceived as premium quality in both its imagery and its flavor profile, and therefore was a good fit with Seagram's new Golden Wine Cooler. So Seagram's Natural Peach Wine Cooler was introduced at the same time. All of this was accomplished in a record-breaking three months, driven by Edgar Bronfman, Jr.'s constant coaching.

In the first year, the new line, which included Seagram's Golden and Seagram's Natural Peach, achieved retail sales of $416 million compared with $163 million the previous year for Seagram's discontinued line. The analysis that followed confirmed that while Seagram's Golden had created the top of the line image, Natural Peach had driven a large part of the volume increase.

"We discovered that flavors were really propelling the business and that we could use flavor names without diminishing the product's premium credentials," Preston says. "So the next year we came up with Wild Berries followed by a series of premium quality fruit flavors."

Adds Mark Taxel: "Consumers were looking for a variety of flavors, and whoever had the most popular flavor of the year won market share."

This key dynamic of the marketplace was reflected in Seagram's evolving product portfolio, which included flavors that created news each season while simultaneously reinforcing the premium image.

This broader portfolio kept Seagram's products at the cutting edge of the cooler market.

(5) Key Profit Drivers

Success in the marketplace, with distributors and consumers, required constant creativity in every aspect of the business. But Seagram found that creativity was just as important when it came to translating growing volume into a solid business that could make money after the initial investment period.

Edgar Bronfman, Jr., had to demonstrate to corporate management that he could do more than create a marketing success out of a product that in its original form had been a failure for Seagram. Making the business profitable for the long term—the ultimate goal—would require learning skills that were new to executives who had grown up in the spirits business. To compound matters, the learning would have to be accomplished in the short time frame imposed by Seagram's corporate management. Recalls Mark Taxel:

> After we introduced the coolers, we realized that we weren't making enough money on them—the margins were simply lower than we thought they should be.
>
> So we assembled a group of people—R&D people, manufacturing people, purchasing people—and we said, "Look, we've gotten the product out, the business is going to run. Now we've got to see if we can make it more profitable." We said "Put together a list of every idea that can possibly take the cost out of this product. I don't want you to limit yourself to things that you think aren't going to affect quality. We're going to look at the quality issue later because we want you to generate a lot of ideas. Also indicate what you think the potential savings would be from them."
>
> We found some extraordinary ways to save money. For instance, we had always insisted that the seams in our four-pack carrier should be lined up exactly. But if we were willing to allow a 5 to 10 percent tolerance on that (without jeopardizing the stability of the carton or the quality of the printing in any way) we could save ten cents a case. By shrinking the

size of the labels by about a quarter inch, we could save another ten cents. And by making changes in the way we purchased flavors, we netted additional savings. The bottom line is that we extracted almost a dollar of cost per case, which at the volumes we were doing at the time (15 million to 18 million cases) proved to be a significant sum.

But cutting costs was more complicated than simply reducing the cost of dry goods, as the following anecdote from John Preston makes clear:

If you want to reduce costs, the largest component is the cost of glass. So what you have to do is find out if you can reduce the weight of the glass, within our safety and quality standards. The problem is that different weights of glass have different specs in terms of the amount of carbonation pressure (pounds per square inch) and torquing force they can withstand. Too much pressure on a weak glass surface will tear the neck right off. Now the bottles come down the line filled with carbonated beverage, and a machine, called a crowner, puts crowns on the bottles. The crowns are twisted on with a certain amount of torque. If the crowner applies too little torque, then the crown will only be halfway on, and you'll lose carbonation. If the crowner is too tight the torquing action will cause the neck of the bottle to break, and you will get what is called a "blowout" on the line. Now we don't have this problem in the whiskey business. So any change in glass thickness meant changing the mechanics of the bottling line as well, so as to meet the Seagram quality and safety standards.

In addition, when you lightweight the glass, you change the outside diameter of the bottle. This, in turn, alters the specifically engineered arms, guards and levers on the bottling line. Also, when you change the diameter of the bottle, you change the cell size of the carrier, which in turn changes the size of the carrier, which can ultimately affect the size of the carton in the truck. So a single change affects the entire system. But the benefits, too, are cumulative: weight, size, corrugated consumption, etc., all of which reduces our total cost.

By focusing on cost cutting while maintaining premium pricing, as well as quality and safety specifications, Seagram was successful in boosting the profitability of the cooler business. Taken individually, each economy measure may have had minimal impact on the bottom line. But collectively, they produced cost savings that significantly boosted net income and generated funds for reinvestment in marketing, manufacturing, product development and other areas that would strengthen Seagram's long-term competitive position and profitability.

Says John Preston: "This is a profitable business. A high cash return on investment continues to make this a viable business for us, and enables us to fund ongoing new product initiatives."

Much like Nintendo, Seagram employed the fundamentals of strategy in an iterative process, integrating the experience with each component and continuously refining and adjusting the others. For example, market research that helped to identify the critical consumer segments also revealed the importance of configuring the product portfolio to stay ahead of the competition on flavor distinctiveness.

The result of Seagram's finely honed strategy for its cooler business was an extraordinary rate of growth. Sales of Seagram coolers tripled from 1985 to 1986, and more than doubled again the following year (figure 4.4). The success of the cooler business was a surprise even to Seagram's management.

Mark Taxel recalls: "Our initial impetus to get into the cooler category was part of a business strategy for the Seagram Wine Company, which had been weak. The emerging wine cooler category seemed to be a business in which we could make money and use excess capacity and product. As it turns out, we ended up dropping the wine business and focusing all of our efforts on building a strong cooler brand."

Another quite different example of the precise definition of strategic fundamentals is that of a European corporation, headquartered in the United Kingdom, Bass PLC. A long-term strategic goal is to build a global corporate presence, from its base in the United Kingdom's traditional brewing business. Under pressure from the U.K. government, Bass's original business analysis was driven by

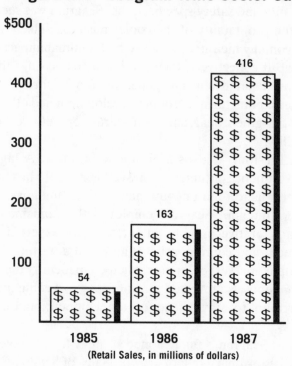

Figure 4.4   Seagram Wine Cooler Sales

(Retail Sales, in millions of dollars)

© Dunham & Marcus International, Inc., 1992.

a need to divest and diversify, but eventually led it to the strategic acquisition of Holiday Inn's worldwide chain of lodging houses.

Holiday Inn: A Global Acquisition and Investment Strategy

The U.K.-based Bass completed its purchase of Holiday Inn, the largest hotel chain in the world (with 1,600 properties and 326,000 rooms worldwide), in 1990. In the process, Bass acquired a company with valuable assets (Holiday Inn's name, locations and Holidex reservation system) but also a significant weakness: Due to poor service conditions at a growing number of its properties, the credentials of the Holiday Inn name had begun to deteriorate.

This decline in quality violated the founding concept underlying the company's leading position in the lodging industry. In the early 1950s, as Americans took to the roads in a postwar travel boom, they found an unappealing selection of available lodgings: At one end of the spectrum a small number of expensive luxury hotels were attractive but beyond their budgets. At the other end a hodge-podge of "mom and pop" properties were reasonably priced but of third-rate quality and questionable safety.

Entrepreneur Kemmon Wilson recognized the opportunity for a chain of moderately priced motels offering a consistently high level of quality service, cleanliness and security. With this in mind, Wilson built the first Holiday Inn in Memphis, Tennessee, in 1952. According to Bass, "Standardized features such as private baths, air conditioning and telephones, coupled with consistently reasonable rates, caused Holiday Inns to grow quickly and to set a standard for the industry against which other motels were judged."[1]

The Holiday Inn juggernaut continued until the mid-1980s when the chain's image and its sales declined. Industry analysts questioned the future growth potential of the Holiday chain.

At this juncture, Bass was having difficulties of its own. Not financial difficulties—the company posted record sales and profits in the 1980s—but regulatory difficulties. In 1989, the U.K. Department of Trade and Industry (DTI) established regulations to reduce potential monopoly positions of companies in beer-brewing and retailing through the ownership of British public houses ("pubs"). With a leading position in the U.K. brewing industry and a national chain of pubs, Bass was forced to restructure its businesses to comply with DTI orders. Bass would have to reduce its presence in one or both industries.

Bass's approach to structuring its future business portfolio was to analyze (using the wealth of detailed data available from operating units) which combination of businesses would optimize shareholder value.

In the words of Ian Prosser, chairman and CEO of Bass PLC:

What we did was to examine the company's divisional plans and cash flows, look at the best and worst case scenarios, factor in the likelihood of each scenario occurring, and then ask: What are the shareholder values of taking different routes? What are the shareholder values of not taking different routes? What are the shareholder values for different arrays or combinations of scenarios?

These analyses, in conjunction with a careful assessment of Bass's particular combination of corporate skills and experience, eventually resulted in a corporate strategy which led to the identification of Holiday Inn as a prime prospect for acquisition.

Bass had previous experience in the lodging industry, as it had managed U.K.-based Crest Hotels since 1969. More recently, Bass acquired Holiday Inn's international business (182 hotels) in 1987 and 1988. Using that acquisition as a stepping stone, and leveraging the financial resources made available from scaling back its British pub business, Bass purchased Holiday Inn's North American operations (1,440 hotels) in February 1990. At a stroke, Bass owned the largest hotel chain in the world.

Why the plunge into hotels? Prosser says,

We believed that we could run large organizations much more effectively than we perceived them as being run. When we looked at Holiday Inn, we found areas where we thought we could substantially improve the management of the business to increase profitability.

We identified specific ways in which our corporate skills would add value to Holiday Inn's operations. One was our ability to run large organizations efficiently. We are also skilled at managing information technology, and felt we could complement Holiday Inn's advanced reservation systems technology. It is not widely known that when Barcrest converted its amusement machines in the mid-seventies, Bass was already, for a period, the largest purchaser of microprocessors. We felt that with our organizational skills, property management skills, technology skills, and of course the marketing and branding skills we learned from our brewing business, we could add significant value to Holiday Inn.

To put more focus on its new acquisition, Bass sold most of the Crest Hotels chain, but retained several properties for conversion to Holiday Inns. A detailed business plan was then developed to revitalize Holiday Inn's growth as a global business.

(1) Competitive Framework

Bass classified its competitors by geographical reach, defining them as global chains, regional chains or individual hotels. Industry consolidation was producing a number of rapidly expanding competitors in the United States. Choice Hotels International (which manages Quality Inn, Comfort Inn, Clarion Hotels, Sleep Inn, Rodeway Inn, Econo Lodge and Friendship Inn) and Hospitality Franchise Systems (which owns Ramada and Howard Johnson), emerged as threats to Holiday Inn's dominance in the U.S. along with Best Western. But Bass determined that none of these chains was positioned to challenge Holiday Inn globally. "There are really only two global brands in the hotel business, one of which is Holiday Inn," says Bryan Langton, chairman and CEO of Holiday Inn Worldwide. "None of the other players are big on a global scale, which gives us a competitive advantage overseas."

(2) Market Target

The lodging-house market can also be subdivided by price into three broad segments: upscale, moderate and economy. Bass set its sights on all three segments, appealing to business and leisure travelers through a mix of properties designed to cater to guests with various budgets, needs and levels of sophistication.

Bass understood its customers well from its prior operating experience. For example, its people knew that there were common requirements among customers at every price point: They expected a quality product which is clean and secure with good service. According to Langton, these are primary benefits which must be delivered to all travelers: "What our customers expect is for quality rooms to be clean and fresh, for the locations and premises to be safe, and for our staff to provide quality service. Our challenge is to meet those expectations when they arrive and throughout their stay with us."

(3) Basis for Perceived Competitive Superiority

Bass identified three factors with the potential to grow Holiday Inn's franchise:

(1)   Consistent, superior delivery of the primary industry benefits of quality, cleanliness, security and service.
(2)   Global branding.
(3)   Worldwide reservation systems.

Bass management set Holiday Inn the goal of establishing competitive superiority in each of these key areas. As a result, the management of Holiday Inn developed a comprehensive plan, encompassing a broad array of investment programs. For example, to address service standards, Bass planned to intensify efforts, through training and capital investment, to deliver the key consumer benefits of quality, cleanliness, security and service. Weak areas, such as the poor caliber of service in the European hotels, were targeted for special attention. Says Langton:

> As soon as we took control of Holiday Inn, we started to demand a higher degree of customer service from everyone. We reminded all of our people that we are in the hospitality business and that top service is critical to our success. Because customers' requirements are becoming more demanding, we had to intensify our training efforts with our employees and our franchises. The ultimate goal is to live up to the highest expectations our customers have for our properties.

To support these efforts, Bass planned to invest $1 billion over a three-year period to expand and upgrade the Holiday Inn system.

In terms of global branding, Ian Prosser and Bass management felt strongly that the travel industry was one of the primary industries in which global branding can be a unique competitive

advantage. "Global branding is absolutely essential for hotels because of the continuing increase in travel between countries," he
says. "Regional lodging companies that fail to tie into this worldwide movement will miss out on the great growth surge in international travel in the 1990s and beyond."

Bass's analysis indicated that few competitors have the credentials of a global brand with the potential to rival Holiday Inn. Also
encouraging from Bass's perspective, was that Holiday Inn had
maintained brand strength on a global basis. "When we bought
Holiday Inn, we relied on the power of the Holiday Inn brand,"
says Prosser.

The third key opportunity for competitive superiority from the
perspective of key customer segments and distributors (travel
agents) was in the worldwide reservations systems, represented by
the proprietary state-of-the-art Holidex system, which was already
processing 26 million reservations per year. Through a satellite-
based computer network, the system could receive and instantly
confirm reservation requests entered on terminals at all Holiday
Inn hotels and reservation centers as well as on terminals in major
corporations and airlines.

(4) Product Portfolio

To target consumers in every segment, Bass developed line exten-
sions to leverage Holiday Inn's brand name across price points and
geographical markets. While Holiday Inn had dominated the mid-
market segment for years, Bass continued to expand into the upscale market with Holiday Inn Crowne Plaza hotels, and by extending the brand into the upper end of the economy segment with
the Holiday Inn Express line. In Europe, the role of Holiday Inn
Garden Court was to strengthen the chain's position in the upper
end of the economy segment (figure 4.5).

In developing Holiday Inn's branded portfolio, Bass planned to
leverage its significant economies of scale by participating in the
important segments of the market with one global megabrand. The
strategy reversed the approach of prior management, which created
new brand names—Embassy Suites, Homewood Suites and Hamp-

FIGURE 4.5. HOLIDAY INN PRODUCT RANGE

PRODUCT LINE	PRICE POINT	LOCATION
Holiday Inn	Moderate	Global
Holiday Inn Crowne Plaza	Upscale	Global
Holiday Inn Garden Court	Economy	Europe
Holiday Inn Express	Economy	U.S.A.

ton Inn—to enter new market segments. Bass's use of the Holiday Inn name was part of the strategy to invest in a brand-driven global business, supported by global technology.

(5) Key Profit Drivers

The role of a strong global brand was central to the financial advantage to be gained by significant economies of scale. But there were also margin advantages. For example, the Garden Court line extension was launched under the Holiday Inn name once Bass management had established the power of its credentials in Europe, which supported higher room rates and occupancy levels, especially compared with the chain's North American properties.[3] Two of Bass's other corporate strengths—its financial controls and its expertise in managing large organizations—were also applied to improving Holiday Inn's profitability.

"Controls throughout the entire financial area are a great strength of Bass and we use this internal discipline to make certain that all of our operations are in sync with our overall goals," Langton says. "In this context, all business or strategic options are evaluated from the viewpoint of shareholder value. For us to make a major move, the potential for that value must be there."

The benefits of Bass's expertise at managing large organizations became apparent immediately.

"In our brewing and pub operations, we were able to squeeze an enormous amount of cash flow and profitability out of businesses that were working within the dynamics of a static market," says Prosser. "Similarly, when we bought Holiday Inn, we immediately stripped out three layers of management and started to refocus the business."

Critical to the success of its cohesive worldwide strategy for Holiday Inn is Bass's ability to motivate its employees.

"Market share, global branding, financial controls—all of these elements are critical to profitability. But equally important is the ability to train and motivate people," Prosser says. "Because in the lodging industry, if you can properly motivate your people—which is something we are very good at—the rest of the factors eventually fall into place."

CHAPTER 5

ACTION WITHOUT STRATEGY

—— • ——

IBM: The Need to Learn a New Set of Fundamentals

In 1955, *Time* magazine published a cover story heralding the dawn of the second industrial revolution, one that would be led by spectacular advances in electronics, specifically the emerging field of computerization. For its cover, *Time* chose a portrait of IBM's Thomas Watson, Jr., with the headline: "Clink. Clank. Think." *Time*'s message, in a nutshell, was that computers would soon change the world, and that IBM would be in the vanguard of that change.

The prediction turned out to be prescient, with IBM proceeding to dominate the computer industry over the next three decades. Fueled by the extraordinary success of its mainframe unit, including the legendary System/360, a standard at corporations worldwide, IBM's sales and profits exploded, soaring from $1 billion in 1957 to $26 billion by 1980.

Given its preoccupation with mainframe technology, IBM was slow to enter the personal computer market pioneered by Apple. But as Big Blue reluctantly accepted the significance of Apple's success, a team of IBM executives engineered a belated entry into personal computing and, to their surprise, established the IBM PC as the standard for office use.

Seeking to capitalize on its unexpected success, but understanding very little about the market it had entered, IBM then set its sights on the personal market, where Apple, the market leader, had focused from the beginning. Launching what it thought was a direct assault on Apple's turf, in 1984 IBM introduced the PC Jr., a unit smaller and lower in cost than the PC, but semicompatible with it. Considering IBM's history of dominating its chosen markets and preempting its opponents, news that the PC Jr. was being launched took a toll on the stock of IBM's competitors, with their shares falling an average of 7 percent the day the new unit was announced.

But Wall Street's anticipation of another product winner—anticipation based in part on IBM's bold and optimistic projections for its follow-up entry into the personal computer market, code-named "Peanut"—proved to be unfounded. Instead of first-year sales of a half million PC Jr.'s, which the company had predicted, the product's major impact was to alienate all of IBM's key constituencies, including the users it was intended for.

In spite of heavy discounting designed to achieve something close to its original sales projection, IBM was hard pressed to come within 50 percent of that figure. By year-end 1984, sales totaled 240,000 units,[1] representing an anemic 5 percent of computers being used in homes instead of offices, which was how IBM had defined the market. During the same period, Apple—IBM's chief competitor—continued to bolster its position as the market leader, shipping a record 750,000 units of its IIe and IIc models, an enormous gain of 30 percent over the previous year.

Despite widespread predictions by computer analysts and the trade press that the PC Jr. would take the home market by storm and become the industry standard, the model flopped so badly that it was discontinued a brief fifteen months after its introduction.

How could IBM, with all its resources and sophistication, let this happen? Why was IBM—which had achieved repeated success in every business computer segment (mainframes, midrange systems, office PCs)—unable to establish itself in the home computer market? The answer was simply that IBM had no framework for strategy, much less an understanding of the issues that would be relevant to developing one. In the case of the PC Jr., the fundamentals of strategy were flouted in every respect.

(1) Competitive Framework

At the outset, IBM had made an accurate assessment of the home computer market's competitive framework, dividing that market into two major groups: In the upscale segment, the business unit identified Apple as its primary competitor; in the more fragmented mass market segment, IBM identified its key competitors as Commodore, Coleco, Atari, Timex and Radio Shack.

But markets are dynamic, not static, and IBM failed to recognize a number of key competitive moves that would redefine the category and directly impact the PC Jr.'s relative position.

Apple made two strategic pricing-related decisions that stole publicity from the PC Jr. and prevented it from gaining significant market share. On the heels of the PC Jr.'s introduction, Apple unveiled its $1,300 IIc, a smaller but more powerful version of its popular IIe. Then, when IBM began discounting the PC Jr. in an attempt to buy market share, Apple matched IBM's price cuts by slashing prices on the IIe to below $1,000. In response to the PC Jr.'s $40 million advertising campaign, Apple more than doubled its spending to promote the IIc and IIe from $14.1 million in 1983 to $29.1 million in 1984.[2] What's more, competitors at the low end of the market—such as Commodore, Coleco and Atari—continued to "change the rules" by introducing new products that were superior to earlier entry-level home computers, but were still priced below the basic PC Jr.

(2) Market Target

IBM studied the dynamics of the home computer market, breaking it into two segments: an upscale-customer segment (that would spend more than $1,000 for a home computer) and a mass-customer segment (that purchased units priced less than $1,000).

But IBM appeared not to understand that there was more involved than dollars and cents. IBM did not recognize precisely how the requirements of consumers in the mass and upscale segments differed from each other and from those of consumers buying PCs for business use (figure 5.1). In fact:

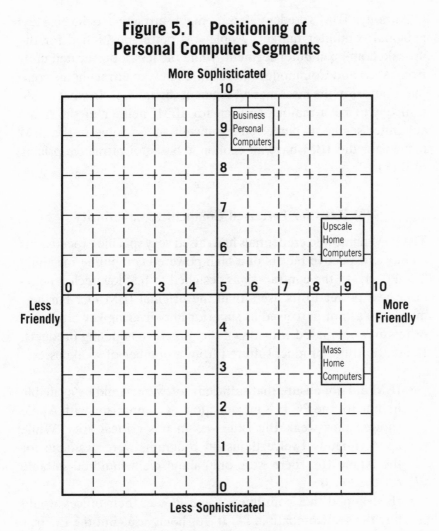

Figure 5.1 Positioning of Personal Computer Segments

Source: Dunham & Marcus International, Inc., Database.

© Dunham & Marcus International, Inc., 1992.

- Upscale consumers of home computers wanted increased user-friendliness with a minimal sacrifice of sophistication.
- Home computer buyers in the mass market segment also valued user-friendliness but looked unfavorably on machines that they perceived as too "complicated."

Although IBM's credentials were highly attractive to the business personal computer market, Apple was better positioned for the upscale home computer segment, while the less sophisticated units from Atari and Commodore were more likely to attract home computer buyers in the mass market segment (figure 5.2). In what would turn out to be a major handicap for IBM, neither of the home computer segments perceived significant added value in the IBM name, nor did IBM have an economic basis for attractive pricing to them.

(3) Basis for Perceived Competitive Superiority

The IBM name and credentials had raised very specific expectations among prospective buyers of a high-powered computing machine. The PC Jr., to the contrary, was designed to be "low-tech," delivering less power to its users than the original IBM PC. Furthermore, it was not perceived as superior in delivering key attributes or features compared with any of the directly competing products. In addition, the product suffered from a number of weaknesses:

- IBM did not ensure that sufficient software would be available in time for the PC Jr.'s introduction. A comparison with Apple showed how weak Big Blue was in this critical area. While approximately twelve thousand programs were available for the Apple IIe, there were only about eight hundred suitable for the PC Jr.[3]
- IBM hoped that consumers using PCs in their offices would buy the semicompatible PC Jr. for home use. But the PC Jr.'s limited memory prevented it from running much of the standard PC's popular business software, including Lotus 1-2-3 and dBASE II.

Figure 5.2 Customer Perception of Personal Computer Market

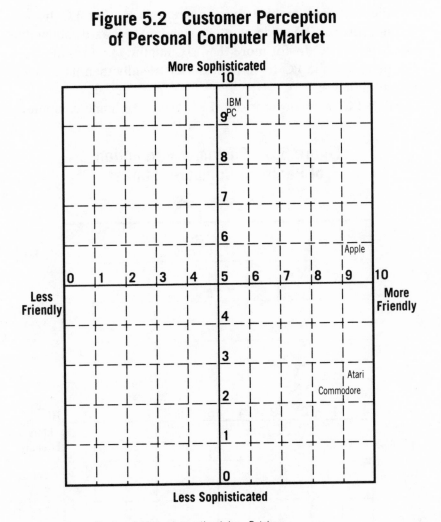

Source: Dunham & Marcus International, Inc., Database.

© Dunham & Marcus International Inc., 1992.

- The PC Jr.'s rubber keyboard (derided by analysts, the media and loyal IBM customers as the "Chicklet keyboard") proved to be more difficult to use than the standard typewriter-style keyboards found on competing home computers. IBM had created the gold standard keyboard with its Selectric typewriter and now had failed to deliver that standard. Although the keyboard problem was apparent soon after PC Jr. was introduced, IBM did not offer a standard keyboard compatible with the PC Jr. for more than six months. As a result, users perceived the PC Jr. to be less user-friendly than its competitors (figure 5.3).

• The PC Jr. was overpriced. Less expensive home computers,

Figure 5.3 Customer Perception
of Personal Computer Market

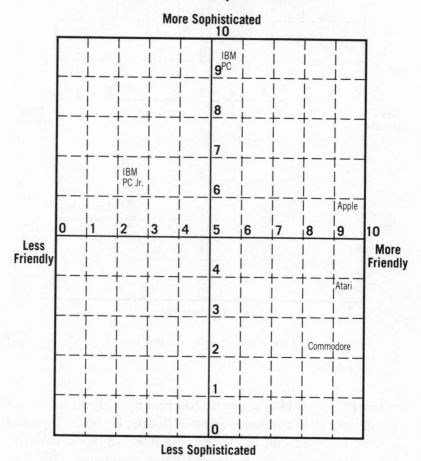

Source: Dunham & Marcus International, Inc., Database.

© Dunham & Marcus International, Inc., 1992.

such as the Commodore 64 ($600) and Coleco's Adam ($750), matched the star-crossed IBM unit in power and capabilities (and in some cases surpassed it in terms of standard features). Contrary to IBM's expectations, the PC Jr.'s limited compatibility with the standard PC was not deemed to be of sufficient benefit to warrant its higher price tag.

(4) Product Portfolio

In an effort to appeal to each segment of the home computer market, IBM sold two versions of the PC Jr.: An upscale model, featuring 128K of memory plus a disk drive, priced at $1,300; and a mass market version, featuring 64K of memory and no disk drive, priced at $700. But neither model met the specific requirements of its target segment.

To compound IBM's problems, consumers were turned off by Big Blue's "à la carte" approach to selling the PC Jr., which treated components such as tape storage units and power cords as options, requiring additional payment. Prospective buyers comparing home computers in the market found that IBM's competitors often included these and other attractive components with their units. For example, Coleco's Adam came equipped with a tape drive and a letter-quality printer for a list price of $750.

(5) Key Profit Drivers

Historically, IBM's profitability had been driven by its installed base of customers to whom it marketed upgrades and new products. While it protected its customers' investments, it also charged premium prices based on its established position, perceived service capabilities and unique user support system. The motto "IBM means service" was a pervasive part of IBM's culture—the heart of its Unique Value strategy for mainframes. In many complex ways, such as its service contracts, personal relationships, education programs, and approach to new products initiatives, IBM locked up its customer base to drive profitability and unit growth throughout its period of dominance.

Tom Watson, Jr., speaking about the early days of IBM computing, remembered when one of the company's first units was coming in over budget and would have to be leased to customers at a far higher cost than the original quotes.

It turned out that the price we'd been quoting to customers was too low—by half. The machine we thought would cost $8,000 a month was actually going to cost somewhere between $12,000 and $18,000. We had no choice but to go around and let the customers know. To my total amazement, we managed to hang on to as many orders as we'd started with. That's when I felt a real Eureka! Clearly, we'd tapped a new and powerful source of demand. Customers wanted computers so badly that we could double the price and still not drive people away.[4]

This kind of thinking, which became endemic to the IBM culture, would prove to be disastrous in PCs and, later, in mainframes. As an early warning of things to come, the PC Jr.'s sales were driven by discounting, in part because customer service was not one of the category's primary drivers. Indeed, IBM relied on its dealer network to reach all PC customers. Before rebates offered in late 1984 lowered the price of the PC Jr.'s top model to below $1,000, only thirty thousand of the units were sold. Although sales picked up under the rebate program, activity dropped substantially once the rebates were discontinued in 1985 (figure 5.4).

Because IBM was unable to charge premium prices for the PC Jr., it was unable to capture the incremental revenue that had traditionally driven its profitability or the loyal customer base that was tied to IBM through systems and service dependence. Moreover, IBM could not sustain heavy discounting because it was not a low-cost producer in the home computer segment. According to industry analysts, IBM's PC Jr. production cost of $375 per unit was double the cost of Apple's IIc.[5]

IBM's strategy for the PC Jr. was incoherent because there was, in the IBM corporation, no framework for dealing with the five fundamentals in an integrated way. For example, a key profit driver

Figure 5.4   PC Jr. Market Share

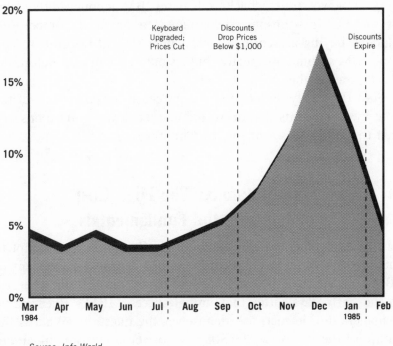

Source: *Info World*

© Dunham & Marcus International, Inc., 1991.

in a cyclical category is the ability to exploit seasonal buying patterns. For home computers, Christmas is the pivotal season, accounting for 40 percent of sales. But IBM mistimed the introduction
of the PC Jr., unveiling it just after Christmas without understanding the significance.

Managers at IBM were taught to assume that the market would
continue to take its lead from IBM. When managers realized they
would not have sufficient stock to meet projected demand for the
1983 Christmas selling season, the company postponed the product
introduction until January 1984. Expecting to put a crimp in its
competitors' Christmas sales, IBM announced in November 1983
that the PC Jr. would not be available until the following January.
Based on its experience with mainframes, the corporation believed
prospective customers would be inclined to put off their purchase

decisions until they could compare competing models with the IBM entry. But the home computer market was not tied to IBM, and the company's strategy backfired. After IBM announced the delay of the PC Jr., consumers continued to purchase competitors' models, buying a record 110,000 Apple IIe's in December. This took IBM's prime prospective buyers out of the market before the PC Jr. was on the shelves.[6]

Had IBM fully understood the purchase considerations of the consumer segments that drove the market, it would have ensured that the PC Jr. was available by Christmas.

Sony Betamax: The High Cost of Ignoring the Fundamentals

The well-documented case of the Sony Corporation's attempt to market its videocassette recorder is one Japanese equivalent of IBM's ignorance in the early stages of the PC market. But whereas, in the early days, after their initial success, IBM's Boca Raton managers did, in fact, ask themselves the question "What is the future of the PC market?"[7] Sony was driven exclusively by an engineering focus. An understanding of the interrelationship of the five fundamentals of strategy would have protected Sony's management from the permanent loss of a valuable market as well as the humiliation of its costly strategic defeat.

Sony (initially the Tokyo Telecommunications Engineering Company and renamed for the Latin word for "sound" [sonus] by its founders Masuru Ibuka and Akio Morita) had its first major success in the American market with miniaturized consumer radios and other electronics built around Western Electric's transistor technology. Their first portable TV was introduced to the American market, with the help of advertising agency Doyle Dane Bernbach, as "Tummy TV." Sony then set the standard for color television with picture tube technology, under the brand name Trinitron.

Sony was an early leader in VCR development, with Ampex and Philips. With its focus on the American consumer electronics market, and its miniaturization technology, it achieved the introduction of the first Japanese consumer video recorder with the Betamax in 1975. Two years later, rival Matsushita introduced a competing system, VHS.

Through cross-licensing agreements, Sony and Matsushita had access to each other's VCR technology. Therefore, each company was capable of manufacturing both Beta and VHS machines. Recognizing the power of standardization, each company tried to persuade the other to adopt its format to create a single VCR standard. But Matsushita was convinced that VHS (which was capable of a longer playing time) was the superior format, while Sony was committed to its technology because it stored information on a tape more efficiently, with the advantage of a smaller cassette. Without the benefit of hindsight, there is no right or wrong answer, although it may be argued that Matsushita was closer to strategic fundamentals. But in both cases, the focus was on marketing a technology, not implementing a strategy. Sony lost the advantage of being first to market and was subsequently routed by Matsushita. Matsushita had captured two-thirds of the market by 1980. Whereas in 1976, every home-use VCR carried the Sony name, by 1983, Sony's share of the U.S. market had dropped to 7 percent.[8]

In terms of the five fundamentals, what went wrong?

(1) Competitive Framework

Sony's primary competitive threat was from Matsushita, but it was a formidable one. The opportunity for Sony was to achieve market dominance with significant penetration before Matsushita entered. But Sony failed to leverage its two-year lead over Matsushita and establish Betamax as the standard VCR format while erecting barriers to entry for future players. Matsushita, on the other hand, had a strategy to ensure that VHS would become the market standard. For example, to grow VHS market share at the expense of Betamax, Matsushita moved quickly to bind major electronics companies to its format by signing up RCA, GE, Magnavox, Sylvania and Mitsubishi to market VHS units under their own brand names (in addition to Matsushita's own Panasonic, Quasar and JVC brands).

Failing to define the nature of Matsushita's threat, in addition to the importance of a standard format, Sony was slow to enlist other manufacturers to market its Betamax machines.

With RCA's guidance, Matsushita identified the consumer requirements that drove the VCR market and designed its VHS units to deliver the category's key benefits. For example, RCA understood that consumers would place a high premium on the longest available playing time per cassette, and thus based its decision to choose VHS's four-hour format over Betamax's two-hour maximum.[9]

Recognizing that VCR sales would be stimulated if per unit prices fell below the $1,000 threshold, Matsushita and RCA priced their entry-level units at $995. Guided by the experienced U.S. marketer, Matsushita made the strategic commitment to grow market share at the expense of short-term profits.

Sony had inadvertently set the stage for Matsushita's success. Having invested $300 to $400 in advertising for each Betamax sold between 1975 and 1977, Sony created awareness and demand for the category—a demand Matsushita would be the first to tap when it priced models below $1,000.[10]

Matsushita fully understood the strategic advantage it had achieved, and as Sony made improvements in its Betamax units, Matsushita matched or exceeded them. When Sony announced a four-and-a-half- to five-hour Betamax cassette, Matsushita responded with a six-hour VHS model. As Sony added "speed search" and other features, Matsushita's units were similarly equipped.

(2) Market Target

Traditionally, much of Sony's success stemmed from its ability to transfer technology to products that created needs in the marketplace, rather than developing products to meet identified consumer needs. Because Ibuka maintained that consumers have difficulty visualizing products that do not yet exist, Sony discounted the idea of using market research in the development of new products.[11]

The lack of such research for the Betamax led to the company's failure to identify the key features consumers sought in home VCRs: video quality, cassette recording and playing time, software availability, compatibility and price. On the basis of its experience with television, Sony management was aware of the importance of video quality and price, but it clearly underestimated the impact the other factors had on consumers' purchasing decisions.

Because of its historical preoccupation with miniaturization, Sony made reducing size the primary focus of its engineering efforts as it developed the Betamax. This management directive had nothing to do with the requirements of the consumers to whom the product would be targeted. Ibuka intuitively felt that size would be critical to the product's success. According to Morita, "When Ibuka was first describing his idea for the Betamax videocassette, he gave the engineers a paperback book and said, 'Make it this size.' Those were his only instructions."[12]

(3) Basis for Perceived Competitive Superiority

Sony had made the decision to stay with the Betamax format for benefits such as more efficient information storage and smaller cassettes, which were not primary consumer benefits. In the delivery of many of the real consumer benefits, VHS was stronger:

- Video quality: The two technologies were equal, so this was not a factor in purchasing decisions.
- Playing time: VHS cassettes had double the playing time of Betamax (four hours versus the latter's two). This proved to be important to consumers, whose primary use for a VCR would be recording and viewing full-length movies.
- Software availability: As videotape rental and sales outlets proliferated, they gravitated toward VHS cassettes, which consumers appeared to favor. Recognizing this trend, retail outlets continued to reduce their inventories of Beta cassettes, which diminished demand for Betamax players. Sony underestimated the role of software in making VCRs valuable to consumers.
- Compatibility: When VHS gained the dominant share position, an even greater number of consumers purchased VHS

units for the benefit of exchanging cassettes with friends, who
were more likely to have the increasingly popular VHS units
as well. While generally recognizing the importance of standardization, Sony still assumed that the market would support
two incompatible VCR formats.

- Price: Betamax's high price deterred many consumers from
  purchasing VCRs until they became more affordable. When
  Matsushita introduced the lower-priced VHS, much of this
  pent-up consumer demand was released in its favor. Although
  Sony was known for producing high-quality, leading-edge
  products, consumers had little reason to pay a premium for
  the Sony name in the VCR market.

What of Betamax's smaller cassette size, which Ibuka valued so
highly? It was irrelevant to consumers.

(4) Product Portfolio

Matsushita's licensing of VHS technology to other manufacturers
was critical to its success. In essence, Matsushita created a portfolio
of businesses and brands to maximize the appeal and availability
of VHS units. The result was a proliferation of VHS models and
subsequent market penetration that ensured that the format became the industry standard. Sony's approach—marketing units
under a limited number of brand names—restricted the availability
of Betamax models.

In terms of market segmentation, the product lines offered by
Sony and Matsushita were nearly identical. When VCRs were first
introduced, there was little variation in price or level of equipment.
As more elaborate, feature-laden models were developed, Sony
and Matsushita tended to match each other in the full range of
models and price points.

The short-term results of Sony's mismanagement of the VCR market in the United States were immediately evident. As category
volume soared from 1979 to 1986, sales of Sony's VCRs remained
depressed (figure 5.5). Over the long term, Sony became a minor
player in the U.S. VCR market (figure 5.6).

Figure 5.5 U.S. VCR Sales 1975–1986

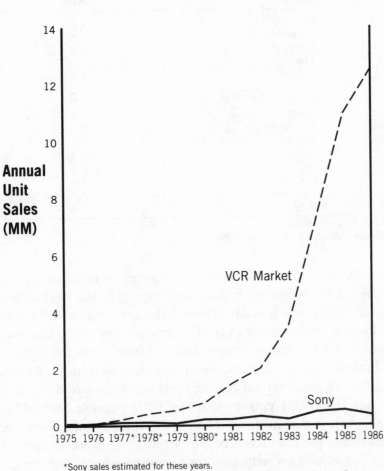

Sony sales estimated for these years.
Sources: Electronic Industries Association; Harvard Business School; *Fortune.*

But the loss was greater than the company's poor performance in the VCR category. The failure of Betamax, coupled with Sony's continued insistence that the product would succeed, eroded Sony's credibility among electronics manufacturers, who failed to follow Sony's lead for the next generation of video technology.

In the early 1980s, Sony introduced the 8-mm videocassette format, which allowed for the development of more compact camcorders and players without sacrificing picture quality or playing

FIGURE 5.6. VCR MARKET SHARE 1989

RANK	BRAND	SHARE
1	RCA	11.0%
2	Panasonic	8.5
3	Emerson	8.0
4	Sharp	7.0
5	Magnavox	6.6
6	GE	5.0
6	Sears	5.0
8	Zenith	4.5
9	Mitsubishi	4.0
10	Toshiba	3.9
11	Fisher	3.3
12	JVC	3.2
13	Goldstar	3.0
14	Samsung	2.7
15	Sony	2.3

Source: Warren Publishing.
©Dunham & Marcus International, Inc., 1992.

time. At first, Matsushita and other Japanese companies appeared to be falling in line with the 8-mm format as the next industry standard. But when rivals achieved the same results with a new VHS-compatible format (VHS-C, introduced in 1986), Matsushita and other VHS manufacturers defected from 8-mm to VHS-C.[13]

In time, Sony has learned the strategic lessons from the Betamax debacle. Its 8-mm format became the leader in the world camcorder market (with a 51 percent share in 1991) because Sony did not repeat two critical mistakes it had made with Betamax. Sony could understand the key drivers of the category, which were camcorder size in conjunction with cassette recording length, and designed the 8-mm with those considerations in mind. As a result, the 8-mm format is comparable in size to VHS-C, but has four times the playing time. Sony also licensed its technology to more than one hundred manufacturers with the specific goal of making 8-mm the industry standard.[14]

(5) Key Profit Drivers

Sony's failure to respond to Matsushita's lower-price policy was partly driven by the corporation's significantly higher cost structure, which was primarily a function of manufacturing costs. When Sony reduced its price to $1,100, its machines still remained at the high end of the price curve—above the psychological barrier of $1,000.

But Sony's pricing strategy was not only a function of profit performance considerations. Sony's corporate philosophy, defined by Ibuka, emphasized the development of unique products from in-house technology over the alternative goals of maximizing financial performance and enhancing shareholder value.[15] "The key to success for Sony," Ibuka said, "and to everything in business, science and technology for that matter, is never to follow the others."[16] This philosophy had guided Sony in the successful development of technological innovations over the years. In a different time and place, had constituted a Unique Value strategy that drove the corporation's business at a time when the openness of American markets, the potential of miniaturization and the lack of direct competitors with comparable products made such a strategy highly opportune. But times had changed. In this case it prevented the company from conceding that Betamax had a flawed strategy and that the product should be terminated to allow corporate resources to be reallocated. Instead, Sony continued to support Betamax, even after 1982, when VHS controlled three-quarters of the world market. Sony would not market VHS models, which it had the technology and capability to produce, until 1988, when it capitulated and joined the VHS mainstream.

CHAPTER 6

HOW TO DEVELOP A UNIQUE VALUE STRATEGY: THE QUESTIONS TO ASK ABOUT YOUR BUSINESS

———— ● ————

When a Unique Value strategy which fully integrates the five fundamentals is in place, it is the framework for managing a business in a coherent, focused way that puts all available resources to their most productive use. Once articulated and translated into the business plan, it enables managers to establish clear and measurable criteria for evaluating the success of the strategy and keeping the business on its strategic track through an array of monitoring mechanisms. It also provides a guide for strategic reinvestment in market share building, operations, training and technology, which will enhance the value of the business and its competitive position.

A Unique Value strategy articulates a business's unique combination of strengths and precisely defines the ways in which they will be leveraged for sustainable growth. Once articulated, it is a roadmap to guide the team responsible for implementation. It is also a training and teaching tool, because the articulation of a Unique Value strategy requires that the business, in all its aspects, be fully understood.

The process of framing a Unique Value strategy, in preparation for its articulation, is an iterative sequence of hypothesis formulation, testing and refinement. Within the process, systematic analyses take place—the Unique Value = ROI (Return on Investment) Model. The Model sets up discrete analytic areas, with the required analyses in each area, reflecting both internal and external perspectives. The learning process is a function of the questions that are asked, and eventually answered, in a process that provides for the integration of all aspects of the business.

For multinational corporations who are managing an array of businesses, each with different characteristics and drivers, it will become essential for corporate management to raise the standard of strategy development at the business-unit level and to standardize strategy recommendations so that the quality of thinking can be evaluated and the likely outcome of a proposed strategy can be discussed objectively. In the healthy enterprises of the future, risks and rewards will be the subject of constructive dialogues between corporate and business-unit management.

Developing technologies make it possible to translate many of the key aspects of a strategy into performance measurements. When performance measures are in place for the total business, corporate management can run a reality check on the quality of market planning, operations, training, technology and competitive initiatives in the context of agreed strategic goals. And when the business falls short, a framework is in place to limit the cost of failure and make productive use of the lessons learned.

In a technologically sophisticated world, the data and mechanisms for evaluating and tracking business results will increasingly be at the fingertips of both business and corporate managers. The opportunity at this moment in time, poised between the previous age of "rule of thumb" decisions and a statistics-driven future, is to structure systems and data so as to an provide a framework for strategic thinking throughout an organization.

Unique Value = ROI Model

The Unique Value = ROI® Model is structured as a pyramid (figure 6.1). At the top of the pyramid is a Unique Value strategy, the informing concept. At the foundation of the pyramid are all the aspects of the business that must be analyzed, structured and fully understood:

- Consumer or Customer.
- Business Systems and Skills.

- Products and Technology.
- Competition.

If the pyramid is looked at from above, so that the Unique Value strategy appears in the center, the foundation is now expressed as four boxes or building blocks, which designate the analyses required (figure 6.2):

- Consumer or Customer Analyses.
- Business System and Skills Analyses.
- Product and Technology Analyses.
- Competitor Analyses.

Figure 6.1   Unique Value = ROI® Model

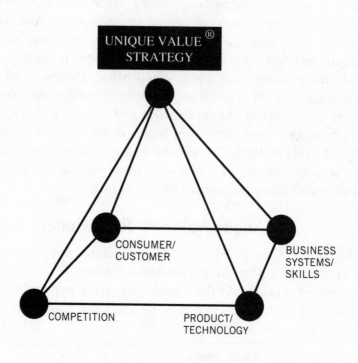

UNIQUE VALUE®
STRATEGY

CONSUMER/
CUSTOMER

BUSINESS
SYSTEMS/
SKILLS

COMPETITION

PRODUCT/
TECHNOLOGY

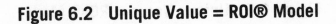

Figure 6.2 Unique Value = ROI® Model

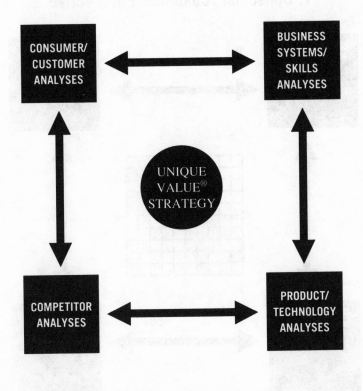

© Dunham & Marcus International, Inc., 1992.

Each of these designated analyses must be performed from two separate perspectives:

- Consumer/Customer Perspective.
- Business/Financial Perspective.

The consumer or customer perspective (figure 6.3) deals with the issue of customer satisfaction. That is, how well is the business performing from the perspective of its key customers? Or, in the case of a business that does not yet exist, what are the requirements of key potential customers or segments?

Each of the analyses must also be performed from the perspec-

Figure 6.3   Unique Value = ROI® Model

1. Consumer /Customer Perspective

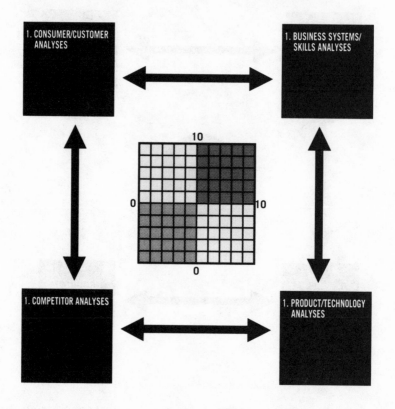

© Dunham & Marcus International, Inc., 1992.

tive of the business and of corporate management (figure 6.4). What are the factors that will drive financial performance to meet management requirements, in accordance with corporate policies, strategies and standards?

Each of these sets of analyses are then interrelated, so that factors can be considered in a way that takes into account both the Consumer/Customer and Business/Financial perspectives (figure 6.5). The result of this integration is an array of rankings, weightings and priorities that can be captured on a strategic map. The

Figure 6.4   Unique Value = ROI® Model

2. Business/Financial Perspective

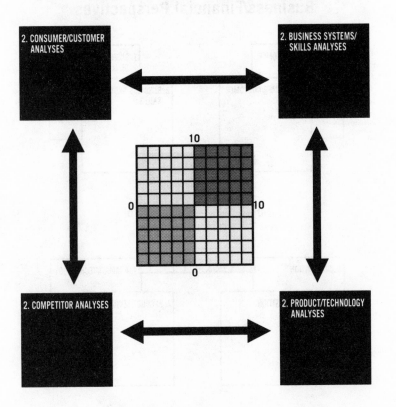

© Dunham & Marcus International, Inc., 1992.

map places the output of the analyses on two scales (figure 6.6). One scale, which reads 0 to 10 horizontally, is perceived value to key consumers and customers. The other scale, which reads 0 to 10 vertically, is value relative to business and financial goals. This structure provides a framework for discussing and prioritizing strategic alternatives. Color coding sensitizes strategists and planners to the implied degrees of risk associated with different options.

High value from both Customer and Business perspectives is coded green, suggesting that the strategy should have a Green Light. Clearly options that fall in the Green Light area are invest-

Figure 6.5   Unique Value = ROI® Model

Integration of Consumer/Customer and Business/Financial Perspectives

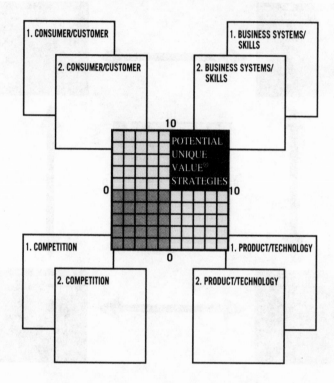

© Dunham & Marcus International, Inc., 1992.

ment priorities for the business and lay the foundation for a Unique Value strategy. Low value from both perspectives is coded red and is an indication not to proceed. In other words, a Red Light. The yellow quadrants represent alternatives that rate high from one perspective but low from the other. These are options that strongly suggest Caution, to be revisited perhaps at a later date if critical factors or assumptions change.

The most attractive options are integrated and articulated as potential Unique Value strategies, structured in terms of the five fundamentals. Substrategies are then developed for each key func-

Figure 6.6   Unique Value = ROI® Model

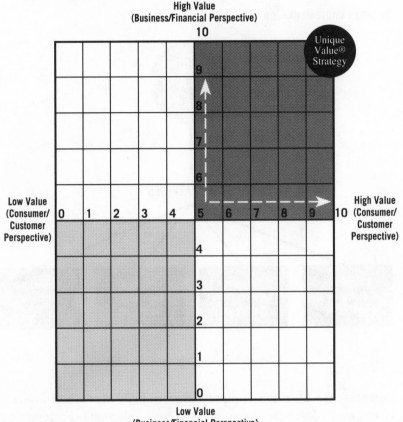

High Value
(Business/Financial Perspective)

Low Value
(Consumer/
Customer
Perspective)

High Value
(Consumer/
Customer
Perspective)

Low Value
(Business/Financial Perspective)

GREEN LIGHT: High Value Consumer/Customer *and* Business/Financial Perspective

CAUTION: High Value Consumer/Customer *or* High Value Business/Financial Perspective

RED LIGHT: Low Value Consumer/Customer *and* Business/Financial Perspective

© Dunham & Marcus International, Inc., 1992.

tional area, such as marketing, manufacturing and R&D, to set priorities and optimize resource allocation over the near and long term (figure 6.7).

Central to the development of a Unique Value strategy is the identification of the key success factors and profit drivers of the

Figure 6.7   Unique Value = ROI® Model

Strategy Implementation

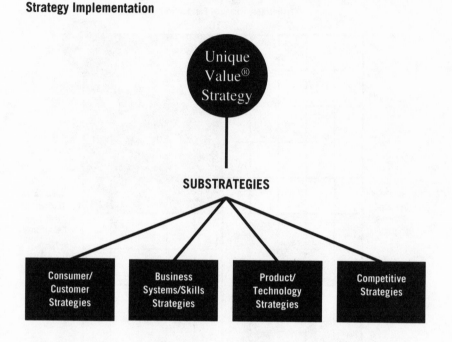

© Dunham & Marcus International, Inc., 1992.

business. Because the Unique Value = ROI Model's analyses are performed iteratively, managers and planners systematically deepen their understanding of these drivers as they revisit the questions and issues raised (figure 6.8).

The process of developing a Unique Value strategy begins by collecting, organizing and analyzing relevant data and information. The information is then structured in the format of the Unique Value = ROI Model. This establishes a foundation or knowledge base that consists of all available data, information and experience. With this foundation in place, preliminary hypotheses can be formulated as to potential Unique Value strategies or alternative scenarios. As knowledge gaps are identified, and more precise information is obtained, preliminary hypotheses are refined, evaluated, compared and tested as investment options.

Figure 6.8 Unique Value = ROI® Model

Key Drivers of Success and Profitability

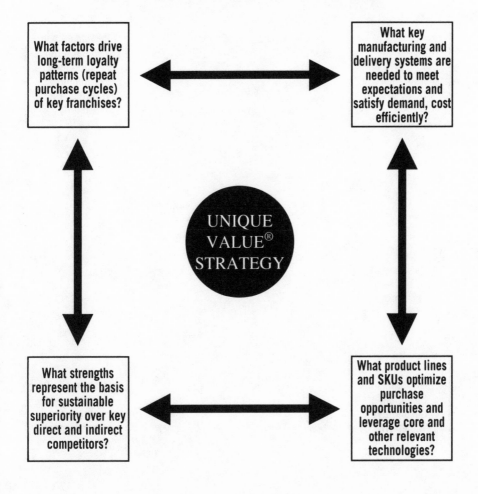

What factors drive long-term loyalty patterns (repeat purchase cycles) of key franchises?

What key manufacturing and delivery systems are needed to meet expectations and satisfy demand, cost efficiently?

UNIQUE VALUE® STRATEGY

What strengths represent the basis for sustainable superiority over key direct and indirect competitors?

What product lines and SKUs optimize purchase opportunities and leverage core and other relevant technologies?

© Dunham & Marcus International, Inc., 1992.

The Green Light options should be tested, since those represent highly attractive investment opportunities for the corporation (figure 6.9). Over the long term, critical factors are measured and tracked to ensure that the business is focusing on the drivers of sustainable success and profitability (figure 6.10).

Figure 6.9 Unique Value = ROI® Model

Investment Priorities

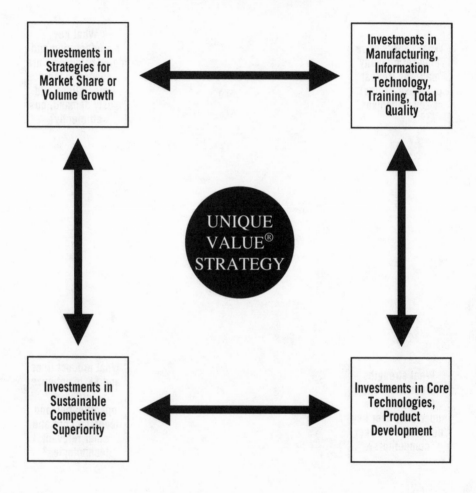

© Dunham & Marcus International, Inc., 1992.

Throughout the process, the Model provides a systematic approach to strategy formulation and implementation (figure 6.11). By encouraging strategists to focus on all relevant aspects of a business, including the factors critical to sustainable success and profitability, the Unique Value = ROI Model brings discipline and shared understanding to strategic decision-making.

Within the framework of the Unique Value = ROI Model, specific sets of issues and questions are addressed.

Figure 6.10　Unique Value = ROI® Model

Measures for Tracking

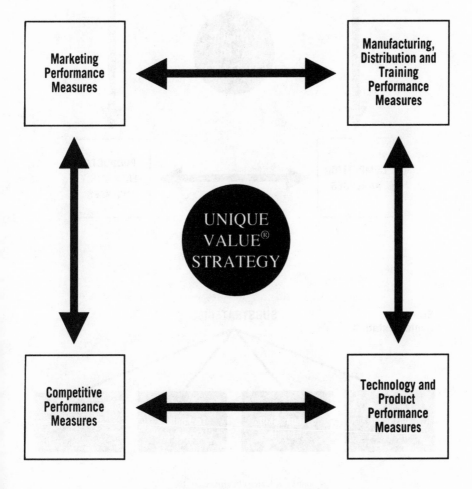

© Dunham & Marcus International, Inc., 1992.

Figure 6.11 Unique Value = ROI® Model

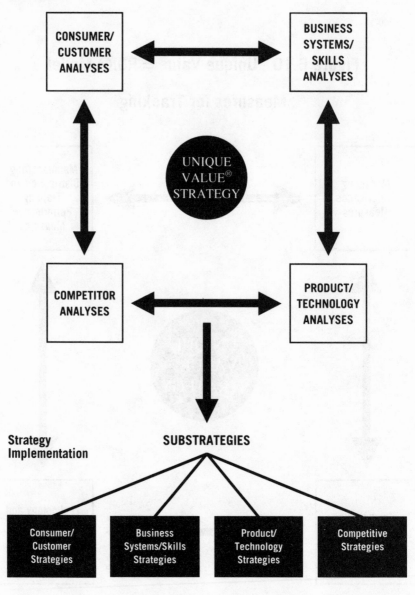

© Dunham & Marcus International, Inc., 1992.

Consumer and Customer Analyses

The consumer (end-user) and customer (trade, distributor, retailer, industrial user) analyses determine the industry and marketplace dynamics, and structure the market into cohesive groups and segments of buyers who share strategic characteristics and behaviors. These analyses differentiate and prioritize the most attractive segments on which to focus R&D, sales and marketing resources and identify the key functional and emotional benefits that must consistently be delivered to sustain consumer or customer loyalty.

Strategic segments are consumer/customer groups that are cohesive and measurable in terms of their relevant business behavior and the sales volume they account for, are accessible to sales and marketing efforts, have unique needs that require different approaches and are large enough in profit potential to justify the incremental costs associated with segmentation.

No customer base is homogeneous. Different segments have different needs and priorities, and their purchase decisions are driven by varying factors and trade-offs.[1] By structuring the market target into strategic segments, managers can identify the most attractive segment opportunities and direct available resources toward them.

The consumer and customer analyses focus on the hierarchy of needs of specific segments that drive market volume; the market trends and factors that are critical to business success; and the advertising and pricing strategies employed. When business managers think and talk about these issues, they do so at many different levels of formality and understanding. For example, Unilever chairman Michael Perry illustrates the value of identifying unmet consumer needs in the development of new products:

> The only way to handle innovation is to put the market and the consumer at the center and have everything else around it. The innovation process is iterative and not linear or sequential. You link in that circle the advertising agency and the marketing company and the research chemist. The re-

search chemist is seeking to satisfy a clear unexpressed consumer need.

Take the hair business. Obviously, the first thing that happened is that people moved from washing their hair with soap
to shampoo. Then someone thought of the idea of a conditioner. That didn't just happen from research chemists sitting
in a lab. It happened through a process of identification of a
whole new application. People had to worry about their hair
being dried out as a result of excessive use of shampoo. Therefore, you had to restore something. This gave birth to a whole
range of treatment products for hair, leading to shampoo and
conditioner in one.

All of this starts off in the consumer consciousness as a
playback to some kind probing marketing research inquiry.

Focusing on the customer is equally important for industrial
product manufacturers and service providers. Dr. Marcus Bierich,
chairman of Robert Bosch, says:

> Over the years, we have established a solid relationship with
> our customers. Most of our products are developed jointly
> with them. Traditionally, our R&D department collaborates
> with our customers to develop products. We often invest mil-
> lions of dollars in these joint projects.
>
> Customer involvement begins at the engineering level, not
> at the executive level. And it rises throughout the
> organization.

As Iain Vallance, chairman and CEO of BT PLC, makes clear,
institutionalizing this focus on the customer must be a strategic
priority:

> One of the most powerful things I've ever learned, I learned
> at the outset of my career. It was then that I spent a year as
> the interface between the customer and the organization.
>
> The experience of serving in that capacity is critical because
> it gives you a gleam of sympathy for what is really important—
> that is, the way the business responds to customer needs. To

institutionalize that experience, that perspective, we have programs designed to initiate regular contact between our top managers and our customers. And this applies not just to our major customers, but to ordinary, run-of-the-day customers as well. A manager will go out with someone whose job it is to maintain an ordinary business telephone. He learns from that experience. He stays in touch. And this is a critical prerequisite for good service.

The Consumer or Customer analyses include asking the following questions:
- What are the key historical and anticipated market performance characteristics associated with strategic product market segments?
  — What is the size of the market, both volume and value?
  — What are the unit/value market shares?
  — What is the relative profitability of manufacturers, suppliers and the trade (customers)?

- What are the strategic customer/consumer segments that will drive future business profitability and growth?
  — From a consumer (end-user) standpoint, which cohesive groups of buyers share strategic characteristics/behaviors?
  — Consumer characteristics
    · Geographic (country, region, city, climate, density)
    · Demographic (age, sex, income, occupation, education)
    · Psychographic (lifestyle, personality traits)
  — Consumer behavior
    · Occasion (regular, special)
    · Use (rate, loyalty, price sensitivity)
    · Attitudes (receptiveness)
  — From a customer (distributor, retailer, industrial user) standpoint, which cohesive groups of buyers share strategic characteristics/behaviors?
  — Geographic
    · Usage concentration (country, region)
    · Distribution (country, region)
  — Customer type

- · Industry type (products, technology)
- · Company type (size, OEM [original equipment manufacturer], user)
- · Capabilities (vertical integration, distribution)
- · Attitudes (loyalty, importance)
- · Usage/volume (high, medium, low)
— Purchase process
- · Purchase criteria (service, quality, features, cost)
- · Organization (centralized, decentralized)
- · Purchase policy (contract, bid, bundling)
— Situational factors
- · Application (basic, specialty, replacement)
- · Order concentration (size, lead time, pattern)
- · Financial strength (credit rating)
— What are the primary functional, emotional and unmet needs of key segments, and how might these change over time?
— How does profitability vary between strategic consumer/customer segments?
— What are the costs associated with each of the strategic segments (shipping, inventory, service)?
— How does current and potential revenue vary among strategic segments in terms of volume and price components?

• What are the purchasing dynamics associated with the product or service?
— How can the adoption process be characterized over time (awareness, trial, repeat, loyalty)?
— Who are the key influencers in the purchase decision (e.g., radiologists and X-ray equipment, children and cereal, breeders and dog food)?
— To what extent is demand wholesaler or retailer focused (push) versus consumer focused (pull), i.e., trade incentives versus consumer advertising?

• How do the strategic customer/consumer segments perceive the organization compared to competition (corporate capabilities, skills, products, services)?

— What is the perceived value of the products/services across key functional/emotional attribute states?

— What images are associated with brands/products?
— What is the overall level of consumer satisfaction?

- What is the consumer/customer franchise in terms of of current and potential strategic segments that can be leveraged for future expansion?
    — Brand or product associations that represent a competitive asset
    — Customer base profile (size, spending behavior)
    — Image (service, premium credentials)
    — Awareness (top of mind, aided levels)
    — Loyalty (share of usage/purchases, switching costs and behavior)
    — Perceived quality (customer satisfaction, product differentiation)

Business Systems and Skills Analyses

The business system represents all of the components of the business related to product or service production and delivery. The business system and skills analyses define the optimal business system and skill base and method of operation to deliver superior value to strategic consumer or customer segments and provide a basis for sustainable operating performance and profitability.

Operating profit is closely linked to business system efficiency. This was one of the primary considerations behind the merger of pharmaceutical giants SmithKline Beckman and Beecham Group PLC, as Fred Kyle, SmithKline Beecham president of commercial operations, described:

> Since the merger of SmithKline and Beecham, we have consolidated the two sales and marketing organizations and have substantially increased the growth rate of those Beecham products that were underpromoted premerger. And that has worked the way we projected it would—almost exactly. Part

of the reason for this is that we shut down duplicate physical facilities for distribution and manufacturing and we achieved a significant reduction in headcount.

These changes have produced a more profitable business. Why? Because we have more volume running through a smaller infrastructure and we are getting much more out of product assets because we have a much more powerful sales operation. Our approach is to work continuously on moving more products through the distribution system and to move them through quicker, while keeping that system lean and efficient.

To generate operating efficiencies in manufacturing, distribution, and other areas of the business system, information technology plays an increasingly important role. But a focus on enhanced productivity must be carefully balanced with the organizational flexibility that today's business environment requires. Because it is critical to bridge the gap between senior management and the marketplace, many corporations have, within corporate guidelines, decentralized decisionmaking to the local level. As Sir Michael Angus, former chairman of Unilever, explained:

> There are certain principles in this company which guide our management philosophy and organization. First of all, we have a flat organizational structure. Indeed, there are normally only four levels between me and a brand manager. Second, we try to devolve decisionmaking down to the lowest possible level where it can be taken with efficiency.

Kan Iwaki, deputy president of Sony, echoes this theme:

> Our past sales organization was rather independent from manufacturing. But as we became active in producing products outside Japan, we started to delegate more of the decisionmaking for manufacturing to the local operating units.
>
> These led to a structure composed of several major divisions: Sony Europa, Sony U.S., and Sony International, based in Singapore. These divisional units, along with Sony head-

quarters in Japan, are responsible for manufacturing and other operational functions.

To help bring cohesion to this, we hold international business meetings twice a year, treating the attendees as members of a strategic decisionmaking body. Top management from Europe, the United States and elsewhere make key strategy decisions at this level, but the routine pricing and quantity decisions are made at the local level. For our record business, these decisions are made in New York; for the movie business, they are made in Hollywood. This is based on a philosophy that the closer to the market decisions are made, the more accurate they are likely to be.

Dr. Hans-Peter Ferslev, group coordinator and executive vice-president of Deutsche Bank, notes that balancing central control with local autonomy is not a simple task:

Deutsche Bank was founded as a corporate bank. In the beginning, it was a bank without branches. Then we grew by acquiring smaller, regional banks throughout Germany. But even as the new banks became part of our organization, they operated with a great deal of autonomy and even retained much of their individual cultures. One of our key strategies was to give as much responsibility as possible to the various local entities that were part of our organization.

We operated this way as long as banking remained relatively simple. We began to notice great change and increasing complexity in the banking world two decades ago—and that we needed to develop a private banking sector (in addition to a corporate sector). The time had come for change. As we developed private banking and strengthened our international corporate and trading capabilities, we had to put, over time, more emphasis on developing a cohesive organization with a more powerful and influential central nucleus. One way to do that was to concentrate know-how in a few places to create critical mass as centers of competence. This was a gradually ongoing evolutionary process with our new structure being the keystone. In essence our new structure is a compromise reflecting our founding organizational structure and our evolving needs.

As Bryan Langton, CEO of Holiday Inn, Worldwide, explains, the balance between localized and centralized authority is tested every time the investment priorities of divisional offices and corporate management differ, and that requires an informed corporation-wide dialogue: "Divisional strategies are formulated by divisional boards. A group requirement for people and money allocation is superimposed on divisional plans to improve total shareholder value. Once the plan is established, divisions operate fairly autonomously within strategic people and financial parameters. With Holiday Inn these will include branding and IT."

Although trends such as decentralized decisionmaking are enhancing the effectiveness or efficiency of the business system, productivity still depends on the quality of individual skills. Bruce Crawford, president and CEO of advertising conglomerate The Omnicom Group, emphasizes the need for effective human resource management:

> The only way to have success is to constantly employ the best people. You have to be good at recruiting them and training them and you also have to create a system of rewards that is performance-oriented. One has to define what good performance is and then one has to reward people accordingly.
>
> People have to know and understand what the company is about, what their role in it is, how they are going to participate and how they are going to gain what they are seeking. In the process, you have to make it possible for people to have some independence and a sense of dignity that so many organizations do not permit. You want to define things so clearly that people can do what they have to do with as little interference as possible.
>
> For most people, the ideal is to be the boss, to own their own company. Of course, in this age of multinational corporations, most people cannot achieve this. But what you want to strive for is to allow people to feel that they are getting as close to that sense of ownership as they can possibly get.

Naoyuki Kondo, executive managing director of Mitsui, describes the procedures Mitsui uses to train and develop effective managers:

> In developing our senior managers, we opt for a dual approach. For most of their careers, they specialize in a particular area of our business, such as chemicals, metals or foods. We are firm believers in the value of specialization.
>
> But we also seek to widen their experience by having them work in overseas offices, where they will oversee a wider range of our activities. As the head of an overseas office, an executive may have responsibility for corporate planning, quality and strategy for many businesses outside the business he was groomed in. Most of the members of our board have had this kind of experience running overseas units such as those in New York, Sydney or London. It adds greatly to their knowledge and perspective.

When performing the Business Systems and Skills analyses, the following issues are addressed:

- What aspects of the business system most efficiently deliver superior value to strategic segments? Which support sustainable sales and operating performance? Which deliver a competitive advantage?
- How are functional areas associated with the business system as it is currently organized?
    - Plant and production operations
        - What is the age and technical sophistication of tools, machinery and production processes?
        - To what extent do the manufacturing operations take advantage of economies of scale (high volume)?
        - To what degree are operations vertically integrated?
        - How flexible are the manufacturing operations to respond to internal and external changes (shifts in demand, new technologies)?
        - How is capacity being effectively utilized or imposing constraints?

- To what extent are the operations focused on minimizing costs?
— Service operations
  - How are the service operations organized (decentralized, vertically integrated, outsourced, integrated with sales or distribution)?
  - What are the cost components of the service operations compared to the overall business system mix?
  - How flexible is the service organization to shifts in capacity and demand?
— Distribution
  - What are the primary and secondary channels of distribution?
  - What are the distribution economics (retail markup, distributor markup)?
  - To what extent is distribution vertically integrated?
  - How is the relationship with the distribution network characterized (exclusive, high interaction/service, good/bad)?
  - What are the drivers of distribution costs (order size, lead time, shipping, inventory)?
  - What is the cost of distribution compared to the overall business system mix?
  - How is the distribution network organized with regard to customers and business location?
— Procurement and suppliers
  - What is the number, concentration and profitability of suppliers?
  - To what extent is procurement vertically integrated?
  - What is the cost structure of procurement and what are the drivers (order size, lead time, shipping)?
  - How are the suppliers integrated into the product development and design process?
— Information systems
  - How is information technology being used to optimize costs, differentiate products or services and create competitive barriers?

- What is the role or status of information technology in the organization and how is it incorporated into the overall strategic planning process?
- How is information technology incorporated into the financial and operational components of the business system?
- To what extent does information technology incorporate internal linkages between functional areas and external linkages with other businesses?
- How is information technology organized (centralized versus decentralized)?

— Finance and accounting
  - What are the corporation's valuation policies (inventory, depreciation)?
  - What is the process for allocating costs to different products, customers and functional areas?
  - What is the relative breakdown of fixed and variable costs?
  - What are the objectives of the management accounting system (i.e., the top management controls that influence behavior)?
  - How is the firm's financial structure characterized (liquidity, leverage, working capital, surplus cash)?

— Sales and marketing
  - How is the sales function organized (customer types, geographically, direct, account focused)?
  - How is the marketing function organized (by function, by category or product line, by customer)?
  - What are the mechanisms for communication with the consumer and customer (direct mail, print media, direct selling, trade advertising)?
  - How are the costs associated with sales and marketing (consumer advertising, consumer promotions, trade promotions, direct mail) broken down?

• What components of the business system represent sources of competitive advantage (i.e., what can the business do better than competitors)?

- How does the business system drive profitability and competitiveness through lower cost, product differentiation, competitive barriers, flexibility?
- How sustainable are the business system advantages?
- What aspects of the business system represent a significant value-added component of the products and services?
- How efficient are business operations compared to competition and the state of the art (benchmarking)?
- How do the business systems compare to the relevant existing or potential competitors in terms of customer value, cost and operationally oriented measures (production/employee, customer complaints, employee turnover, selling costs)?

- How are the experience curve effects in the components of the business system being managed and utilized?
  - What opportunities exist for improved efficiency through improved information flow, automation, increased focus, process reengineering and increased labor productivity?
  - How effectively are control mechanisms integrated into the business system (costs, operations, quality, centralized control)?
    - What business skills are required to respond to emerging needs of strategic consumer or customer segments?
  - What are the unique skills tied to the underlying business operations that have driven business performance?
    - Functional skills (quality techniques, technical expertise)
    - Corporate skills (flexibility, quality of personnel)
- How can the components of culture be characterized?
  - How suitable is the culture to the current business environment and emerging customer and consumer trends?
  - Human resources
    - Are there corporate policies or principles related to the management of human resources (lifetime employment, promotion from within, job rotation)?
    - What is the profile of the labor force (gender, education, age)?

- What are the primary sources of employee personnel?
- What is the structure of the compensation system (wages, benefits, equity incentives)?
- What is the role of employee and trade unions?
- How effectively is training incorporated in employee development?

Product and Technology Analyses

The Product and Technology analyses determine the specific product or service attributes and technologies required to deliver competitively superior benefits that meet consumer or customer needs and maximize sales volume and margin potential over the near and long term. Says Seagram president and chief operating officer Edgar Bronfman, Jr.:

There are two kinds of products. Those that provide a functional benefit—brighten your teeth, clean your shirt, take the dandruff out of your hair. And those products that deliver an emotional benefit—they make you feel better about yourself.

Procter & Gamble is the best company in the world at creating and delivering functional benefits. But it is a very different approach to deliver an emotional benefit, as do Chanel and Chivas Regal.

No company can be all things to all people. At Seagram, we couldn't market a detergent well. Nor could we market a toothpaste well. Procter and Unilever know how to do that.

By the same token, where Procter and Unilever have fallen down is in trying to deliver products that have an emotional benefit rather than a functional benefit. Procter marketed Citrus Hill orange juice on the basis of health claims—that it makes you healthy and your bones stronger. But people don't drink orange juice to make their bones healthy. They drink milk for that. The point is that Procter's functional approach, which works for 95 percent of their businesses, ultimately didn't work for orange juice, and they withdrew the product from the market.

Because different consumer segments have different needs, tastes and usage patterns, businesses often seek to develop a portfolio of products to maximize product appeal and selling opportunities.

Building a portfolio of products serves to minimize risks for the corporation. This applies to all industries, whether consumer products, industrial engineering or financial services. Says Mitsui's Kondo:

> In all of our trading activities, we prefer to hedge our risks. We do this in part by being very selective in the investments we make and the trading activities we enter. Always, our goal is to maintain a well-balanced portfolio of products. This balance, we have found, has a stabilizing impact through the economic cycles. While we have had losses in some components of our portfolio, we have usually had gains in other components to offset those losses.
>
> We try to keep this kind of balance as a form of insurance. If we make an investment in one product area, we look for a compensating investment in another area. This strategy has worked well for us.

Developing products that are competitively superior in their delivery of the benefits that customers and consumers demand requires staying ahead of technological innovation. But maintaining competitive advantage is a continual challenge. For a company to expand or even retain its customer base, preserving the status quo is not sufficient; it must have active quality improvement programs in place for the current product line while introducing new products that either deliver superior consumer value in established segments or deliver relevant new benefits. Burnell Roberts, former chairman and CEO of Mead Paper, describes his experience:

> We believe that the most effective means of competing in the marketplace is to satisfy our customers. That means more than simply smiling and saying "thank you." It means determining what the customer really wants from us—in terms of

product, service, credit, delivery and price—and delivering it to him.

But of course in the real world there are always complications. Assume that we are providing the customer with a good product, service, delivery and price but a competitor introduces an innovative product that is clearly superior to ours. Certainly, our customers will be tempted to gravitate toward that superior product. But it need not be that way. We have found that by intensifying service during this period and by assuring the customer that we are working on a product of our own that is even better than the competition's, we can protect our most important customer relationships.

Thus the ongoing importance of technology. Once there is a new product introduced into the market, we believe it is inadequate to match that product. Instead, we think we must leapfrog it. The idea is to reward our loyal customers with a product that goes the competition one better.

We did just that in the case of our top grade of coated printing papers a few years ago. Our number-one grade had lost ground to the competition. The decision to leapfrog the competition with a new number one required not just reformulating the paper and coating but rebuilding and modernizing paper machines, coaters and finishing equipment. When we introduced the new grade, "Signature," it exceeded all the normal standards for a number-one grade. It not only leapfrogged its competition, it began to attract orders from those who had been buying highly expensive, super-premium grades.

Burnell Roberts's perspective is that to innovate successfully and continually, a corporation's management must encourage entrepreneurial activity:

When our R&D people come to us with ideas or innovations that do not qualify for capital on the basis of furthering the strategic plan, we may authorize limited expenditures to pursue the projects further. We hope the projects develop strategic significance, but part of our rationale is to keep our people motivated. The most dangerous thing a company can do is to cut off people with good ideas. Although it may cost us a modest sum to support some of these ancillary projects, the trade-off in keeping our good people with us, and keeping them motivated, is well worth it.

In a recent case, one of our R&D people came to us with a good idea involving paper that could be encapsulated with chemicals which produce electric energy. The idea had come, in part, from our involvement with the coating of paper with encapsulated dyes for making carbonless paper.

In order to keep the idea alive and evaluate it further, we approved a seed capital investment of $500,000. As the product developed, we determined that it fell outside our strategic area. Still, when the innovator asked for additional capital in order to develop a plant for the project, we agreed to make the investment. Part of our reason for proceeding was to maintain a culture that attracts innovators and encourages the formation of new ideas. Saying the company does this through a memo is one thing. Backing it up with dollars is something else.

In consumer financial services, Citibank has long been a technology leader. In the United States, from its branch network base in the New York market, Citibank pioneered sophisticated automatic teller machines (ATMs).

In the words of Pei-Yian Chia, Citibank's senior executive vice president for global consumer banking:

Starting out, it wasn't an ATM program. An ATM was the solution. One of the possible solutions. At the time, it was one of the most controversial solutions. We were trying to solve two severe problems. One was that we were the largest bank in New York, and we were all things to all people, but we didn't have an specific product that could claim uniqueness. Second, our branches were crowded, because we had too many customers for each branch to handle. The branches were unautomated and very inefficient. Call it the 1939 banking operation existing in 1974. Customers waiting on line were very unhappy with the service.

When we started looking at ATMs, most of the ATM projects we studied were managed by technologists, or by operations managers. The ATM was seen as a cost-saving device, not a marketing tool. But we saw the ATM as a way to improve customer service. So, in 1975, we set up a consumer laboratory, to start to understand what an ATM should be like from the customer's point of view. When we showed them the existing ATMs, consumer feedback was universally negative. They were frightened by the machine.

With our goal of improving customer service, we determined that the machine had to do more than just give cash. Cash is only one transaction. If you start doing transaction analysis in the branches, this is one of the largest. The next is transferring money. If we could move a certain percentage onto this machine, what kind of capacity would it open up, and how would it increase service? A key thing was capacity.

When we went to order the machine, there were three: IBM, Diebold and Docutel. I talked to IBM, and I offered them a contract of five hundred units. I was asking them to work with us to develop the machine, to change the way they did business by working to our specifications. They said they would never do that, and we would probably fail trying to do it ourselves. But John Reed appointed a task force, which I headed, to make this happen. When I needed a decision from John, I could pick up the phone and get one quickly.

Once we had this idea of setting up the special force, we just used common sense. First of all, this was a marketing project, so the marketing department was the ongoing form of support. We were using technology to deliver "Easy Banking," as we called it then. The ATM was only one of the many elements. Bringing the machine indoors, instead of sticking it out into the street, where early ATMs had been placed, was important because it offered safety and comfort to the consumer. We put the ATM contiguous with the teller station. We wanted the teller to feel that this is your companion, not your threat. We had 1,200 tellers, and we built 1,200 teller stations. Every teller got a new chair, new station, new work flow. This assured them that they would not be replaced. Why else would we buy them furniture?

We had two machines for each branch. In the state of engineering at that time, each machine would deliver 95 percent reliability. And 95 percent of the time, they were running. The five percent would compute to eight hours a week. But we had to promise seven days, twenty-four hours. You end up with eight hours down and their not being able to get it would destroy the credibility of the program. It has to be always available. You can't fool around with this. We hired a statistician to determine the conditional probability of a failure at each site if we installed two machines at one location. It was computed as 99 percent availability.

Another good reason for having two machines in place was if you had a long weekend in New York, a location might run out of cash with only one machine. Each machine had a load of $25,000 to $30,000. Two machines double the load. Today, if you see a Citibank sign, you don't have to think which branch is twenty-four hours, and will it have cash? Anytime you see a sign, it is open. That is "Citibanking."

Today, technology, supported by service training and driven by marketing, is central to Citibank's increasingly global service standard. The internal code word we use is "Citibanking" for our worldwide retail banking strategy. All major markets are executing the strategy. Singapore is the most advanced. We experiment a lot in Singapore. Today we have ATMs of our own design around the world in countries like in Germany, Belgium, Spain, France, Greece, Singapore, Taiwan and Korea, and we're adding to the list Australia and Mexico. A New York customer can go to an ATM, stick his card in the machine and ask for deutsch marks. I was there three weeks ago, and I was transacting with my New York account. The German customer can go to Spain and get money. A Spaniard can go to Belgium or Greece. We are the only bank where a customer can go across a border and get cash from his home bank account.

The ATM service is only one part of Citibanking. The banking distribution system we are building will mean you can do everything you want to, any way you want to, in the future. Go to the teller, pick up the phone, and call, and you will get the same information, the same service. The telephone will be a branch. You should be able to do everything on the phone as if you were in a branch. That is the key to what we have been doing in technology—developing a new standard of worldwide customer service for banking.

Questions encompassed by the Product and Technology analyses include:

- What is the optimal product portfolio configuration to most profitably address current and emerging needs?
  — How can the performance/opportunity of each product line be characterized in terms of market share, profitability and growth?
  — How can the product portfolio/key lines be characterized from a lifecycle perspective?
    · What is the shape of the lifecycle (classical, rapid penetration, stable maturity)?
    · What are the products positioned from a lifecycle perspective (stage of the lifecycle)?
    · How is the lifecycle being managed (lengthened, modified, investment patterns, pricing)?
  — How are the resources currently being allocated to products/SKUs (stock keeping units)?
  — What is the current and anticipated role of price?
    · What are the industry segmentation trends (generic, low-end, mid, premium, super-premium)?
    · How is the product portfolio positioned compared to industry price segmentation?
    · What is the impact of price on the consumer or customer (elasticity, perceived quality)?
    · To what extent does the product portfolio compete on price?
  — What new product strategies can be incorporated into the product mix?
    · How can existing products be improved or redesigned?
    · How can new products effectively capitalize on emerging needs or segmentation?

- · How can new products be used to create competitive barriers and protect market position?

- What unique product portfolio attributes are sources of current and future competitive advantage?
  — How are product designs or attributes segmented or differentiated?
  — What are the product attributes representing the greatest added value?
  — How do product design and quality compare with competitive products?
    · Benchmarking relative to competition or state of the art
  — What is the rate and nature of product changes and improvements within the marketplace?
    · Standardization versus differentiation
    · What is the role of packaging and visual design; its cost, configuration, graphics and size from customer, distributor and competitive perspectives?

- How can technological assets and capabilities be efficiently developed and incorporated into the product portfolio and business operations?
  — How is technology being utilized in the overall business?
    · Product designs
    · Production processes
    · Business operations
  — How does technology represent a sustainable competitive advantage?
    · How do patents or proprietary technology support or insulate business performance?
    · How can the management of these assets be improved or modified?
  — What opportunities exist to expand the utilization of existing technologies into different areas?
  — What opportunities exist to develop or acquire (joint venture, licensing) new technologies that complement existing technologies or business operations?

- How can research and development enhance long-term performance?
  — What is the role of research and development within the overall organization (goals, mission, status)?
  — How will emerging technologies affect R&D?
  — What is the role of basic research?
  — How can the performance of R&D be characterized, and how can it be improved?
    · How are R&D resources focused?
      — Core versus peripheral technologies
      — Driven by market demand or internally driven innovation
    · How is R&D organized?
      — Centralized versus decentralized
      — Communication infrastructure (from corporate to R&D line management)
      — To what extent are organization linkages (with manufacturing, marketing) utilized?
    · How can R&D productivity be characterized?
      — Product and patent yields
      — Costs and process development
      — Product development cycle time

Competitor Analyses

The Competitor analyses structure the competitive environment, define the relevant competitive set and evaluate current and anticipated sources of advantage or disadvantage (in terms of customer franchises, business systems and skills, products and technologies). This determines the key factors necessary to maximize competitive differentiation and insulation. At the center of a business's competitive position is the identification of its core capabilities compared with those of its competitors, and the knowledge of how to leverage them for a marketplace advantage. Konica's Managing Director, Sho Kamiiisaka, says that it was this rationale that influenced Konica's decision to focus on the color copier segment of the market:

As we look to the immediate future, we see that office technology—including graphics, facsimile machines and printers—will shift increasingly from black and white to color. One of our great strengths is that we have leading technology in color imaging, so we are at the vanguard in developing new generations of color machines. Providing a full line of color products will give our distributors an edge, which in turn will bolster Konica's sales.

The decision to focus our resources and efforts in the color product area was a direct result of our strategic planning process. We asked ourselves, "Who are our strongest competitors? What major advantages do they have? What direction should we go in to give us the advantage?" The answer to the last question—an answer we arrived at five years ago—was that capitalizing on our color technology would be the best approach. We believe it was the appropriate approach and that it will lead to strong performance in the marketplace.

The importance of competitive position varies widely from industry to industry. Being the low-cost producer is critical in some cases. For example, SmithKline Beecham's policy is explicitly stated in key documents:

In support of our purpose to provide products and services of superior value, SmithKline Beecham aims to become the low-cost competitor in the pharmaceutical and health care industry. Achieving this status requires placing an absolute priority on the efficiency and productivity of employees and capital at all levels and in all areas of our company. The benefits of a sustained, low-cost position are manifold, but they include a higher share value, the generation of more cash flow for reinvestment in the business and the ability to achieve and defend leading market shares within our products, including, if necessary, taking a low-price strategy.

Yet attaining a low-cost position by itself may not be the ideal strategy in every industry or competitive situation. The key is to understand the competitive framework, determine strengths and vulnerabilities compared to specific competitors, and integrate this knowledge to develop a strategy that produces a long-term defensible competitive advantage. As David Sainsbury, chairman and CFO of U.K. supermarket chain Sainsbury's, said:

At Sainsbury, our philosophy since the founding of this business is to combine what are often viewed as polar opposites: the finest quality at very competitive prices. The driving concept of our business is value for money. That doesn't mean we want to be the cheapest producer or the highest-quality producer. We believe, in theory, that if you seek to sell on the basis of price alone, you will always find a competitor willing to undercut you and thus find a new bottom. If you only strive for ultimate quality, someone will do the same to you on that end as well. By balancing this price-quality relationship and giving our customers better value for money than anyone else, we want to find a position in the marketplace which is difficult for our competitors to match.

Motorola's philosophy was succinctly defined in the December 1992 issue of the company's internal training and education publication by Gary Tooker, president and chief operating officer:

The importance of time as a competitive advantage is well documented. Shelves are full of 'how-to' books that explore time issues from every angle. At Motorola, our time-based advantage is not something we can pull off the shelf in a standard package. We are building this advantage through experience, and learning by managing the process, not the result. We are learning the critical importance of eliminating nonvalue-added factors that add up to time lost.

In 1991, we introduced the concept of EXCELERATION—combining the qualities of empowered action, excellence and speed. During the last year, we have fine-tuned the definition of exceleration to combine empowerment and excellence with acceleration, changing our focus to the rate of change of speed.

We are learning that the real edge in time-based competition comes not from a steady pace of improvement but from improvement at an increasing pace.

Gary Tooker then goes on to say,

Until now, our goal to improve customer responsiveness has focused on cycle time alone. But the measurement of cycle time alone is static. It overlooks the most important phenomenon of short cycle times—they improve upon themselves. Increasing the number of cycles in a given time period increases the number of learning opportunities to improve quality and cost and thereby achieve even short cycle times.

A learning opportunity becomes a cycle of learning only when we provide a feedback loop for each cycle. This feedback loop must contain creative improvements in the process for the next repetition of the cycle. Without this feedback loop, the opportunity is only a cycle of history, not a cycle of learning.[2]

George Fisher, CEO, explains how this pursuit of speed as a key competitive advantage works in relation to management and motivation of the entire organization:

The best example of this was when we set a quality level which was an extremely 'reach out' goal about five years ago, and at the time nobody knew quite how to get to it. We had just finished a quality drive in the years 1981–86 that talked a tenfold improvement in five years. That expectation level was thought by our people to be unachievable and tough. But five years later, we found we had achieved it. We thought our competitors were moving as fast. In fact, we had to be moving faster. In 1986, our new goal asked for a tenfold improvement in two years, a hundredfold improvement in four years, leading to virtual defect-free performance in five years (our 6 Sigma program). That program has been amazingly successful but the thought of that, when it started, was unbelievable to our people. Gradually we had one success after another and we enhanced our training program to set up skills that would maintain this momentum.

A large part of the CEO's responsibility, in addition to developing the core of competencies and driving initiative throughout the company, is to set proper expectations. Often we don't expect a lot of our people—and we get what we ask for.

The Competitor analyses require asking:

- What is the nature of industry competition and how does it affect business performance in terms of profitability, market position and growth?
  - How can the existing competitive framework be characterized?
    - Who are the relevant direct and indirect competitors who are sources of business?
    - What are the strategic groupings (competitive segmentation based on similar business characteristics, such as customer segments, image, distribution channels)?
    - How has the competitive framework evolved (shakeout, consolidation, new entrants and so forth)?
  - What is the impact of industry competitive dynamics on business economics?
    - Volume
    - Pricing flexibility
    - Cost advantages
    - Entry and exit barriers
    - Market power
  - How is the competitive framework expected to evolve in the near and long term?
    - What is the impact of projected industry growth?
    - What is the potential impact of consolidation through merger and acquisitions?
    - What companies are vulnerable to a shakeout or industry decline?
    - What is the likelihood of vertical integration by buyers and suppliers?
    - To what extent do substitutes and new entrants represent potential competitors?

- What are the strengths and weaknesses within the relevant existing and potential competitive set regarding marketplace dynamics and emerging consumer and customer needs?
  — What are the corporate capabilities of the relevant existing or potential competitors that represent significant competitive assets?
    · Consumer/Customer franchise (loyal customers, premium image, quality associations)
    · Business Systems/Skills (distribution network, information technology utilization, marketing expertise, responsive organization or culture, financial resources)
    · Product/Technology (patents, proprietary technology, superior product design or quality, R&D capability)
  — What is the time horizon/sustainability of these assets?
  — What will be the impact of shifting consumer or customer needs and external dynamics on relative competitive strengths and weaknesses?

- What are the current and anticipated strategies of the relevant existing or potential competitors that affect business performance and profitability?
  — What are the strategies of relevant existing and potential competitors?
  — How are the strategies and positioning of competitors expected to change?
    · How have competitive strategies and positioning affected business profitability and relative market shares?
    · How are competitors' financial, marketplace and organizational goals characterized and what is the time horizon?
    · What are the most likely strategies that the competitors will use to meet business goals?
    · How vulnerable is the business to anticipated competitive strategies and positioning?
    · How effectively can the business respond to the anticipated competitive strategic initiatives?
  — How does the anticipated competitive response to strategic

alternatives affect projected profitability or attractiveness?

- · How vulnerable is competition to a given strategy?
- · What strategic initiatives are likely to result in a competitive response?
  - — What is the reputation of competitors in similar situations?
  - — What are the drivers of competitive strategic decisionmaking?
- · How effectively can competition respond to a given strategy?
- · How will the likely competitive response affect business profitability and growth?

Business-unit management and corporate management must both ask these questions continually. The answers and the issues raised should be uppermost in a manager's mind if he or she is to have the business in strategic focus. No general manager should consider himself or herself a strategist if this knowledge base is not in place as a foundation for decisionmaking.

See Appendix B: Unique Value = ROI Model ®; Analyses to Be Performed, for further information.

CHAPTER 7

WHAT HAPPENS
WHEN YOU DON'T ASK
THE RIGHT QUESTIONS

— ● —

Sometimes businesspeople don't know what questions to ask. Sometimes they think they know all the answers. The result, either way, will be an underperforming business.

In large, complex multinational corporations, significant business failures, which could have been averted by informed managements who asked the right questions at the right time, can be swept under the rug of a corporate write-off. Procter & Gamble, for example, took an $800 million write-off in the year they withdrew from the Duncan Hines ready-to-eat cookie business, included in which was an estimated $100 million of investments in the cookie business. Brown-Forman did the equivalent with California Coolers when they sold what remained of a business they had paid over $100 million for to a beer company for a token amount, just a few years later.

Knowing what questions to ask is essential to good management, and yet very little in the training of most managers equips them to ask intelligent questions outside their special areas of competency. As a result, marketers, sales managers, engineers, technologists and finance managers become general managers without the tools to become business strategists. And when they are charged with the management of a complex business in complex times, the entire enterprise and all the investments in it are placed at risk.

In some cases, the corporate parent is weakened as a result. In the case of a stand-alone business, it may be wiped out, disappearing into bankruptcy, or sold out.

To manage a business strategically, the questions framed by the Unique Value = ROI Model must be interrelated.

A Unique Value strategy integrates all the key factors so that the fundamentals are built on a unique combination of strengths and capabilities. But in the absence of any strategy, not only are the fundamentals absent, but key questions, central to keeping the business on track, are neither asked nor answered.

What follows is a set of specific situations where extraordinary mismanagement was demonstrated by a conspicuous failure to ask the most obvious questions. As a result, the issues that were central to the health of the business were never addressed.

Questions That Were Not Asked About Consumers and Customers

From the 1920s through the 1960s, Cadillac was considered the king of the American road—the gold standard against which all other automobiles were measured. Fulfilling the marketing strategy developed by legendary General Motors CEO Alfred Sloan, Cadillac had built its reputation by delivering the key benefits that luxury car consumers most valued: a powerful engine, a smooth ride, a soft, plush interior, spaciousness and the prestige of the Cadillac name, as well as Cadillac's distinctive design and styling.

For nearly half a century, Cadillac's heritage was intact. But in the 1970s, triggered by the first oil crisis, rising fuel costs and mounting pressure for America to become more energy efficient, a dramatic change took place in the marketplace. To a new generation of younger, upscale consumers, luxury came to be defined as performance, road handling, fuel economy, reliability and quality rather than the yachtlike size and gas-guzzling ride that was synonymous with the Cadillac experience.

Reflecting these dramatic political and economic changes, and stimulated by European competitors who were able to meet the need with new standards of luxury, style and efficiency, young, affluent American car buyers changed their standards over a relatively brief period. A new segment of "contemporary luxury cars," dominated by such European leaders as Mercedes and BMW, emerged as the growing market—one in which the American manufacturers, including Cadillac, had no presence.

Responding to the loss of its dominant position, Cadillac introduced the Cimarron in 1981 to compete in the contemporary luxury segment, with the expectation that it would attract younger consumers whose needs could not be met by a traditional Cadillac. But GM had failed to assess needs of the market. To young, affluent import car buyers, the Cimarron did not represent quality and did not deliver any of their basic requirements (figure 7.1). Fewer than 20 percent of Cimarron buyers traded in imports, suggesting that its consumers were primarily domestic car users.[1] Moreover, Cimarron consumers averaged fifty years of age—about eight years younger than buyers of other Cadillacs, but far older than purchasers of its import competitors in the contemporary segment (figure 7.2).[2] The Cadillac Division of General Motors had not asked the most basic marketing questions—questions that were critical to success with the younger, affluent luxury car buyers in the United States, such as, What are their key purchase criteria? What are their emotional and functional needs? What will drive their trial, repeat purchase patterns, and loyalty?

While sales of the Cimarron remained depressed, loyal Cadillac buyers were embarrassed by its failure, much as loyal IBM customers were embarrassed by the introduction of the IBM PC Jr. Meanwhile, the market for expensive European luxury cars continued to grow (figure 7.3). The long-term effect was that the negative publicity surrounding the Cimarron's failure eroded Cadillac's credentials among its core consumer franchise (figure 7.4). In the marketplace, Cadillac's sales, compared to those of Lincoln, its primary competitor in the traditional luxury segment, declined steadily from 1983 to 1989, when the Cimarron was discontinued (figure 7.5).

Procter & Gamble failed to ask many of the same questions when the company introduced Duncan Hines cookies in 1987. One of the key drivers of profitability at Procter & Gamble is the power of "the Brand" to command the respect of the grocery trade and the loyalty of consumers. To maintain the power of the Brand,

Figure 7.1 Competitive Framework from the Perspective of Young Affluent Import Consumers

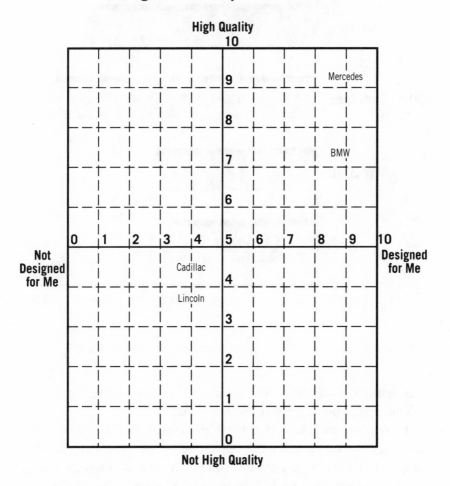

Source: Dunham & Marcus International, Inc., Database.

© Dunham & Marcus International, Inc., 1992.

P&G is single-minded about the Brand's equity (the key benefits it is associated with in the minds of users of the category of products in which it competes) and the quality of the product itself in terms of the key attributes it is perceived to deliver better than category

Figure 7.2 Average Age of Luxury Car Consumers

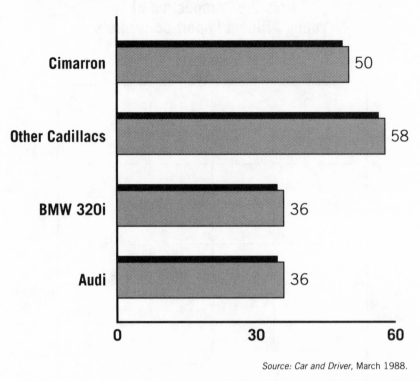

Cimarron — 50

Other Cadillacs — 58

BMW 320i — 36

Audi — 36

0   30   60

Source: Car and Driver, March 1988.

© Dunham & Marcus International, Inc., 1992.

competitors. P&G also believes in the central role of technology in delivering meaningful consumer benefits.

Thus a patentable technology breakthrough that could make packaged cookies much more appealing to consumers appeared to justify a significant capital investment in manufacturing capacity and in product and market development, when supported by the powerful "home-baked" credentials of the Duncan Hines brand name.

The superior product was not, however, evaluated from the perspective of the consumer segment that drives the bulk of mainstream packaged cookie consumption—that is, children. And for consumption by children, the product technology and P&G's need to recoup its investment made the product too expensive. P&G is

Figure 7.3 Contemporary Luxury Market Sales

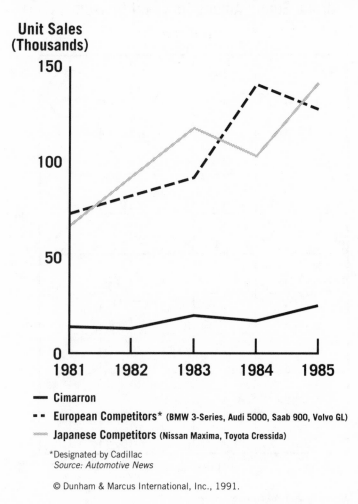

Unit Sales (Thousands)

— Cimarron

- - European Competitors* (BMW 3-Series, Audi 5000, Saab 900, Volvo GL)

Japanese Competitors (Nissan Maxima, Toyota Cressida)

*Designated by Cadillac
Source: Automotive News

© Dunham & Marcus International, Inc., 1991.

seldom the low-cost producer in a category. Its profitability is driven by the higher margins that strong brands command and the high volumes and economies of scale that its mainstream, "basic need" product categories generate.

But in the United States the ready-to-eat cookie market is dominated by RJR Nabisco. Nabisco is not only the low-cost producer, but it also owns the most powerful brand name in the mainstream market for the kinds of cookies children eat every day.

Figure 7.4 Cimarron's Impact on Cadillac's Brand Equity Among Its Loyal Consumers

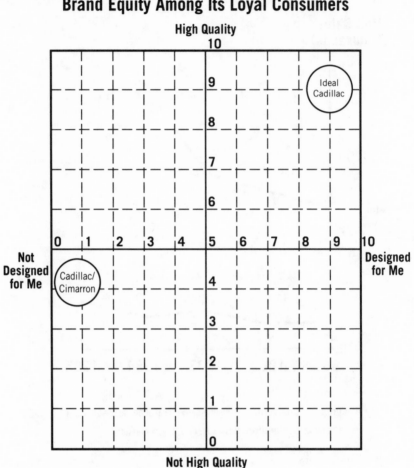

Source: Dunham & Marcus International, Inc., Database

© Dunham & Marcus International, Inc., 1992.

Procter & Gamble's product superiority was relatively unimportant in a purchase decision driven by children's tastes and a homemaker's need for affordable value. P&G did not evaluate the relevance of its technology to the strategic market target, or the role of price and value. The questions that were not asked included:

Figure 7.5 Traditional Luxury Market Sales

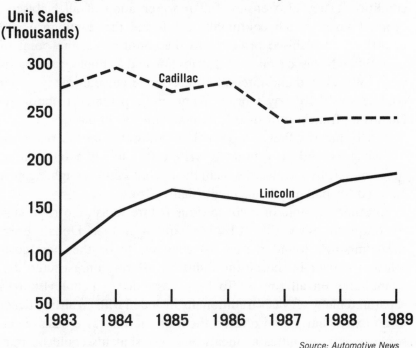

Source: Automotive News

Who will be the primary consumer? Who will be the primary purchaser? What cookie-eating occasions will drive high-volume consumption? What are the dynamics of those occasions in terms of price and volume, perceived superiority and unmet needs?

Procter & Gamble assumed that it had enormous power with every class of the grocery trade. The power was demonstrated every day in the ability to get instant distribution for almost any product on the dry grocery shelf. But the distribution system for most packaged goods involves classic warehousing, whereas bakery products with a shorter shelf life are delivered to the store directly every day, when stale products are picked up and replaced.

Driven by a "direct-to-store door" (DSD) system of distribution, Nabisco maintains an army of salespeople to man their delivery system. Because DSD teams are in stores so frequently, they maintain Nabisco's shelf space and product lines in immaculate condition. They also ensure full representation of all Nabisco's product lines, which continually reinforces the dominance and quality of all Nabisco products to the consumer at the point of sale. While Nabisco's market, distribution and technology strengths were fully aligned and integrated, P&G's initiative in ready-to-eat cookies was driven by a brand name and a patented technology. No strong franchise or distribution system was in place.

The result was P&G's eventual withdrawal from the ready-to-eat category and an estimated write-off of nearly $100 million, offset in part by the award won in the lawsuit P&G brought against Nabisco for patent infringement (figure 7.6).

Another example of a conspicious failure to ask the right customer questions was that of People Express. In 1980, Donald Burr, the company's founder, said his goal was to be the most cost-efficient carrier in the airline industry, offering unrestricted discount fares on all routes. To keep costs down, People Express separated many services traditionally included with an airline ticket at no extra charge and offered them on an à la carte basis. Such services and amenities as meals and refreshments could be purchased at the passenger's discretion, thus allowing consumers to choose those options that appealed to them.

People Express attracted a large volume of initial traffic, but developed no brand loyalty from its consumers, who were mostly pleasure travelers and therefore price-sensitive and willing to fly any airline offering lower fares. In an attempt to develop a more loyal following, People Express began to target business travelers in 1984. But business travelers, who had very different needs, including on-time arrival and on-board service, were not willing to sacrifice quality or reliability to save money. They didn't want to pay three dollars for a snack on board or for each piece of baggage they wished to check, and they were extremely intolerant of the delays, lost luggage or other mishaps which became associated with People Express.

Questions that People Express failed to ask about its customers included: What are the key considerations for vacation travelers, as

Figure 7.6 Duncan Hines Cookies
1987 Write-Off: Estimated $100 Million

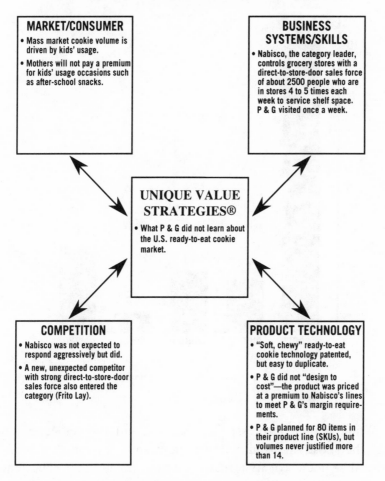

MARKET/CONSUMER
- Mass market cookie volume is driven by kids' usage.
- Mothers will not pay a premium for kids' usage occasions such as after-school snacks.

BUSINESS SYSTEMS/SKILLS
- Nabisco, the category leader, controls grocery stores with a direct-to-store-door sales force of about 2500 people who are in stores 4 to 5 times each week to service shelf space. P & G visited once a week.

UNIQUE VALUE STRATEGIES®
- What P & G did not learn about the U.S. ready-to-eat cookie market.

COMPETITION
- Nabisco was not expected to respond aggressively but did.
- A new, unexpected competitor with strong direct-to-store-door sales force also entered the category (Frito Lay).

PRODUCT TECHNOLOGY
- "Soft, chewy" ready-to-eat cookie technology patented, but easy to duplicate.
- P & G did not "design to cost"—the product was priced at a premium to Nabisco's lines to meet P & G's margin requirements.
- P & G planned for 80 items in their product line (SKUs), but volumes never justified more than 14.

© Dunham & Marcus International, Inc., 1992.

opposed to business travelers? What represents good service? What aspects of service are most likely to lead to repeat purchases? As a result, the carrier was known as an "adventure" to fly and was nicknamed "Poverty Express" and "People Distress" among business travelers. Indeed, passenger complaints for the airline ran triple the industry average (figure 7.7).

Figure 7.7   Complaints per 100,000 Passengers

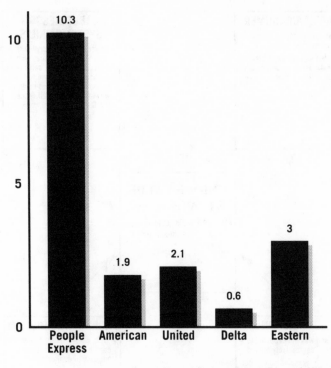

Source: Harvard Business School; Friesen & Mills

While People Express, like Cadillac and Procter & Gamble, launched costly new initiatives without understanding the needs of critical segments of its targeted market, many other experienced managers around the world have disenfranchised the constituencies on which their business depended. For example, German-based Nixdorf Computer, established in 1952, built its reputation on customer service. Under the direction of founder Heinz Nixdorf, the firm for many years was the industry leader in customer service, marketing agility and ability to create user-friendly machines.

But as personal computers gained popularity in the 1980s, Nixdorf was unable to match the customer-responsiveness of rivals with more flexible and cost-effective PCs. When Nixdorf posted a substantial loss in 1989, the one asset the company had left—its customer loyalty—was allowed to erode:

> Nixdorf's problems became self-fueling. The worse its losses became, the less confidence its customers had. For a company whose strength has been its people—its technical people and its loyal customer base—that was life threatening. Nixdorf was going to go bust unless it found strong (customer) support very quickly.[3]

Questions Nixdorf management never asked included: How do customers perceive their options? What alternatives are becoming available? How important are computers in the management of customers' business? How robust is the relationship with customers? What would jeopardize it?

Nixdorf was acquired by Siemens in 1990, bringing one of Germany's great postwar entrepreneurial success stories to an end.

Questions That Were Not Asked About Business Systems and Skills

People Express's management failed to ask strategically important questions about its business systems and skills, as well as about its customers. It sought the cost advantage needed to offer bargain fares by financing aircraft through then-revolutionary sale and leaseback arrangements, which became a financial drain on the company. And to maximize its operating efficiency, People Express organized its route structure through a unique hub and spoke network that allowed aircraft to be utilized more efficiently than the traditional route systems used throughout the industry. As a result, People's planes were in the air 50 percent more per day than the industry average.[4]

Separately, Burr worked toward developing a unique corporate culture designed to achieve an unprecedented level of labor-management harmony and, in turn, of employee productivity, by, for example:

- Offering employees generous stock rights that would induce them to accept below-standard salaries (35 percent below the industry average) and to beat back attempts at unionization.[5]
- Increasing morale and productivity among employees by supplementing wages with nonmonetary rewards (such as important-sounding titles); by frequently rotating job assignments; and by creating an egalitarian organization with minimal perks (such as expense accounts and private secretaries) for executives. In addition to the psychological impact, this helped to keep operating costs to a minimum (figure 7.8).

Figure 7.8   Cost per Available Seat Mile–1981*

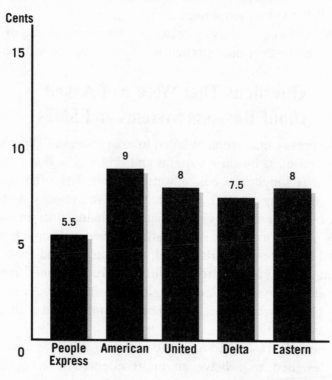

* Figures are approximate

Source: Harvard Business School; Whitestone & Schlesinger

Burr believed that the pride and loyalty generated by People's unique employee-owner arrangement was crucial to the airline's success. "People Express was a lesson in freedom in corporate behavior," Burr maintains. "Yet people say to me all the time: 'That stuff doesn't work. That's all touchy-feely.' But that's why we came out of nowhere and grew to be the fifth largest airline in the country."[6]

Using these business system and operations principles, People became a major force in the airline industry's eastern U.S. market. Starting in April, 1981, with service to four cities, People Express expanded rapidly. In little more than a year, People had seventeen planes and an enthusiastic workforce of twelve hundred, serviced thirteen destinations and reported a quarterly profit.

But as Donald Burr pursued his personal beliefs and values in the early days of the venture, no foundation was put in place to sustain growth. The corporate culture, designed to reduce operating expenses, did so at the expense of consistent service and management experience that would be critical to remaining competitive as the airline sought to sustain its growth. Several factors contributed:

- People Express relied heavily on part-time employees and interns who were poorly trained and lacked motivation.
- The company's job rotation policy contradicted widely accepted principles of improved efficiency through specialization.
- People's lack of middle management left the company devoid of expertise for developing financial, marketing and route expansion strategies.

After the initial burst of success and rapid growth, the open management style thought to be People's asset proved to be a liability. The airline became chronically understaffed as the hiring and training of new employees failed to keep up with the carrier's growth. To cope with the increased organizational and administrative duties resulting from People's expansion, Burr added an additional layer of management. This proved to be a double negative,

increasing costs (a cardinal sin for a low-cost competitor) and diminishing employee morale—morale that would plunge even further as People's stock was battered. As events spiraled downward,
service deteriorated further, thus accentuating the company's
weaknesses in the marketplace.

There was also an ill-conceived $300 million acquisition of fi-
nancially ailing Frontier Airlines in 1985. Not only did People
Express overpay, thus adding to an already high debt load and, in
turn, further inhibiting financial flexibility to deliver the promised
low fares, but by merging Frontier's unionized workforce, hide-
bound corporate bureaucracy and full-service philosophy with People's radically different system and culture, People Express
demonstrated conclusively its lack of a cohesive and implementable
strategy.

Business systems and skills questions that People Express failed
to ask included: What operating systems, if any, will allow us to
deliver quality service at a lower price on a sustainable basis? What
kind of people do we need to hire to deliver quality service? What
systems or training approaches will lower costs and deliver superior
service? What organizational structures could improve airlines
operations?

"I practiced a number of things that were ideological but not
practical," Donald Burr admitted, with the lessons of failure behind him. "If I were doing it over, I would hire from the outside
and amend our compensation terms to attract good people. You
couldn't get a chief financial officer for a $1 billion company for
$75,000 a year [Burr's salary]."[7]

Questions That Were Not Asked
About Products and Technologies

Nixdorf Computer's demise as a leader in Germany's computer
industry may seem inevitable given the changes in the global industry, but as with Wang in the United States, which filed for
bankruptcy in August 1992, the founder's lack of interest in putting
a long-term strategy in place was the real problem.

After the death of Founder Heinz Nixdorf in 1986, industry analysts put the blame on his successor, Klaus Luft, for subsequent failures and for not providing badly needed leadership. *The Economist* reported:

> [Luft] succumbed to self-doubt as the competition from personal computers increased.
>
> Despite, or perhaps because of, his 20 years at Mr. Nixdorf's knee, Mr. Luft's changes were too little, too late. Attempts to adopt industry-standard technologies like the Unix operating system raised R&D costs and complicated the product line. Repeated reorganizations helped spread Mr. Luft's uncertainty to others in the organization.[8]

In reality, Nixdorf's research and development group had long been allowed to deteriorate, losing the innovativeness that paved the way for the firm's early technological prowess. In 1962, Nixdorf had developed the world's first electronic desktop printing calculator, and it pioneered the first semiconductor-based small computer in 1965. In 1968 it introduced compact computer work stations, which were far less expensive than mainframes and therefore could meet the needs of organizations that until then could not afford to invest in powerful computers.

But in a relatively short period of time, it lost this edge. While competitors were continually introducing faster, more powerful machines, Nixdorf began to have trouble keeping pace. Nixdorf's products were also limited in terms of compatibility, a critical consideration as personal computers became ubiquitous and were required to interact with other brands and systems.

Nixdorf's approach, like many, had been to offer a "full-solution" product—hardware, software and service. But because Nixdorf's hardware was incompatible with other systems, independent software designers did not produce leading-edge software for Nixdorf's machines, and the firm's declining R&D capability could not match the software being developed externally. With no technological or cost advantage in hardware and deteriorating customer service, Nixdorf's product was no longer viable. Questions

Nixdorf's founder failed to ask included: What is the next generation of technology? How must technology be managed internally to stay current and meet customer needs? What technology strengths can Nixdorf build on?

The failure of the Cimarron was symptomatic of a failure to ask the same kinds of questions. To minimize development costs, General Motors routinely designed its cars to share as many components as possible with other GM products. Cadillac's Cimarron was based on GM's J-car family, which was composed of the Chevrolet Cavalier, Pontiac J2000/Sunbird, Buick Skyhawk and Oldsmobile Firenza. As a result, the Cimarron closely resembled its less expensive J-car relatives, and consumers correctly perceived it to be no more than a dressed-up version of those lower-priced models. While the J-car platform was sufficiently advanced to compete in the entry-level compact segment, it lacked the technology and refinement of the Cimarron's competitors in the contemporary luxury segment—such as the BMW 320i and Audi 4000.

Questions That Were Not Asked About Competitors

In the early 1980s, Yamaha attempted to overtake Honda as Japan's leading motorcycle manufacturer after years of steadily gaining on its long-time rival. With Honda focusing primarily on its growing automobile business, Yamaha's management believed that with sufficient production capacity, it could dethrone Honda as the world motorcycle leader. In 1981, Yamaha's president, Hisao Koike, was quoted as saying: "As primarily a motorcycle producer, you cannot expect us to remain in our present number two position forever. If we only had enough capacity we could beat Honda."[9]

The same year, Yamaha announced the construction of a new manufacturing facility that would increase its capacity by 33 percent, to 4 million units. Yamaha also continued to invest heavily in new product development and, in 1981, introduced more new models than Honda.

But Yamaha had seriously underestimated the competition, just as P&G had underestimated Nabisco's franchise and business strengths.[10] Honda, which had been focused on building its automotive operations during the 1970s, responded to the Yamaha threat by inundating the market with new models and product innovations and aggressively cutting prices. In eighteen months, Honda increased its domestic market share from 38 percent to 43 percent, while Yamaha's share dropped from 37 percent to 23 percent.[11] It was certainly true that Yamaha was free to focus all its resources on motorcycles. However, its revenue from motorcycle sales could not fund the high levels of investment needed to match Honda's product development capabilities. And Honda generated substantial income from its other business units, giving it marketing, operations and financial flexibility.

P&G, on the other hand, did not underestimate Nabisco. It simply did not take Nabisco's competitive strengths into account. In a comparable case years earlier, P&G made the same strategic error. It did not take regional potato-chip makers into account when it introduced Pringles Potato Chips and set off a firestorm of reaction from local "chippers" (potato chip manufacturers).

In the case of People Express, disregard of the competitive structure of the airline industry led not only to management errors in judgment, but also stimulated a creative response from competitors.

With P&G and the ready-to-eat cookie category, Nabisco merely lowered its annual earnings projections by $50 million and invested the money in marketing its own soft cookie entry, Almost Home.

With People Express, local and regional carriers took steps to strengthen their competitive position in a variety of ways. For example, small airlines started forming partnerships with larger carriers to increase their traffic flow and to gain needed capital investment. Regional carriers also made efforts to slash their costs, by identifying and eliminating operating inefficiencies and seeking out cheaper labor agreements, so that they could afford to match People's lower fares.

The major airlines also responded as People Express began to enter their primary markets. Across the board, larger carriers matched People's cheap fares, thereby allowing consumers to fly established full-service airlines for the same price as flying People Express. Simultaneously, the major airlines initiated or expanded frequent-flyer programs to increase loyalty among the business travelers that People Express was targeting and improved their operating efficiency by reorganizing their route systems into the same hub-and-spoke networks pioneered by People Express.

One critical competitive disadvantage People Express faced was its lack of a sophisticated computer reservation system that would allow it to maximize revenue by offering a range of fares on every flight. This concept, known as "yield management," conflicted with People's basic premise: to offer across-the-board low prices that varied only by flight time (peak or off-peak).

While People was trapped in its inflexible pricing structure, airlines with more sophisticated computer systems (such as American Airlines and its SABRE system) were able to increase revenue by incrementally pricing seats according to flight time, season and purchase factors (such as advance bookings and minimum length of stay). Because it lacked the technology to do this, and because it set a pricing schedule designed to undercut its competitors, People Express earned the lowest revenue yield in the industry (figure 7.9).

Before People Express challenged the major carriers, its simple reservation system proved sufficient, since local and regional airlines lacked this technology and therefore could not match People's fares. But when a full-scale price war erupted, the major carriers were able to match People's lower fares while maintaining superior margins. This was accomplished, in part, by charging full fares to consumers not booking in advance and to business travelers seeking unrestricted tickets. Questions that People Express, Procter & Gamble and Yamaha all failed to ask about the competition included: What strategies drive the actions of our competitors? How are they likely to respond given an attack to their core business? What strategies and tactics are available to them? What are their available resources? What could they do that would put us at a disadvantage? How costly would that be? Can we afford it?

Whether the questions not asked are about consumers, customers, business systems, skills, products, technologies or competitors, the

Figure 7.9 Revenue Per Passenger Mile–1981*

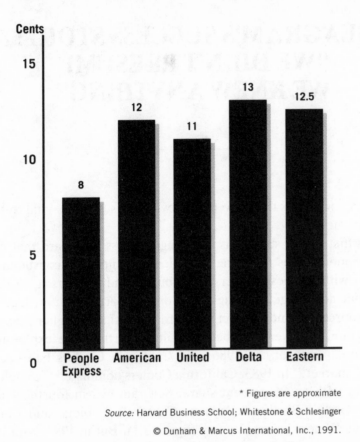

* Figures are approximate

Source: Harvard Business School; Whitestone & Schlesinger

© Dunham & Marcus International, Inc., 1991.

result will affect the entire management of the business, its financial performance and its return on investment. In a complex and dynamic environment one or all of these variables may be evolving. Assumptions must therefore be checked and updated again and again.

No manager can afford to think he or she has all the answers. In any manager that is a fatal flaw.

Knowing what questions to ask, and asking them all the time, is a precondition for strategic solutions to complex business problems. It is also the only way to avoid the financial and human costs associated with catastrophic business failure.

CHAPTER 8

SEAGRAM'S SUCCESS STORY: "WE DIDN'T PRESUME WE KNEW ANYTHING"

———— • ————

In academic circles the conventional wisdom is that it is vital to be "first to market."

This first-mover status has advantages across the board that include opportunities to define the rules; lock up loyal consumers; partner with the best brokers, distributors and retailers; gain the economic advantage of being ahead on the learning curve; secure key resources; define product standards; and charge higher prices.

Seagram, however, had been a failing fourth in the exploding wine cooler category in 1986, and California Coolers had been "first to market." In 1983, California Coolers dominated the cooler category with an 86 percent share. Seagram was in fourth place behind Gallo's Bartles & Jaymes, California Coolers, and Canandaigua Winery's Sun Country (figure 8.1). But in 1987, with its reentry strategy, Seagram more than doubled its market share and gained category leadership in just one year with sales of $416 million, while California Coolers slipped from its previous 86 percent share to 21 percent (figure 8.2).

Seagram's turnaround in the cooler category had required not only a new strategy, but also a new attitude, which included a commitment to learn new skills and develop new systems to manage a business that was fundamentally different from its established spirits business. Dick Coffey, former president of Seagram Beverage Company, explains how this learning attitude was instilled throughout the organization:

Figure 8.1   Wine Cooler Market Share
1986

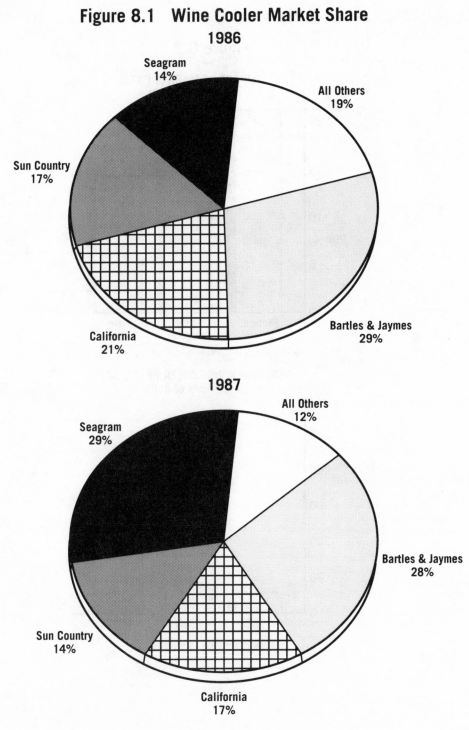

Source: Beverage Marketing, 1987 U.S. Wine Market Report.

UNIQUE VALUE

Figure 8.2

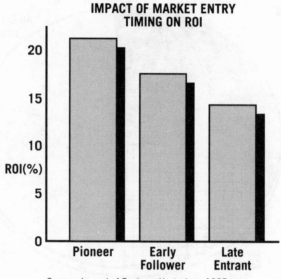

IMPACT OF MARKET ENTRY TIMING ON ROI

Source: Journal of Business Venturings, 1985.

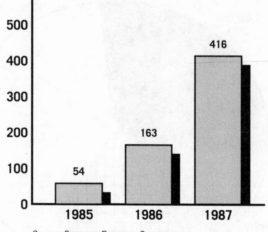

SEAGRAM WINE COOLER RETAIL SALES (in millions of dollars)

Source: Seagram Beverage Company

When we got back into coolers (the reentry in 1986), we didn't presume we knew anything. The business maxim that I like to practice is "ninety days to perfection." Give us ninety days to do anything and we'll do it right. You don't always have ninety days in this process, but you have to keep probing and trying to find out. You cannot presume anything. I can't presume my distribution system is right. I can't presume my purchasing system is right. I can't presume my manufacturing system is right. I can't presume my marketing is right.

We got into broadcast media. This company had no experience in broadcast media. Suddenly we were buying millions of dollars in television. Were we doing it correctly? That depends on your point of view. This was a brand new experience for us. We had to eat a lot of humble pie. I couldn't go in and say, "I've got twenty-five years of experience in this business." I didn't. I had one month or two months, because this was an entirely different business from spirits.

With no disrespect for Brown-Forman—they're a very respected company and I have the highest regard for them—they didn't make the cultural shift with California Coolers that we made in this company.

What were the building blocks of the strategic knowledge base Seagram established as a foundation for its reentry strategy?

Consumer/Customer Learning

To become a success in the cooler business, Seagram had to recognize that it could not rely on the consumer profile it knew from generations in the spirits business. Says Coffey:

We made a significant investment in consumer information. And we learned that we could not deal in subjectivity. That's why we've been able to sail in front of our major competitor, because we've been the innovator in the marketplace—in packaging, in flavors. But we learned the importance of understanding the consumer the hard way.

At one point, we put wine coolers in cans. We didn't ask consumers what they thought about our innovation, we just did it, and those same consumers rejected it, saying, "Wine doesn't come in cans." Then one of our people said it wasn't the wine cooler in a can that bothered consumers, but that the graphics were wrong, so we spent a lot of money designing new graphics. At that point, we went back to the market and consumers told us again, "Wine doesn't belong in cans."

We ran into a consumer perception that can be a difficult thing to shake. Let's say there is a Campbell's soup and a Campbell's ketchup: Who knows of the latter? Let's say there is a Heinz ketchup and a Heinz soup: Ask consumers about soup and they'll say Campbell's.

The point is that you have to keep focused on the fundamentals and you have to keep learning and relearning them. That's why I go into stores all the time. I look at jams. I look at jellies, I look at yogurt. I look at juice drinks. I look to see what flavors people are buying, what kind of packaging they are attracted to. You can conduct all kinds of elaborate research—which we do—but there's no substitute for following people down supermarket aisles to see what they buy.

When consumers enter a convenience store, they want to be in and out of there in three minutes. It's snowing out, the kids are crying and they don't want to intellectualize about the purchase decision. The product either grabs them or it doesn't; they either need it or they don't. And we learned the hard way that we had to scrap the wine cooler in the can because that didn't grab them. Period.

I have to make my people realize that we can never accept that what we are doing is the best way to do it. Because there's always a better way. If you don't recognize that, history is going to teach you a lesson the hard way.

One thing that Seagram learned was that coolers represented a unique opportunity for the company to grow its business. Says Seagram Beverage Company executive vice president of marketing Mark Taxel:

Brands were growing. Companies were spending money, and there was a real alternative alcohol beverage product being presented to the American public. The trial rates for coolers were incredible. A 1985 Attitude and Usage study showed that the category had already attracted about 50 percent of all adults under the age of forty-nine. By 1987 that figure had jumped to 70 percent. That's quite a trial rate.

Through careful market research, Seagram identified a unique way to enter the category that its competitors had not addressed. Says Taxel:

> Our competition, which were mostly wineries, felt that coolers would provide an introductory wine product from which people would trade up to more sophisticated wines. Coolers were being presented as a new fun way to drink wine. But our research revealed a different usage pattern. We saw a new beverage category developing, one which was not actually based on wine. Tests showed, in fact, that coolers were being substituted for beer much more than wine. We initially hypothesized, and eventually concluded, that from the consumer's perspective coolers were not an adjunct to the wine business, but shared certain characteristics of the beer business.

Business Systems/Skills Learning

When Seagram entered the cooler business, it had to meet a number of requirements that were dramatically different from its spirits business. Foremost among these was learning to manage a copacking network for production instead of building new bottling facilities. Seagram treasurer John Preston recalls:

> We used copackers for two principal reasons. First, we minimized our asset base by not owning facilities. Second, by using outside production we increased our flexibility to respond to changing market conditions because we would be able to adjust production capacity to meet volume and geographic needs by changing our arrangements with copackers when necessary.

While using copackers had advantages over company-owned plants, it presented some significant challenges as well. According to John Preston:

> The huge downside to using copackers is that copacking, by its very nature, is a "bare light bulb from the ceiling" kind of business. It's a tough business—skinny, skinny margins force them to cut every corner that they can. Among the reasons that we have traditionally owned our facilities is to ensure quality; the company was founded on quality and is run on quality. We won't compromise on that. So to achieve the benefits of low capital expenditure, production capacity flexibility and cost competitiveness, without a sacrifice in quality, we had to work as a team to ensure that the copackers met our quality standard.

Seagram's management organized a joint effort among its R&D, operations, quality assurance and purchasing departments that would allow the firm to translate its precise quality requirements to the cooler business. This challenge was heightened by the difficulties of controlling quality at five to seven different bottling locations simultaneously, while Seagram's technical staff was still learning about a new technology: Cooler bottling lines run at much higher speeds than those for traditional spirits. Preston says:

> Keep in mind that this is not the spirits business. It is a cyclical business characterized by tremendous peaks in production, flat-out production, days on end. You're asking people to go like hell—you've got distributors screaming for the product. Our whiskey bottle line runs at 200 to 300 bottles a minute, at the most. The specialty bottles, like the Frangelico, or Drambuie, or square bottles are something like 150 bottles a minute. Compare this to a cooler line, which runs at 900 bottles a minute.
>
> The speed of the line affects the way in which we measure and monitor the quality of our product. On the whiskey line, a lot of what we do to sustain quality is visual. We have people on the line looking at the label, looking at the fill level, looking

at the bottle to see if it looks right. When the bottle speeds by at 900 bottles a minute, you have to rely upon more sophisticated technology to achieve Seagram quality standards. As a result, your procedures for label application and for crowning are very, very different.

The team had to discover new ways of gauging and monitoring quality on the line. This introduced a different type of challenge to our group of technical experts. Yet, they took—and ultimately met—the challenge of producing a product to specific Seagram quality standards at a specific cost.

As was the case with manufacturing, Seagram had to learn the dynamics of a totally new distribution system. Wine and spirits distributors were typically unfamiliar with such practices as:

- Setting up a cold box in retail outlets
- Merchandising and in-store displays
- Using scanner data as a sales tool
- Making money on a high volume, fast turnover product

According to Taxel, this transition was demanding for some of their traditional distributors: "The wine and spirits distributors had to accept the challenge to learn. Because of this pressure to learn, we lost some of our distributors who felt that they couldn't adjust to the new requirements. Those who made an effort to learn these trade channels gained the ability to take on other lines and do a creditable job. We enlisted beer and soda distributors to fill in the blanks. Today, 50 percent of our distributors are wine and spirits and 50 percent are beer and/or soda."

The beer and soda distributors were well-equipped to handle coolers. Says Preston:

Our new breed of distributor knew all about stock rotation, which was a new concept for our traditional distributor. Unlike spirits, coolers have a limited shelf life, which means that we must continually rotate the oldest product up front first. This helped our cost structure because we had a distribution network which could turn its inventory faster than our traditional

distributor, and faster than Gallo's. And whereas the wine and spirits distributor is used to calling on a customer once, maybe twice a week, a beer distributor is in the account every other day—every day in the summer, which is our peak season. In addition, beer distributors were used to running on thin margins and tig
tories.

While Seagram was learning a new set of skills specifically related to the production and distribution of coolers, it was also undergoing an organizational transformation that allowed this learning to take place. Perhaps the most difficult feat in making a company responsive is to ensure an adaptive culture. At Seagram, this meant changing the nature of the organization from a rigid, hierarchical structure to a flexible, cooperative environment.

Edgar Bronfman, Jr., held a "red light, green light" meeting in December 1985. At this meeting, it was either going to be Stop or Go for a restaged Seagram cooler business. The evidence assembled strongly supported a "Go." And when the decision was made, based on that evidence, a crash program had to be developed, working through the holiday season. Says Bronfman:

> In order to meet the tight production deadlines of the cooler business, we had to learn to work together. I'm talking about a schedule whereby we had to deliver our first order to supermarkets on May 6, 1986, and that product was bottled on May 5.
>
> To make this work, we needed a much flatter organization. The Seagram culture didn't favor that but our timetable demanded it and we made it happen. In the past, any time there were more than seven people in a meeting it was considered a mob. But with coolers, we would have thirty, forty, fifty people in a meeting. That's because there was no time to go talk to everybody individually, as had been the practice in the past.
>
> In the new environment, people collaborated by bringing their peers from other departments together and making them feel part of the team. This helped to instill a singular challenge

and a sense of a single objective. The change in organization
that occurred here was a real-world case of necessity being
the mother of invention. If we were going to succeed in a new
business, we needed a new type of organization to make it
work.

To make this happen in an established corporation with a long
tradition of departmental autonomy, Bronfman played the role of
"Mission Czar" armed with the power and the mandate to break
through the inevitable squabbling and logjams and to keep all
divisions and departments moving toward the common mission.
Says Taxel:

People throughout the company had been working fever-
ishly to get our wine cooler ready for months. Just when it
seemed that we had all the logistics in place, we had this big
interdepartmental meeting to conduct a last-minute check of
the systems. That's when I asked, "Does anyone here know
of any reason why we should have a problem meeting our
deadline?" At that point, a guy in the back of the room raised
his hand and said, "Yes, I have a big problem. We haven't
ordered the flavors yet."

I was incredulous. "We've been working for months and
you haven't ordered the flavors yet! Why?" He said, "Because
I don't have an approved company formula signed off and
ready to go. And I'm not allowed to order anything unless I
have that in my hand." All of a sudden, I thought I was in
the army. When I asked how much lead time was involved in
ordering the flavors, he said a couple of weeks, which was
more time than we had.

From there the plot thickened. An R&D guy, who was
responsible for making the formula, said it was company policy
that he couldn't make it until he got an approval from BATF
(the Bureau of Alcohol, Tobacco and Firearms). When I asked
how long that would take, he said about two weeks before
production. That's when I kind of blew up.

"Wait a minute. How many dollars do these flavors cost?"

"About $50,000," the R&D guy said.

"We have $4 million in glass being produced, $4 million of

advertising being bought, $1 million of sales promotion materials ready to be sent out, we've already invested $X million in plant and equipment and you're telling me that we're allowing $50,000 worth of formula to jeopardize all of that?"

To which the R&D guy responded:

"I'm just telling you what I'm allowed to do and what I'm not allowed to do. And I can't produce a formula until I get a signoff."

That's where the mission czar had to flex his muscles, not as a power play but as a means of integrating the critical elements and, in turn, of achieving the corporate objectives.

Taxel continues:

At the outset of the cooler project, Edgar said, "If you ever need help making this work, get me in on the problem if you can't handle yourself." So when I informed him of the problem I was having in getting the flavors, he brought in the senior VP for worldwide manufacturing. After conversing with that executive, I told the R&D guy, "I understand the rule you've been complying with, but I want you to prepare all the papers you need to order the flavors because within a half hour of getting back to your office, you're going to get the authorization to do just that."

And sure enough the call came through and we moved ahead.

One example of how the Seagram organization changed to manage the cooler business is that purchasing was brought under the control of the Seagram Beverage Company chief financial officer John Preston. This would accomplish dual objectives:

(1) As the company was acquiring a new skill set as a low-cost, low-margin producer, all purchasing decisions filtered through the CFO would bring new discipline to corporate spending.

(2) In appointing the beverage company's CFO as the maestro of the cooler business, Seagram was creating a system for having a senior executive integrate all the elements and keep them focused on the corporate mission.

Preston recalls:

> In 1987, we had conducted market research on new flavors and found the best candidates to be wild berries and apple cranberry. As it turned out, we were half right: wild berries took off and apple cranberry languished, producing our first inventory problem in the cooler business. Based on optimistic projections for both flavors, the purchasing people went out and bought a year's supply of cardboard carriers and labels. Much of these materials for the apple cranberry flavor had to be written off.

After swallowing that bitter pill, Seagram announced that the purchasing people would no longer be allowed to buy what they alone deemed appropriate. Starting immediately, their decisions would have to be filtered through the beverage company's CFO. Says John Preston:

> Each month I would sit with them and we would forecast by flavor and SKU on a rolling basis for the coming months. We would then look at the expected production plan and finished goods inventory over the next 90 to 180 days. With this as our target, the purchasing people would propose various levels of production by the glass company and by the label company. Those are two big variables. Because there is constant experimentation and constant change, overproducing components could mean we would be stuck with six to eight months of labels and carrying containers when a product had to be discontinued. Given the slim margins we were working with, that kind of waste couldn't be tolerated.
>
> We had to learn that purchasing can't overorder from suppliers just to ensure that enough supplies are on hand to meet unexpected demand. Sales can't overinflate demand forecasts to prevent out-of-stocks—after all, their department would not get charged for write-offs of obsolete packaging, so over-estimating had not been perceived to be a problem. Similarly, we learned that marketing can't second guess volume figures to boost their advertising and promotional dollars.

As Preston recognized, cost-cutting was more than simply a means of bringing added profitability to the cooler line. It was the spearhead of a new strategic focus that Seagram's had to adopt to be successful in the marketplace. Preston says:

> We had to have the strategic vision of an innovative, high-quality producer that would be competitive in price and product. We had to know our customers, we had to know our costs, we had to know our competition and we had to develop the business systems that would enable us to deal effectively with all of these factors. We did so, in part, because we knew that if we lost our focus, Gallo would eat us for lunch.

Product/Technology Learning

Before entering the wine cooler business, Seagram had very little experience outside cordials in developing flavor systems. So the company had to build expertise in flavoring technology and development. This too was a critical part of the learning process. Preston recalls:

> We had to learn how the flavor companies look at their economics. They produce what's called a flavor key, and put it in a solvent such as juice or water. If you were capable of buying or developing a flavor key, you could eliminate about 50 percent of the cost.
>
> Take, for example, our most successful wine cooler flavor, wild berries. We had a couple of scientists at our R&D facility go to work on the project and they were successful in determining the essence and what solvent was used. Then we could go back to the flavor suppliers and renegotiate prices.
>
> Not only did their technology reduce our cost of goods, but it also wound up playing a big part in the development of new flavors on an ongoing basis. Their work represented a new area of learning for our organization.

The process of continually developing and introducing new products was also new for Seagram. Preston continues:

Before coolers, we rarely introduced new products or flankers, so our purchasing was routine and component inventories weren't critical. And now we were continually introducing new flavors to create news in the marketplace. Keeping the shelves stocked with a string of new flavors to maintain retail excitement and interest was an essential part of our strategy. But that involved purchasing critically sensitive materials with each new introduction.

Not only did this require Seagram to monitor inventories and supplies of dry goods much more closely in order to keep costs down, it was a new experience for Seagram in terms of transferring new formulas from R&D to production. Explains Preston:

The scale-up from lab quantity to production quantity is laden with hiccups. This is not a "formula to production" business. For example, you can end up with ingredients that worked right in the lab, but you can't get to work right on the bottling line. What worked in R&D might result in foaming on the line. Why? A sample from the flavor house may have been just right in the lab, but when they supply it in quantity for the run, it might be slightly different. The difference from a biological or molecular point of view can cause precipitation. These were all things that our R&D department had to learn from square one.

Competitor Learning

The intensity of competition in the cooler business required Seagram to track the activities of Gallo, the giant privately held corporation that dominates the California wine industry with its unparalleled purchasing, manufacturing and distribution strengths. Gallo had created Bartles & Jaymes as an integral part of its strategy to maintain control of every aspect of the California wine industry. Seagram carefully monitored Gallo's product initiatives and its business system and capabilities. Says Preston:

Gallo followed our product introductions on a number of occasions. We did wild berries, they did a berry. We did a tropical, they did a tropical. They followed us on peach.

In competing with them flavor by flavor, market by market, we had to understand what drives their business. Their manufacturing is totally vertically integrated. They make their own glass. They make their own crowns and caps. They have the largest winery in the state of California and are, therefore, the largest purchaser of grapes. So for instance, they can use excess white wine for inventory balancing and blend it off against cooler flavors.

In the words of Dick Coffey:

One of the major competitive elements they employ in many cases is that they're the principal supplier to their distributor, as opposed to being a minority supplier. A Gallo distributor, for the most part, is either an exclusive Gallo distributor or they're an exclusive division that markets Gallo products. The product that competes against our product is a member of that particular family. Frequently it's sold with it; frequently it's discounted with it. It's certainly merchandised with it and they have very good trade access.

The second thing is, the Gallo company is very retail-account-oriented. They have excellent coverage at the retail level but we think we've been able to do a superior job of competing against that. We're not as strong as they are in every market, in every channel of trade, but again, statistically, we're now very, very good in that area.

They're a tough competitor. It's as clear as Coke and Pepsi, as Miller and Bud. In this particular product line, it's Seagram and Gallo.

The knowledge base that Seagram had built before the "red light, green light" meeting on December 20, 1985, had laid a strategic foundation for Edgar Bronfman, Jr.'s management decision to reenter the category in 1986. Partly because Seagram was already distributing a cooler product, even though it was failing, and partly because of a systematic set of studies and analyses, as well as exhaustive internal discussions, the management team was in full agreement about the right questions and issues surrounding strategies for marketing, distribution, skills, technologies and competitors. Substrategies for every aspect of the business flowed from this shared understanding.

Examples of key conclusions from the situation analysis that led to the formulation of Seagram wine coolers reentry strategy, crystallized in the Unique Value = ROI Model format, are shown in Figure 8.3. With the strategy for reentry in place and fully understood by all members of the team responsible for executing it, specific substrategies became the responsibility of Seagram's functional experts. Mark Taxel led the marketing effort to develop a product line with the level of sophistication the strategy required; Dick Coffey led the effort to build a distribution network, focus the sales force and achieve the necessary "ubiquity" to execute the strategy (that is, being everywhere a potential consumer would want to buy the product); John Preston led the effort to manage operating costs and profit margins; and Edgar Bronfman, Jr., provided continuous input, probing and prodding, while focusing on the requirements of competing with a force as formidable as Gallo.

Throughout the year of 1986 and beyond, the foundation of knowledge that had been put in place to formulate the reentry strategy was constantly reviewed, revised and built upon. In the subsequent years, the Seagram Beverage Company consciously became a learning organization which paid attention to every detail of strategy and execution. As Mark Taxel said:

> We met our strategic objectives within two years by managing the business in a learning environment. I mean that we had to learn to learn. We had to learn that to carve out a business in this category, you must first build a strong brand with premium credentials, and then build the business, because our margins are driven by the strength of our brand. We had to learn from the past, and from each other. We had to learn from our competitors, and we had to learn from other segments of the beverage business. We're still learning. Our desire and ability to learn will be a common denominator for all of our future efforts.

Figure 8.3 What Seagram Learned about the Wine Cooler Business

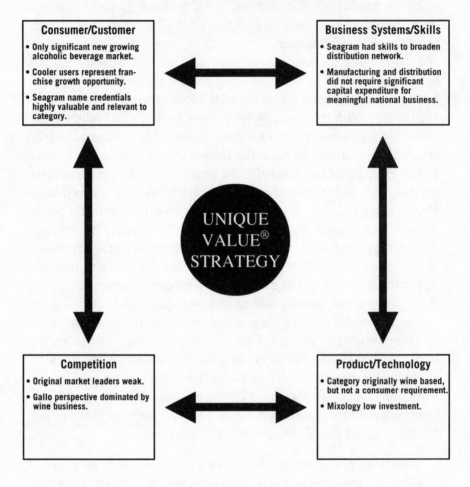

© Dunham & Marcus International, Inc., 1992.

Seagram's success in wine coolers was a strategic triumph for the corporation. It was an important part of the parent company's hoped-for transformation from a North American whiskey company, known historically for Seagram's V.O., Seagram's 7-Crown and Chivas Regal, to a more broadly based beverage company. By learning to shave costs, to distribute to mass merchandisers, to innovate and to compete aggressively for cold box as well as standard shelf space, Seagram had built expertise that could potentially be leveraged across a wide range of premium branded products.

An opportunity to make a quantum leap as a diversified beverage business came when Kohlberg, Kravis & Roberts, then the owners of Tropicana, put the juice company up for sale in 1987.

"At first, KKR wanted to sell Tropicana only as part of the Beatrice Foods business," recalls Edgar Bronfman, Jr., whose success with wine coolers gave him the corporate support for making a major nonspirits acquisition.

> We told them we weren't interested in the other Beatrice companies and so the talks were put on the back burner.
>
> But after the market crash of '87 it became harder to sell businesses and KKR decided to sell off some of the more attractive Beatrice companies. So in the early part of 1988, I called Henry Kravis, telling him I'd like to buy Tropicana. The conversation went like this:
>
> Edgar Bronfman: "I want an exclusive on Tropicana. You name a price, give me two weeks to consider it, and I'll either say yes or no. If I don't meet your price, you can go back to your auction."
>
> Henry Kravis: "Why should I give you an exclusive?"
>
> Edgar Bronfman: "Because you get to name your price. You have no risk of falling short. Give us two weeks and you'll either get the price or you won't, at which point you can go to an auction. If you go straight to an auction, it's going to take three or four weeks for each company to do their due diligence, you won't get to name your price and the process may be much slower. I'm giving you a chance to make a good deal very quickly."

Ultimately Kravis agreed to the two-week exclusive, during which time Seagram reached an assessment of Tropicana's value. But the rub was that KKR's investment bankers made it clear that to be successful, the preemptive bid would have to be $1.2 billion, which was more than Seagram's valuation. Although the debate over whether to meet that price was intense within Seagram's senior management, Bronfman pushed to accept KKR's price, arguing that if the deal made sense at $1 billion, the same was true at $1.2 billion. Says Bronfman:

> I had a strategic vision that this was a business we should be in, and in which we could be successful. So I wasn't going to risk losing it at an auction. We paid the price, and it has proven to be an extraordinary investment for us, both in terms of the company's appreciation—if we sold it today we'd probably get over $2 billion—and in the fact that it has enhanced our potential to be a diversified, premium branded beverage company.
>
> And that's where we see our future.
>
> Of course, we had to prove to the board that we could manage and grow a business that was very unlike our traditional spirits. The success of Seagram's Wine Coolers was the proof.

CHAPTER 9

TAKING STRATEGY
TO MARKET

— • —

A Unique Value strategy focuses the business unit on what matters most for successful execution as well as near- and long-term profitability. A business plan driven by a Unique Value strategy allocates resources and functional responsibilities to the places where they are most valuable, where they can be most productively utilized over the near and long term.

The plan translates the strategy into a road map for execution and defines a set of functional substrategies for marketing, operations and product development. Substrategies set targets and measurable performance criteria for all relevant functions so that day-to-day, quarter-to-quarter or year-to-year results can be looked at in the context of the Unique Value strategy and its five fundamentals. Problems can then be diagnosed in terms of strategic assumptions, made during the original analyses, or issues of implementation. When substrategies are formulated, they reflect the analyses conducted to build the Unique Value = ROI Model (figure 9.1). What follows is a description of the issues each substrategy addresses.

Consumer and Customer Substrategies

With an increased understanding of the role of customer satisfaction and loyalty in superior business results, corporations around the world have been sensitized to the need for more sophisticated market research. Market data continues to proliferate, and feedback from the marketplace can be obtained overnight, as, for ex-

Figure 9.1

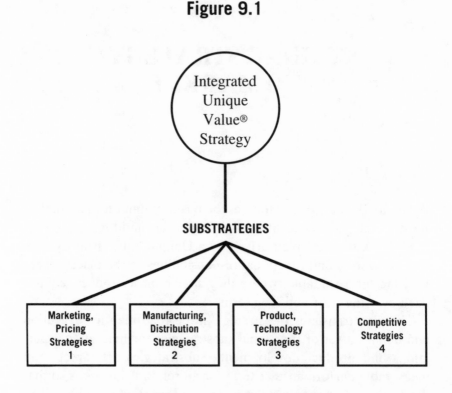

SUBSTRATEGIES

| Marketing, Pricing Strategies 1 | Manufacturing, Distribution Strategies 2 | Product, Technology Strategies 3 | Competitive Strategies 4 |

ample, in the case of Frito-Lay, the Pepsico unit that sells snack chips in the United States, or in the case of the movie industry, which can evaluate potential success or failure based on a weekend of box office receipts. A marketing substrategy should reflect a long-term commitment to a specific basis for competitive superiority and insulation. For example, in the case of Frito-Lay, this involves superior delivery of the product freshness that is critical to a key product attribute, crunchiness, which, in turn, is critical to satisfying the physiological requirements of regular snack food eaters (figure 9.2).

The marketing substrategy must be built upon a precise knowledge of key competitors, key prospects and the tangible or intangible benefit(s) that will establish a value-added product's or service's competitive superiority, in the context of the business's

Figure 9.2 Frito-Lay's Decision Support System

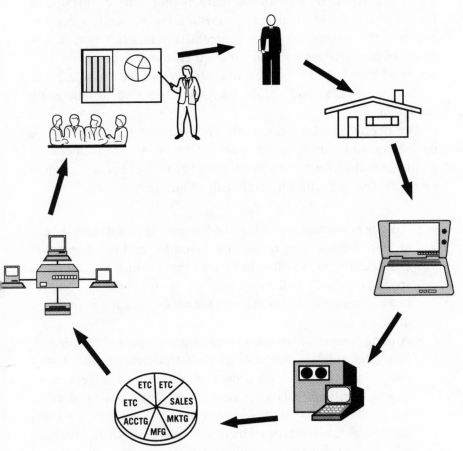

© Dunham & Marcus International, Inc., 1992.

overall Unique Value strategy. All aspects of the marketing sub-strategy—pricing, merchandising, advertising and promotion—should reflect this focus.

When markets are in transition, as, for example, in the case of PCs and consumer electronics, many of the specifics will be changing. New competitive frameworks are evolving; new patterns of customer behavior, attitudes and needs are emerging. But even in the most predictable of times, the future of markets is not pre-determined. Markets are built by marketers who identify and invest in important new benefits that appeal to specific consumer or customer segments. By structuring markets into cohesive groups of buyers who share strategic characteristics, businesses can develop products that are perceived as competitively superior in their delivery of key benefits by their targeted customer segments. Their potential to deliver the consistent customer satisfaction that is the basis for loyalty and profitability is therefore dramatically improved.

The definition of a strategically focused target segment varies by market. One fundamental basis for structure is consumer segments (people who buy to meet personal needs) versus business segments (people who buy on behalf of an organization):

- Among consumer segments, the basis for segmentation should at least include geographic, demographic and psychographic characteristics (as well as behavior breaks, which are category-specific), benefit structures and key price points. A comprehensive range of consumer segmentation options is outlined in figure 9.3.
- Among business customers, segmentation options include volume (the number and scale of their transactions with a supplier), internal purchase processes (the way customers make buying decisions, including how many people are involved in the decision and what the hierarchy is in making that decision), customer location, type of business, type of product, purchase criteria and the relative value of their business. A comprehensive range of "business to business" segmentation options is outlined in figure 9.4.

Market targeting is a key element of the marketing substrategy, and plays a critical role in:

- Building customer loyalty.
- Justifying higher margins.
- Focusing product line and R&D programs.
- Providing competitive insulation.

Figure 9.3

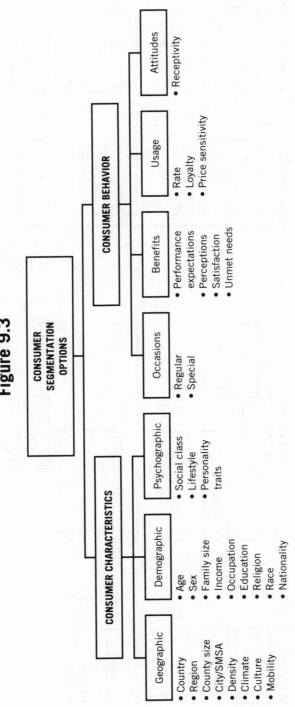

Dunham & Marcus International, Inc., 1992

Fig. 9.4

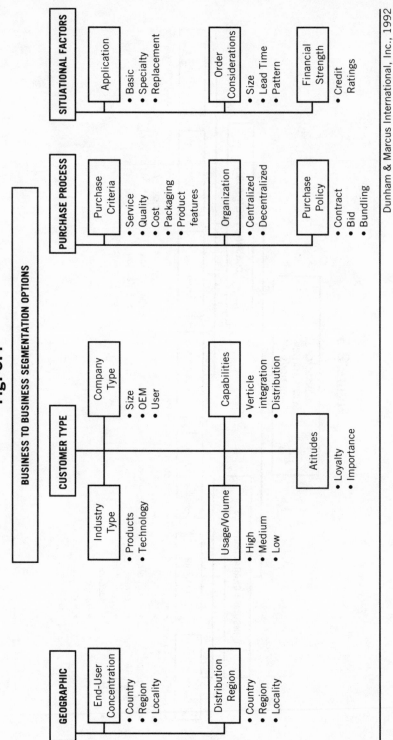

BUSINESS TO BUSINESS SEGMENTATION OPTIONS

GEOGRAPHIC

End-User Concentration
- Country
- Region
- Locality

Distribution Region
- Country
- Region
- Locality

CUSTOMER TYPE

Company Type
- Size
- OEM
- User

Industry Type
- Products
- Technology

Capabilities
- Verticle integration
- Distribution

Usage/Volume
- High
- Medium
- Low

Atitudes
- Loyalty
- Importance

PURCHASE PROCESS

Purchase Criteria
- Service
- Quality
- Cost
- Packaging
- Product features

Organization
- Centralized
- Decentralized

Purchase Policy
- Contract
- Bid
- Bundling

SITUATIONAL FACTORS

Application
- Basic
- Specialty
- Replacement

Order Considerations
- Size
- Lead Time
- Pattern

Financial Strength
- Credit Ratings

Dunham & Marcus International, Inc., 1992

Precise segmentation builds customer loyalty by focusing on key customer segments that drive volume and profit, and deepening the understanding of their needs, their priorities and the trade-offs they make. Segmentation protects margins in three ways: by identifying the key customer segments that are willing to pay a premium for superior value; by focusing business systems and skills on satisfying the needs of those customers; and by redirecting efforts and funds for strategic priorities.

Precise segmentation focuses product lines and technology development by enhancing the business's understanding of the needs and strategies of the customer segments that drive growth.

Segmentation leads to:

- Product lines targeted to loyal customer segments or franchises, resulting in franchise enhancement.
- Well-defined customer benefit structures that guide short- and long-term applied research programs.
- Consistent long-term strategies that provide a framework for basic research.

No business can be all things to all people in a way that is competitively superior. If marketing, selling and service substrategies are focused on superior delivery of the key benefits articulated in the business's Unique Value strategy (for example, in the case of IBM mainframes, service; in the case of the American Express card, prestige, service, security; in the case of Alfred Sloan's General Motors, a car for every level of affluence; in the case of the original Rolls-Royce, handcrafted quality), competitive insulation will be established and reinforced.

Over the short and long term, precise segmentation maximizes financial performance because it focuses investment and all resources (ideas, assets, skill sets, products and technologies) on the most attractive customer segments for profitable growth. Not all customers are equally valuable and not all customers are equally important to a business. The 80/20 rule, which states that 80 percent of revenue is accounted for by 20 percent of customers, is a simplification but indicates a principle: The customer segments that are critical to business performance are the ones to concentrate on in delivering superior value. These are a business's key strategic segments.

American Express, for example, built its original T&E (Travel and Entertainment) card business on an in-depth understanding of the needs of business travelers.

American Express saw its cardmembers as people who had a special set of expectations of its service quality and professionalism. From a behavioral and demographic point of view, American Express defined the cardmember as a business person with a high need for travel and entertainment services. In the United States, since these business expenses are tax deductible, American Express cardmembers were often less limited in their travel and entertainment budgets than leisure travelers. Part of American Express's winning formula is still its interrelated business and personal cardmember businesses. In the case of the corporate card, American Express also serves the need of corporate comptrollers by providing services such as tracking and recording expense account activities.

By contrast, the bank card business has a very different set of dynamics and a very different user base. Profitability is driven by interest charged for credit and by very high volume, not by high annual fees and service charges to establishments where the card is used. Thus, when Americn Express entered the credit card business with its Optima card, designed to compete directly with bank cards, it needed a carefully designed set of strategies to manage a new set of business risks, such as credit exposure and a different pattern of usage. American Express assumed the skills were in place to succeed because Optima was offered only to American Express cardmembers. But its initial market entry was a costly failure, resulting in 1991's write-off of $265 million—a humbling experience and a lesson in terms of the need for strategies tailored to the realities of markets, consumers and customers.[1]

Seagram had also rushed to market with its original wine cooler entry. But the second time around, the realities of the marketplace were carefully addressed. In Mark Taxel's words:

We felt that nobody had really gotten the category right; that fun must be combined with relative sophistication. So we made sure that the name was sophisticated: Seagram's Golden Wine Cooler. And the package was black and gold, which looked very sophisticated relative to the competition.

The advertising strategy also became clear—we needed a spokesperson who could simultaneously communicate sophistication and fun. Here's what we wanted to communicate:

- We wanted to be seen as the drink to be had where real drinks were being served; the competition was viewed as being imbibed on the beach.
- We wanted to be seen as the drink to be enjoyed in bars; not beer-chugging bars, and not your ultrasophisticated bars, either. Places where sociable people gathered; it was to be a social drink.
- We wanted the product to be seen as a drink consumed in more sophisticated circumstances than they were actually being consumed. Our product was to be served in a glass and on ice.

Bruce Willis gave us that image of contemporary urbanity; he was definitely not a yuppie.

Since ads and displays are so important, we invented a national program which we called "national ad week." Everybody in our company and all our distributors went out selling retailers on advertising our product at a time when they normally wouldn't. We got retailers to run full-page ads at their expense, motivated by the national television advertising campaign we showed them. We got executions that exceded our wildest expectations.

Business Systems and Skills Substrategies

A new line of products may take an enterprise into a business that is quite different in key aspects from the one it knows, one in which all the elements of a Unique Value strategy are in place. American Express's Optima card was an example, and so was the IBM PC, which required a different distribution system with very different economics compared with the mainframe National Accounts business IBM knew so well and managed so profitably.

In the Unique Value = ROI Model, the Business Systems and

Skills analyses examine all aspects of operations, including manufacturing, distribution, information systems, human resources and organizational structures in relation to financial performance and ROI. When a business is driven by a Unique Value strategy, its business systems will be aligned with corporate and business-unit assets, skills and experience to leverage a unique combination of capabilities.

Operations and organization management provide an array of examples of the role, in a Unique Value strategy, of innovative investments in manufacturing, distribution networks and skill sets designed to enhance the productivity of the entire enterprise. Toyota, for example, pioneered lean production. American Airlines pioneered the SABRE systems. McDonalds pioneered franchised quality. Frito-Lay and Federal Express pioneered state-of-the-art distribution systems to deliver superior customer satisfaction in alignment with premium pricing and attractive profit margins. At Federal Express this approach was executed internally and externally and expressed in an elegant articulation of strategy: "people, service, profit."

Lean production at Toyota began in the 1950s when Toyota began to design and implement a manufacturing strategy that it believed would redefine the standard for quality and productivity in the automotive industry. Toyota revolutionized the manufacturing and supply processes that American automobile manufacturers had developed:

- Assembly: Western mass production emphasized output over quality, with mistakes expected to be identified and corrected in a rework area at the end of the line. Toyota's approach was to correct problems as they were discovered, and then to question why the error occurred and how it could be prevented in the future. As a result, Toyota, and other Japanese auto manufacturers who emulated Toyota's system, have been able to achieve benchmark quality levels with almost no rework and repair —historically Western manufacturers dedicated 25 percent of their time and 20 percent of plant area to postassembly rework, yet their quality levels did not approach those of the Japanese.

- Supply System: Toyota pioneered the use of just-in-time manufacturing to eliminate inventory costs. While American assembly plants store, on average, three days' worth of parts,
  inventories at Japanese facilities average three hours' worth.
  Moreover, Toyota vertically integrated its suppliers so that they
  became involved in every step of the engineering and product
  development process. Traditionally, Western manufacturers
  designed their vehicles, developed specifications for the necessary parts, asked suppliers for bids on a particular quantity
  of parts at a given quality level (defect rate) and selected supply
  firms on a cost-quality basis. Toyota recognized that involving
  suppliers in the product development cycle would enable them
  to provide valuable input to part and product design to ease
  assembly, enhance quality and lower long-term engineering
  and manufacturing costs.[2]

Not only has lean production enabled Japanese auto manufacturers to set new standards for quality control and productivity, it
has also allowed them to shorten product development time and
thereby increase their responsiveness to changes in consumer and
customer (dealer) demand. Today, world-class corporations in Europe and America are developing manufacturing strategies that
extend lean production techniques into other industries.

In terms of business skills, Deutsche Bank's commercial banking
operation is an example of training and human resource strategies
that are clearly in alignment with the drivers of the bank's success
and profitability—its Unique Value strategy. Knowing that trust is
what drives healthy, long-term fiscal relationships and that pre-
dictability and recognition are the underpinnings of trust, the bank
presents a seamless uniformity of style to its customers in its home
and overseas markets. Putting German nationals in place in the
United States may not be desirable, but it is far preferable to
American bankers who don't understand the Deutsche Bank way,
according to Detlev Staecker, U.S. executive vice-president. Historically, to better serve its customers, Deutsche Bank was structured internally by regional areas of responsibility, where regional
bankers provided customers with a wide array of banking services,

and individuals in each office specialized in specific services, such as Private Banking or Corporate Trust. With its expansion into commercial retail banking, Deutsche Bank came to recognize that it had to restructure in order to coordinate national retail banking operations and provide the array of services its corporate customers demanded, without sacrificing the high level of personalized service loyal customers had come to expect.

As a result of a client-focused organizational structure, Deutsche Bank was quick to learn that its regional bankers were not providing the depth of expertise and range of financing demanded by increasingly sophisticated customers. The bank needed to provide these enhanced services without abrogating the unique relationship its regional bankers had with their customers, and at the same time provide central coordination for technology-driven retail banking services, such as ATMs. Deutsche Bank's solution was to place more emphasis on areas of expertise and less emphasis on regional affiliations.

Executive Vice-President Dr. Hans-Peter Ferslev notes: "We have gradually rotated the matrix ninety degrees. Managers specialize in an area of expertise such as private retail banking while continuing to maintain relationships with the most important corporate clients."

The shift in emphasis from regional to divisional extended from the various branch offices to the board of directors. In an increasingly competitive market Deutsche Bank has remained at the forefront of the European banking industry, well placed to take advantage of the new European structures and alignments. For example, a strategic imperative is its position in what used to be East Germany. As of November 1990, Deutsche Bank had more than $10 billion in deposits there. On the asset side, it had $6 billion in credits to East German companies, a number estimated to be 40 to 50 percent of the corporate lending market in that part of Germany.

According to Dr. Hans-Peter Ferslev:

To successfully establish a position as a Western Europe bank, we must expand into the former GDR and enhance our position in France to supplement our operations in Spain, Italy and the U.K. We need to run these foreign operations as national, domestic institutions headed by local country nationals. This will take time, but the coming European Economic Community developments demand our attention.

That is not to say that the organizational changes were made without pain. The emphasis on functional areas of expertise within the matrix reporting structure took time and significant effort to work through the organization without compromising the professionalism that tied loyal clients to Deutsche Bank.

Today's corporate structure enables the bank to be responsive to the needs of retail and corporate customers while accommodating the need for expansion. For example, the acquisition of Morgan Grenfell added a range of international investment-banking skills such as mergers and acquisitions to a healthy commercial bank. The objective was to establish Deutsche Bank as a true merchant bank. The successful merger of two disparate organizations—an Anglo-Saxon investment bank and a German commercial bank—was driven by a clearly articulated strategy.

A well-established global player, Pepsico, is also at the cutting edge of management change with a view to long-term competitive advantage. In the case of subsidiary Frito-Lay's Dallas snack-food operation, the organization is committed to state-of-the-art information systems, which establish the model for its overseas operations. Information-systems technology is executed in the field by Frito-Lay's direct sales force, which implements the direct-to-store door delivery system (DSD). DSD bypasses brokers, wholesalers and warehouses and allows Frito-Lay to control quality standards for its products in the market by removing damaged and stale goods from the racks before consumers are exposed to any less-than-fresh product. Frito's three-thousand-strong sales force is equipped with hand-held computers, to provide accurate and cost-efficient tracking of daily inventory movement at the local store level. While competitors such as Borden and Eagle Snacks also have a DSD distribution network, sales forces are smaller, less well equipped and not backed up by Frito-Lay's sophisticated systems technology.

How can today's multinationals acquire the competitive business skills they need to operate in sophisticated new markets? Some opportunities are offered by licensing agreements, strategic alliances and joint ventures. For example, Kirin Brewery of Japan now brews its beer at Molson's plants in Canada to provide expanded, cost-effective distribution for its brands in North America. Through a distribution relationship with Whitbread, a leading British brewer, Heineken increased sales volume by 7 percent in Great Britain from 1989 to 1990 by leveraging Whitbread's investment in market presence. Both Kirin and Heineken are examples of extensive cross-distribution relationships in the global beverage industry, where competitors commonly work with each other to leverage local distribution strengths for economies of scale.

World-class corporations such as Coca-Cola and Nestlé are joint venturing to produce and market a portfolio of canned beverages, using the Nestlé brands Nestea and Nescafé, and Coca-Cola's bottler network in the United States. Coca-Cola will provide the bottling and its formidable, ubiquitous distribution network, and Nestlé will bring tea and coffee technology and the equity of its brands to the table.

In the case of Seagram's Wine Coolers, a new business system and distribution network was built by piecing together a patchwork of the best bottlers and distributors across the United States, region by region. Seagram's strategic goal was 100 percent distribution. As Mark Taxel describes it:

> We recognized that we had to take a page from the successful beer brands, and be available wherever beverage alcohol was available. As an example, we sold coolers in kegs, and sold the kegs to stadiums, so they could sell the product on tap. We did not make real money this way, but we generated a lot of interest and consumer trial.
>
> We recognized that we had to be very visible at convenience stores. To do this we had to provide merchandising support and consumer promotion, which would help turn the goods.

We recognized that in the grocery store channel, mass merchandising was crucial. We had to theme it for things like football. So we became the NFL licensee for the cooler category.

With the beer industry's business systems and skills as a model for coolers, Seagram learned how to manage local promotional events such as concerts and sporting activities, including the Rose Bowl. It was all part of learning how to be ubiquitous.

Product and Technology Substrategies

Innovation does not guarantee marketplace success. Technological gains must be translated into products that deliver superior consumer value to strategically important segments. With a Unique Value strategy, a business's technology and product portfolio strategies are inextricably interrelated. The role of technology in a Unique Value strategy is to provide the technical programs and resources to generate new products, quality improvements and cost reductions that support the near- and long-term focus of the strategy. The business's translation of technology into product portfolios is crafted to maximize the return on that investment.

Empirical evidence links R&D expenditures and innovation to enhanced profitability. And a 1982 analysis of PIMS (Profit Impact of Market Strategy) member businesses suggested that on average, one dollar of R&D spending generated over three dollars in future gross profit (figure 9.5), with a time lag of 4.2 years before the average outlay reached fruition.[3] By maintaining high levels of R&D spending, companies theoretically strengthen their long-term financial position (figure 9.6). Another PIMS study found that R&D spending enhanced long-term shareholder value.[4] And a study by Rosabeth Moss Kanter of the Harvard Business School suggested that over a twenty-year period, companies perceived as innovative consistently outperformed less progressive competitors in financial growth and performance.[5]

How do world-class corporations with Unique Value strategies in place ensure that technology management is an expression of a

Figure 9.5   Each Dollar of R & D Expenditure Generates over Three Dollars of Future Profit.

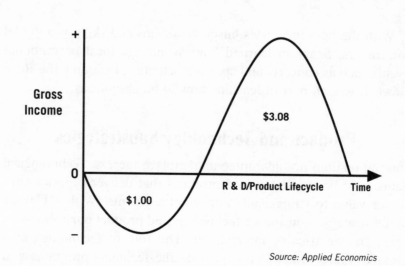

Source: Applied Economics

cohesive business strategy? The clearer the strategy, the more successful specific development efforts will be in meeting business and market goals and enhancing corporate performance. The strategic approaches employed by R&D must be interdependent with a business's unique customer or consumer franchises, its business systems and skills and its position relative to key competitors.

For example, Sharp, the electronics company, achieved its position as the benchmark for efficient design and production by organizing for a fully integrated R&D function. R&D, manufacturing and product development were put under the supervision of one executive.[6] Hitachi, with an R&D budget six times larger than Sharp's, manages its numerous research and development departments through a single office, which coordinates information flow and project priorities with corporate strategies, goals and budget considerations clearly defined.[7]

Ampex, on the other hand, surrendered its pioneering lead in video recording to Sony and Matsushita as a result of their superior ability to translate technology initiatives into commercial successes.

Figure 9.6 Continual R & D Outlays Enhance Long-Term Profitability.

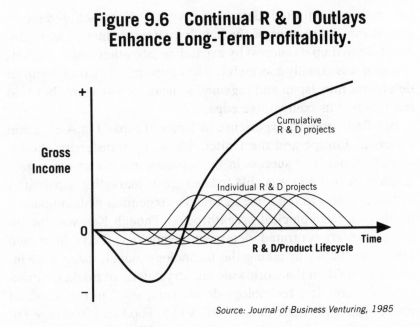

Source: Journal of Business Venturing, 1985

And U.K. engineering firm John Brown lost its technological advantage in two of its primary industries, shipbuilding and machine tools, because of a lack of strategic focus.[8] For the same reason, American manufacturers lost the U.S. color television market (falling from 90 percent to less than 10 percent share since 1970), and the domestic semiconductor market (90 percent to 60 percent),[9] and are now rethinking their links with R&D. The goal is manage the innovation process in a way that is tied to future business performance. To enhance the productivity of basic and applied research, AT&T has shortened the channels of communication between researchers at Bell Labs and product management. And, to ensure that innovation remains a priority, 3M and Corning have policies requiring that one-quarter of each year's revenue comes from new products.

Where technology is strategically aligned with other business strengths, it becomes a key competitive advantage. For example, Procter & Gamble used concentration in detergents to increase its worldwide laundry detergent share, despite the fact that P&G was not first to market. In fact, it was Kao of Japan that introduced the first concentrated detergent, Attack. Compact detergents gained over 80 percent of the laundry detergent market in Japan. Kao followed up its success by expanding into other Asian markets where it was equally successful. P&G introduced its own compact detergents into Japan and regained some of its lost share, but Kao has retained its competitive edge.

But P&G used its experience in Japan to expand in Asia, Latin America, Europe and the United States. By transferring the essential elements of success in the Japanese market to other geographic areas, P&G was able to leverage its marketing capabilities with consumers to reinforce its brand's credentials with announcements of a technological breakthrough. Though Kao was the innovator in concentrated detergent technology, P&G leveraged other capabilities in taking the technology global, using it to increase its hold on the worldwide laundry detergent market. "Procter & Gamble is a technology-driven company," in the words of Frank Weise, former CFO of P&G's U.S. Food and Beverage Division, and now senior vice-president and CFO of Campbell Soup Company. He believes there is a strategic imperative to transfer technology around the world, not only for Procter & Gamble, but for every future-focused business. His model is P&G:

> The thing that Procter has been able to do that probably far exceeds almost any other consumer products company is, once new technology is developed, P&G has the ability, because now it has set up the infrastructure, to redeploy that technology in a matter of months. It used to be a matter of years, now it's a matter of months. It's happened in the last couple of years. The time frame is continually condensed from the time that new technology is developed until it's reapplied around the world. At a number of different levels there's a technology exchange that goes on every day around the world. There are also formal, structured meetings that happen on a frequent basis.

Lois Juliber, chief technology officer of Colgate-Palmolive, which competes in many categories with P&G around the world, says that, since "speed to market" is a global imperative today, successful companies have "got to have science on the shelf" ready to go, at a few months' notice, as well as programs of "constant discovery."

Balancing incremental and radical innovation is a critical component of strategy. The ability of Japanese companies continually to improve on successful products results from a commitment to both incremental and radical innovation. About two-thirds of Japanese R&D spending goes to improving existing products and technology, compared with one-half of R&D funding by U.S. industry.[10] But while incremental innovation is necessary to generate minor product improvements or further market share growth, it is not sufficient to maintain technological leadership. When NCR attempted to advance its electromechanical cash registers incrementally, it suffered a serious blow. Competitors leapfrogged its technology by introducing fully electronic machines.[11]

Corporations with long-term core technologies consistently demonstrate the leverage that strategic focus represents. Procter & Gamble and Du Pont are two American examples of corporations that have grown their core businesses by a consistent focus on their core technologies (figures 9.7 and 9.8).

Since core technologies are an integral part of long-term success, they must be clearly identified and recognized as such. Pharmaceutical manufacturer Richardson-Vicks is an example of the failure to do this. In 1981, the firm sold Merrill Laboratories, its primary research and product development facility. Afterwards, it could no longer generate new products and therefore tried to compensate by acquiring established or emerging brands from other pharmaceutical firms. From 1981 to 1985, as a result, the company's stock underperformed the market as sales failed to meet expectations and profits dwindled. The firm became a primary takeover target, valued for its extensive distribution system, strong brands and low share price (which reflected its lack of R&D). In 1985, it was acquired by P&G.

Japanese companies were the initiators of holistic (concurrent) techniques that improve communication between functional groups such as marketing, engineering and packaging. By organizing prod-

Figure 9.7   The Procter & Gamble Company
Core Technology: Fats & Oils

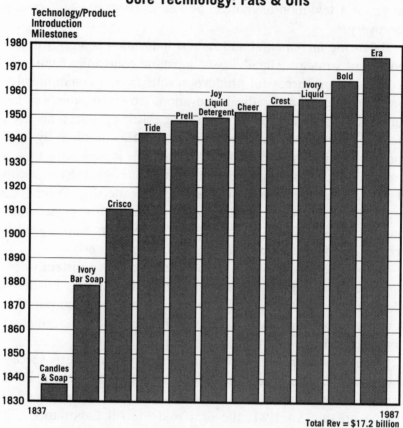

Source: R & D Scoreboard 1987; Businessweek, June 1988
"Eyes on Tomorrow," Oscar Schisgall, 1981;
P & G's Annual Report, 1987.

uct development teams holistically, Fuji-Xerox cut the development time for its FX-3500 copier in half, from four years to two. Learning from its joint venture with Fuji Film, Xerox, which lost its lead in copiers because it was unable to introduce new products as quickly as Canon, copied holistic techniques to reduce the development time for its 9900 copier from five years to three.[12]

Xerox created a case study on how to beat the Japanese:

Figure 9.8   Du Pont

Core Technology: Chemicals

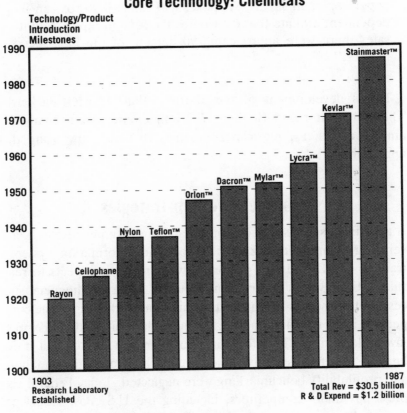

Technology/Product
Introduction
Milestones

1903
Research Laboratory
Established

1987
Total Rev = $30.5 billion
R & D Expend = $1.2 billion

Source: Du Pont Annual Report, 1987;
R & D Scoreboard 1987; *Businessweek*, June 1988.

When the Xerox Corporation began designing its new high-speed photocopying machine, the Model 5100, it had world markets in mind, especially the Japanese.

But it took a different tack from American automakers, which, in pursuit of Japanese markets, tried to sell cars with steering wheels on the wrong side. Xerox took great pains to understand the needs of its foreign customers, developing a machine for the Japanese that would duplicate the delicate kanji language characters, for instance, or would handle the flimsy papers used in Japan.

Now the American machine, capable of producing high-quality reproductions faster than anything made by Japanese manufacturers, has become the biggest-selling high-speed paper copier in Japan. A spokesman for Fuji Xerox, an independent affiliate that distributes the 5100 in Japan, said its sales there were approaching 90 percent of the high-speed market.[13]

Ford's development of the Taurus sedan, Hewlett-Packard's Thinkjet printer and Boeing's 777 jetliner are among many examples of other American companies that are now using this approach.

Competitive Substrategies

If a business spends millions of dollars on consumer research, advertising, manufacturing distribution and information systems, training, R&D and new product development, it expects to reap substantial rewards in the form of market share and financial success. Yet investing without the thorough understanding of the competition is a formula for failure. For example, while Federal Express invested heavily in MIS to deliver superior benefits to what it defined as the "time-sensitive" package market, competitor analyses and profitability benchmarking were neglected. Today Federal Express has many competitors, including the U.S. Postal Service. Sustainable success requires a superior formula for profitability that integrates all the issues the business must deal with, including the nature of the competition.

Historically, competitive strategies have been classified as either preemptive or responsive. A preemptive strategy is employed in anticipation of competitive moves; a responsive strategy is implemented in reaction to competitive action.

By contrast, a Unique Value strategy looks at the competitive framework in terms of a cohesive set of strategic issues and is designed to leverage a business's unique combination of assets and capabilities at the expense of key competitors.

In the case of Matsushita's battle with Sony in the VCR industry, the considerations were unique to those competitors, in that particular time and market. Whether or not Sony had been "first to market," the specifics of the competitive arena unfolded gradually. The appropriate competitive strategy for Sony was not clear at the beginning—what the situation requires was close and consistent monitoring. On the other hand, IBM's competitive strategy for marketing the System/360 series computer straightforward. In the early 1960s, IBM controlled two-thirds of the computer market. To maintain its competitive position, IBM made its own products obsolete in 1964 by launching the revolutionary System/360. As a complete line of compatible and expandable computers, the System/360 made switching between manufacturers unnecessary.[14] The model was an overwhelming success, solidifying IBM's position as dominant competitor. By leveraging the benefits of compatibility, IBM reinforced its base of long-term customers and preempted competitors from further eroding its market share.

Honda's attack on Yamaha in the Japanese motorcycle market was also a unique strategy for unique circumstances. It was a specific reaction to Yamaha's announced intention to supersede Honda as the world's leading motorcycle manufacturer and a reaffirmation of Honda's commitment to its base business. Nabisco's response to Procter & Gamble's Duncan Hines cookies initiative, as well as the fare cutting practiced by the major U.S. airlines in the face of People Express's challenge are classic responses to attacks on a base business. However, in each case, the characteristics of the underlying business strategy were unique and dealt with the specifics of the situation in a particular time and place.

In the global cosmetics industry, Revlon is also in a unique position. As the "American color authority," it is recognized by women in every country. But as Jerry Levin, president and CEO, points out, it was a position the company had abandoned for twenty years. Today, Revlon's competitive challenge is to take back its position with the utmost speed in a world where "countries keep getting added every day." To start to do that, management distributed a one-page vision statement and a one-page strategy statement simultaneously to 130 countries. According to Jerry Levin, the strategy is simple, but every Revlon employee around the world had to be given the opportunity to hear it directly from management. "A lot of people responded—some wrote me letters, some wrote little notes—but now they all understand. It's incredible the power the Revlon name has, after so many years of misdirection. As the American color authority, we have no competition."

With Seagram's Wine Coolers, the attention to competitor issues allowed the company to change the rules of the game so as to lay the foundation for category leadership, even with a competitor as tough as Gallo. John Preston explains how Seagram's competitive focus delivered to the bottom line.

By using copackers we were able to disperse our production around the country. This gave us a competitive advantage, since we were closer to the retailers' markets than Gallo. Gallo produces everything in Modesto, then they ship the product all over the country. So, our economics were better than Gallo's.

The distributors help provide the accurate forecast that we need to manage our competitive effort. You start thinking in August about new flavor introductions for the following May. And when you do that, you know where you are and which of your flavors on shelf are not the winners. At that point, you have a sense of your exposure. You ask how many facings you have, does Gallo have, so you are always measuring what is moving and how the buyer at their retail chains perceives your product versus your competition.

The reason that our strategies worked was that we managed our risks as a team. Team building was not something we set out to do; it was the result of necessity, the need to manage a new, fast-paced business. It was the result of having to learn. We managed risks and we tackled our challenges by tearing down the walls between functional areas, and that was an important part of our competitive advantage against Gallo.

CHAPTER 10

STRATEGY FORMULATION USING THE UNIQUE VALUE = ROI MODEL: A CASE STUDY

——— • ———

The pyramid of the Unique Value = ROI Model provides a framework for an iterative process. Initially it puts the necessary building blocks in place for strategy formulation. Eventually it establishes the knowledge base for the strategic management of the business. The management team and key departments participate. The process starts with agreement as to a meaningful and valuable business goal, which ideally should be measurable—for example, "Double volume in two to five years," or "Reverse a profit decline within one to two years," or "Penetrate a new market and achieve a 30 percent share" within a specified time. The agreed goal provides the focus for all the subsequent knowledge gathering, analyses and hypothesis formulation. When articulated, potential Unique Value strategies focus on achieving the defined goal. Issues to be addressed are then framed by the Unique Value = ROI Model. In schematic form, the process is shown in figure 10.1.

With the process laid out in diagrammatic form, the specifics of a Unique Value strategy formulation process, which will address a complex business problem, can be addressed. Key learning will be reviewed and preliminary strategic hypotheses refined or dropped until the optimal strategy is identified. Throughout this chapter, examples of the strategy formulation process are based on a real-life case that has been modified for illustrative purposes. The case deals with an American rental car company, renamed Triple A,

Fig. 10.1

STRATEGY FORMULATION PROCESS

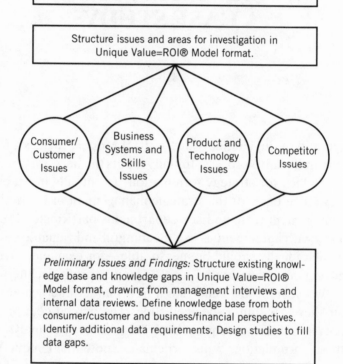

Goal Definition and Assessment of Key Issues: Gain management agreement to a business goal, which the Unique Value® strategy formulation process will address.

Structure issues and areas for investigation in Unique Value=ROI® Model format.

Consumer/ Customer Issues

Business Systems and Skills Issues

Product and Technology Issues

Competitor Issues

Preliminary Issues and Findings: Structure existing knowledge base and knowledge gaps in Unique Value=ROI® Model format, drawing from management interviews and internal data reviews. Define knowledge base from both consumer/customer and business/financial perspectives. Identify additional data requirements. Design studies to fill data gaps.

Fig. 10.1 (cont'd)

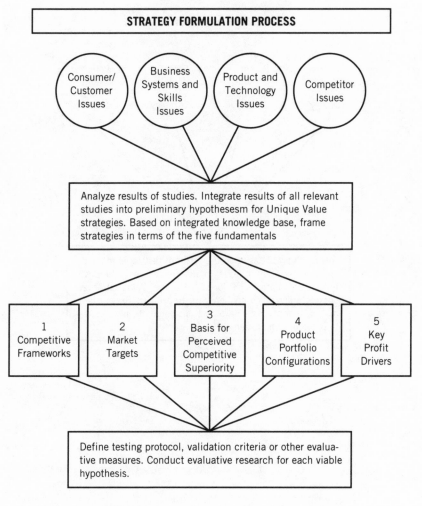

STRATEGY FORMULATION PROCESS

Consumer/ Customer Issues

Business Systems and Skills Issues

Product and Technology Issues

Competitor Issues

Analyze results of studies. Integrate results of all relevant studies into preliminary hypothesesm for Unique Value strategies. Based on integrated knowledge base, frame strategies in terms of the five fundamentals

| 1 Competitive Frameworks | 2 Market Targets | 3 Basis for Perceived Competitive Superiority | 4 Product Portfolio Configurations | 5 Key Profit Drivers |

Define testing protocol, validation criteria or other evaluative measures. Conduct evaluative research for each viable hypothesis.

Fig. 10.1 (cont'd)

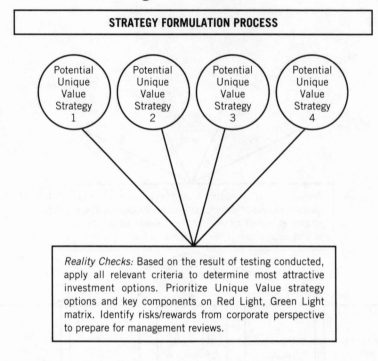

STRATEGY FORMULATION PROCESS

Potential Unique Value Strategy 1

Potential Unique Value Strategy 2

Potential Unique Value Strategy 3

Potential Unique Value Strategy 4

Reality Checks: Based on the result of testing conducted, apply all relevant criteria to determine most attractive investment options. Prioritize Unique Value strategy options and key components on Red Light, Green Light matrix. Identify risks/rewards from corporate perspective to prepare for management reviews.

Fig. 10.1 (cont'd)

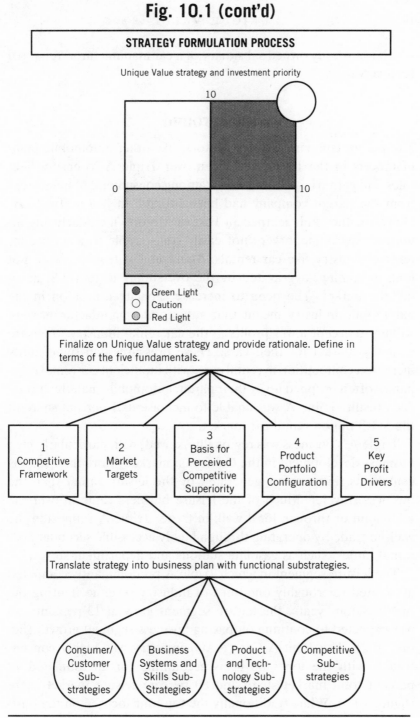

STRATEGY FORMULATION PROCESS

Unique Value strategy and investment priority

- ● Green Light
- ○ Caution
- ◐ Red Light

Finalize on Unique Value strategy and provide rationale. Define in terms of the five fundamentals.

| 1 Competitive Framework | 2 Market Targets | 3 Basis for Perceived Competitive Superiority | 4 Product Portfolio Configuration | 5 Key Profit Drivers |

Translate strategy into business plan with functional substrategies.

Consumer/ Customer Sub-strategies

Business Systems and Skills Sub-Strategies

Product and Tech-nology Sub-strategies

Competitive Sub-strategies

which is a wholly owned subsidiary of a car manufacturer, renamed
Festiva Motors.

Background

The parent company, Festiva Motors, like other automobile manufacturers in the 1990s, had taken over Triple A to ensure fleet
sales and gain trial and awareness among consumers. Management
from the parent company had been brought in to run Triple A.
However, the skills learned in Festiva Motors' manufacturing-intensive environment were not easily transferable to a service-intensive industry like car rentals. Management troubles were not
long in coming, aggravated by the oversupply in the U.S. automobile market. The need to increase capacity utilization in the
automobile industry meant that automobile manufacturers were
willing to accept lower profits in the car rental industry to ensure
a steady market for their cars. These pressures had significantly
increased competition in rental cars, with inefficient car rental companies often propped up by their parent automobile manufacturers.
As a result, Triple A was unable to increase its 1 percent share of
the $11.3 billion rental car market.

Triple A's business was regionally skewed, with particularly high
business development in the California market. More than 95 percent of its revenue was generated by the leisure rather than the
business traveler. Much of the leisure business came in over the
telephone or through local walk-in trade. Triple A supported the
walk-in trade by operating through highly accessible secondary car
rental outlets such as gasoline stations and department stores.

The leisure segment in which Triple A predominantly competed
accounted for roughly one-third of industry revenue. During the
previous four years, the leisure segment grew at 13 percent and
was expected to continue outpacing business segment growth (figure 10.2). The Rent-A-Car (RAC) industry was highly concentrated, with the top nine firms accounting for an estimated 72
percent total market share and 80 percent leisure market share
(figure 10.3). While traditionally the top four focused on the busi-

FIGURE 10.2.   U.S. CAR RENTAL REVENUES

REVENUE	1987		1991		Annual Growth %
	$B	%	$B	%	
Business	4.3	52%	5.4	47%	6%
Leisure	2.3	28%	3.8	34%	13%
Replacement	1.7	20%	2.1	19%	5%
Total U.S. Car Rental	8.3	100%	11.3	100%	8%

Source: *Auto Rental News, Fact Book 1991–1992;* Charles Finnie, Alex. Brown & Sons Dunham & Marcus Database.

FIGURE 10.3.   U.S. CAR RENTAL MARKET SHARE

ESTIMATED 1991 DOLLAR SHARE

	TOTAL MARKET SHARE (%)	LEISURE ONLY MARKET SHARE (%)
Total Top 14	78	85
All Others (third tier)	22	15
Total RAC	100	100

ness market, slower growth and continued price discounting in this area fueled interest and investment in the leisure segment.

While growth in air travel continued to fuel increased rental car demand, an automobile industry leader's decision to downsize plant production, in line with unit share levels in the mid to low 30 percent range, was expected to greatly reduce supply. As a result, vehicle manufacturers would be more selective with their production output. Unstable and smaller third-tier operators would have reduced bargaining leverage in this environment. This competitive disadvantage, combined with the poor business climate experienced over the previous eighteen months, was expected to force marginal competitors out of the market, creating a void for Triple A to fill.

Preliminary Assessment of Key Issues

As part of the preliminary assessment, the strategy team gained management agreement to the business goal that a Unique Value strategy would meet. The agreed goal: Make the Triple A business profitable on a stand-alone basis within one year. The deliverables of the process were structured in the format of the Unique Value = ROI Model.

In addition to a recommended strategy, supplementary deliverables were defined as follows:

(1) Consumer/Customer
   a. Determine feasibility for national leisure versus local business and expansion.
   b. Determine optimal locations for Triple A as they relate to leisure and local market segment customers.
   c. Determine optimum strategy to convert travel operators to represent Triple A to the leisure market.

(2) Business Systems and Skills
   a. Determine strategic and structural changes necessary to achieve goals.
   b. Assess current locations.
   c. Assess new locations.
   d. Assess current internal and external barriers to utilizing the current asset base.
   e. Determine which components of the business need to be restructured.

(3) Product and Technology
   a. Determine the viability of airport counter locations and off-airport locations.
   b. Assess the effect of current computer technology on market share.

(4) Competition
   a. Define the competitive framework for the leisure and local market segments by regional markets.
   b. Determine services Triple A can provide to its market segments (travel operators or customers) that give Triple A competitive leverage to specific competitors.

Preliminary Issues and Findings

The existing knowledge base was structured in accordance with the Unique Value = ROI Model, to ensure a comprehensive review of all factors relevant to the business goal. The source of this knowledge base was primarily management interviews and formal and informal data reviews.

Each of the four areas were addressed from two perspectives: the Consumer/Customer perspective and the Business/Financial perspective—that is, how customers and other constituencies, including industry experts, view Triple A and the issues, and how the business itself and its key managers, including the corporate parent's management, view Triple A and the issues. This ensures that both internal and external perspectives are compared and contrasted as a basis for strategy formulation. The list below illustrates how findings and key issues from external and internal interviews and the data review were organized as a preliminary knowledge base for Triple A.

(1) Consumer/Customer
   a. Consumer/Customer Perspective: More leisure travelers than business travelers use Triple A. Leisure travelers account for more than 95 percent of Triple A's business, and leisure travelers indicate that price is their most important consideration.
   b. Business/Financial Perspective: Triple A's business is regionally skewed, with particularly high business development in the California market.
(2) Business Systems and Skills
   a. Consumer/Customer Perspective: Much of the leisure business comes in over the telephone or through local walk-in trade, and Triple A supports the walk-in trade by operating through highly accessible secondary car rental outlets such as gasoline stations and department stores.
   b. Business/Financial Perspective: Festiva Motors personnel with extensive general management experience have been brought in to run Triple A. However, many of the

skills learned in the manufacturing-intensive environment are not transferable to a service-intensive industry like car rentals.

(3) Product and Technology: Early in the process, some areas for investigation may not yield relevant findings. However, the role of sophisticated reservation systems is a relevant technology issue.

(4) Competition
   a. Consumer/Customer Perspective: The top four rental car companies have refocused their marketing and promotion efforts to concentrate on the leisure segment—price discounting has become common.
   b. Business/Financial Perspective: Due to the sudden intense competition in the rental car business, Triple A has been unable to increase volume. Each of Triple A's competitors has close ownership ties to a major automobile manufacturer. The need to increase capacity utilization in the automobile industry means that automobile manufacturers are willing to accept lower profits in the car rental industry to ensure a steady market for their automobiles. As a result, inefficient car rental companies are being propped up by the automobile manufacturers and Triple A seems unlikely to be able to increase its 1 percent share.

Once preliminary issues and findings have been identified, preliminary strategic hypotheses can be formulated.

Preliminary Hypotheses and Potential Unique Value Strategies

The strategy team regrouped after the information and issues had been structured to discuss preliminary hypotheses. The most attractive alternatives were put to the test of the five fundamentals: At whose expense could Triple A get share growth? What customer profile could it target? What basis of perceived competitive superiority could attract the targeted segment from competitors? Does Triple A have to modify the product? What are the economics of each potential unqiue value strategy defined in terms of the Competitive Framework, Market Target, Basis for Perceived Competitive Superiority, Product Portfolio Configuration, and Key Profit Drivers? Below are sample Triple A hypotheses structured in terms of the five fundamentals.

Hypothesis One: "Local Leisure Market Strategy."
Fundamentals of Potential Unique Value Strategy:

1. Competitive Framework: Triple A could grow at the expense of unstable and smaller operators who will be forced out of the market by the recent poor business climate.
2. Market Target: Triple A could single-mindedly target the California leisure traveler.
3. Basis for Perceived Competitive Superiority: Triple A could provide superior service and convenience through its network of satellite (department stores and gas stations) rental centers.
4. Product Portfolio Configuration: Triple A could offer the full array of Festiva cars.
5. Key Profit Drivers: Triple A could meet financial goals by building loyal customers among leisure travelers, despite the fact that they tend to buy on price.

Hypothesis Two: "Exit Strategy."
Fundamentals of Potential Unique Value Strategy:

1. Competitive Framework: Triple A could stabilize its current share of the total business.
2. Market Target: Triple A could maintain its current mix of customers.
3. Basis for Perceived Competitive Superiority: Triple A could seek out a strategic partner to enhance its service.
4. Product Portfolio Configuration: Triple A could offer the full array of Festiva cars.
5. Key Profit Drivers: Triple A could lower its costs by stream-

lining operations through a partner and maximizing cash flow to service debt.

Hypothesis Three: "Change the Rules Strategy."
Fundamentals of Potential Unique Value Strategy:

1. Competitive Framework: Triple A could create barriers to competition by changing the game in rental cars. Possibilities would include changing the competitive environment, changing the target, meeting new consumer needs, opening new distribution channels and forming a strategic alliance with a major player in the travel industry.
2. Market Target: To be determined.
3. Basis for Perceived Competitive Superiority: To be determined.
4. Product Portfolio Configuration: Triple A could offer the full array of Festiva cars.
5. Key Profit Drivers: To be determined.

Hypothesis Four: "Full Service Agency Strategy."
Fundamentals of Potential Unique Value Strategy:

1. Competitive Framework: Triple A could grow at the expense of unstable and smaller operators who will be forced out of the market by the recent poor business climate.
2. Market Target: Triple A could expand beyond its strong California base.
3. Basis for Perceived Competitive Superiority: Triple A would provide superior service and convenience through its expanding network of satellite (department stores and gas stations) rental centers.
4. Product Portfolio Configuration: Triple A would offer the full array of Festiva cars.
5. Key Profit Drivers: Achieve economies of scale.

Strategic hypotheses may be incomplete at this point. However, they are sufficiently developed to provide guidance for the next phase, which requires primary research studies to fill information gaps and address the most pressing and significant questions and issues.

In-Depth Research to Test and Refine Hypotheses

The Unique Value = ROI Model requires a carefully crafted approach to primary research. Studies are designed to address each building block of the Model from the perspective of the consumer or customer and from the perspective of the business unit and the corporate parent. Below is a list of studies conducted to determine the viability of alternative preliminary hypotheses for Triple A.

(1) Consumer/Customer
   a. Consumer/Customer Perspective
      Travel agent interviews: In-depth interviews to determine their perception of customer needs.
      Consumer interviews: In-depth interviews to determine met and unmet, functional and emotional needs using appropriate market research methodologies.
   b. Business/Financial Perspective
      Internal data review: A detailed review of Triple A's internal consumer, market and financial data.

(2) Business Systems and Skills
   a. Consumer/Customer Perspective
      Triple A management/field interviews: In-depth interviews across functions, including sales, operations, systems, service and financial personnel in various geographic regions to benchmark Triple A capabilities and probe options.
   b. Business/Financial Perspective
      Industry expert interviews: In-depth interviews to determine state-of-the-art business management skills relevant to Triple A's particular issues.

(3) Product and Technology
   a. Consumer/Customer Perspective
      Technology review: Investigation of data systems

used in-house and by competition to determine impact of technology on service levels and profitability
and customer perspectives of product and service offerings and alternatives.
  b. Business/Financial Perspective
      Technology review: A cost assessment of various sys-
      tems options available to the business unit.
(4) Competition
  a. Consumer/Customer Perspective
      Industry review: A review of trends and competitors
      in the industry.
      Competitive benchmarking: Analysis of high-growth
      competitors including service, marketing and busi-
      ness technology skills and key customer perspective
      of competitive options, strengths, weaknesses and
      key factors driving choice.
  b. Business/Financial Perspective
      Secondary data review: A review of publicly available
      information on the travel services industry.

Figure 10.4 shows the analyses from the Consumer/Customer
perspective, while figure 10.5 shows the analyses from the Business/
Financial perspective. These analyses were then interrelated as
findings were compiled and implications were determined for strategy. Integrating the Consumer/Customer and Business/Financial
perspectives of the four sets of analyses leads to reassessments and
refinements of the four initial strategic hypotheses.

Integrated Findings

The accompanying table (figure 10.6) summarizes some key issues
and their respective impact on aspects of the rent-a-car business.

Key Findings

(1) Consumer/Customer
     • Consumers have relatively low loyalty to any one brand,

Figure 10.4 Unique Value = ROI® Model

Consumer/Customer Perspective

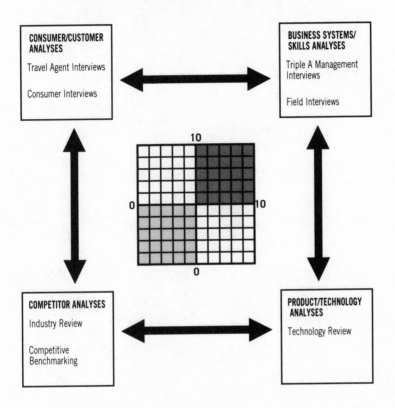

© Dunham & Marcus International, Inc., 1992.

but make the purchase decision among a relevant set of RAC companies based on price. Relevant set is determined by service level in past experience. Consumers want low prices and expect high quality.

- Pricing actions are not taken in response to market conditions or fleet availability.
- The leisure market has outpaced and is expected to continue to outpace business segment growth in key regions. This suggests that major and second-tier operators will employ aggressive leisure market initiatives.

Figure 10.5   Unique Value = ROI® Model

Business/Financial Perspective

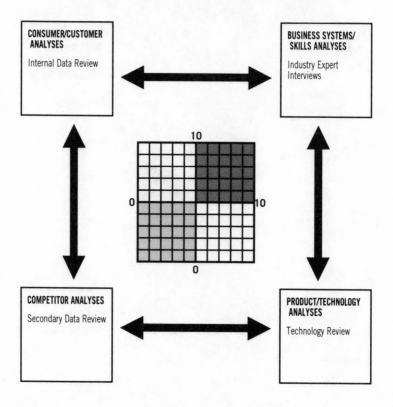

© Dunham & Marcus International, Inc., 1992.

- The travel agent segment is large and penetrable. As a small operator, Triple A must address a number of issues in order to fully attain travel agency support, namely:
  — Sales and marketing support
  — Number of locations
  — Automation
  — Guaranteed vehicle availability
- Tour operator and direct telephone consumer segments are highly price-sensitive. Walk-in traffic is less price-sensitive.

FIGURE 10.6   ESTIMATED IMPACT OF KEY ISSUES ON THE RENT-A-CAR BUSINESS

ESTIMATED DEGREE OF IMPACT ON RAC
BUSINESS RESULTS (H-M-L)

KEY ISSUES	CUSTOMER SALES/ SERVICE	PRODUCTIVITY/ COST	OPTIMAL DECISIONMAKING	FLEXIBILITY (INTERNAL/ EXTERNAL)
No formalized pricing strategy/standards exist		M	H	
Lack of daily focus	H	H	H	M
Pricing does not reflect true market/ internal demand considerations	H	H	H	
Expanded rate structure does not exist (daily, weekend, week and modified day rate)	H	H	H	H
Time to execute rate changes/closeouts	H	H	H	H
Competitive intelligence not managed daily, near and long term	H		M	H
No tracking of walk-in rates at corporate		L	L	

Key: H = High
    M = Medium
    L = Low

•

The majority of Triple A's customers are concentrated in three origin markets, suggesting management must focus resources to maintain or retain business in these areas.

• Triple A's nonexistent repeat purchase cycle clearly signals a problem. Triple A must focus on customer service. Consumers will not repeat based on poor service.

• The California market offers significant opportunity for growth driven by:

— Domestic and international in-bound air travel growth

— Key destinations in relation to key Triple A locations

— The likelihood that visitors will rent cars and a

strong potential to repeat assuming acceptable service

- The local market in California is relatively stable compared with "all other United States," suggesting that local initiatives can provide constant incremental rental volume in the long term.

(2) Business Systems and Skills

- The current planning process is not efficient from a day-to-day or long-term perspective. There appear to be opportunities to better increase capacity utilization based on the experience of successful leisure competitors.
- The utilization levels and poor profitability of many Triple A locations are driven by poor fleet management, particularly an inability to forecast.
- Flexibility and profit accountability at the local level are critical to Triple A's future success.
- Advertising spending levels in planning years one and two appear to be too high, given:
    — Category spending
    — Underdeveloped travel agent base
- The condition of some facilities suggests major loss of business unless they are brought to reasonable standards.
- Customer service should be sharply improved through training and measurement systems.
- Labor, rent and mortgage rates are key drivers of cost, which must be managed aggressively.

(3) Product and Technology

- Triple A is behind on the automation curve and needs to invest in systems that generate incremental revenue through better:
    — Reservation control
    — Pricing and yield management
    — Reporting and tracking
- Most revenue comes from Triple A customers who use a limited number of models, thus reduced fleet mix appears

to be a potential opportunity for more efficient fleet utilization.

(4) Competition
   • The leisure class leader's success is a result of doing a lot of little things right, rather than doing one major thing outstandingly.

The results of in-depth research were used to discard some hypotheses and refine others that could more reasonably be expected to deliver a Unique Value strategy to meet the agreed goal. Figure 10.7 was the strategic map produced by the Triple A team to discuss potential Unique Value strategies, while figure 10.8 summarizes the qualitative inputs used to generate the map.

Refined Strategies and Hypotheses

Potential Unique Value strategies were reformulated to reflect a more sophisticated knowledge base and understanding of the issues.

Hypothesis One: "Local Leisure Market Strategy."
Fundamentals of Refined Unique Value Strategy:
1. Competitive Framework: Triple A will grow at the expense of unstable and smaller operators who will be forced out of the market by the recent poor business climate.
2. Market Target: Triple A will focus on the California leisure traveler.
3. Basis for Perceived Competitive Superiority: Triple A will increase its level of service to exceed industry norms and shut down its network of satellite (department stores and gas stations) rental centers.
4. Product Portfolio Configuration: Triple A will re-focus to emphasize service, not the cars being offered to consumers.
5. Key Profit Drivers: Triple A will improve profit margins by

Figure 10.7 : Unique Value = ROI® Model

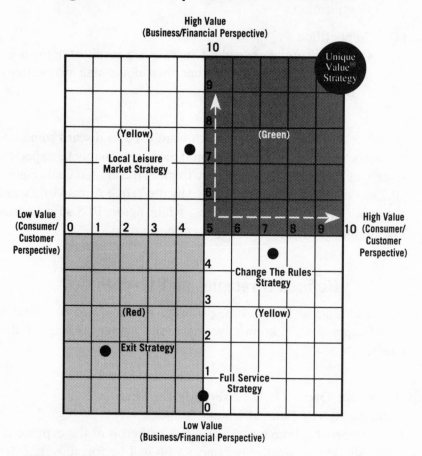

© Dunham & Marcus International, Inc., 1992.

focusing marketing efforts on travel agents, who are the major influencers in the decision on which rental car company to use. In addition, Triple A will adjust the number of car models rented to meet consumer preferences.

FIGURE 10.8   SUMMARY CHART OF POTENTIAL UNIQUE VALUE® STRATEGIES

POTENTIAL UNIQUE VALUE STRATEGY	RESULT OF INTEGRATED ANALYSIS	IMPLICATION FOR UNIQUE VALUE STRATEGY
1. Local Leisure Market Strategy	•Competitive benchmarking shows that the most successful of Triple A competitors is attacking the leisure market. •Field interviews and travel agent interviews show that Triple A currently provides inferior service. Thus, this is a source of competitive disadvantage. •Internal data review shows that the current use of satellite locations does not constitute a barrier to competition.	Refine strategy. Achieve growth by focusing on the leisure market segment only.
2. Exit Strategy	•Industry review and secondary data review show that the rental car market is expected to continue growing. •Industry review shows that with current saturation in market, there is no demand for acquisition of rental car companies.	Drop this as a strategic option.
3. Change the Rules Strategy	•Triple A management interviews showed that many of the options for changing the rules in the rental car industry had already been considered and discarded. •The technology review shows that updated systems were available that could increase the efficiency of Triple A's order taking and cost-allocation process.	Pursue this option by further investigating cost-allocation and systems options
4. Full Service Agency Strategy	•Triple A management interviews showed that they were unwilling to pursue the costs involved in this option.	Drop this as a strategic option.

Hypothesis Two: "Exit Strategy."
Dropped from further consideration.

Hypothesis Three: "Change the Rules Strategy."
Fundamentals of Refined Unique Value Strategy:
1.   Competitive Framework: Efficient cost allocation will allow

Triple A to underbid competition, offering the lowest prices to increase capacity utilization.

2. Market Target: To be determined.
3. Basis for Perceived Competitive Superiority: A superior cost-allocation and bidding system.
4. Product Portfolio Configuration: Triple A will re-focus to emphasize service, not the cars being offered to consumers.
5. Key Profit Drivers: Full capacity utilization will allow Triple A to gain marginal revenue even on very low-priced rentals.

Hypothesis Four: "Full Service Agency Strategy."
Dropped from further consideration.

Reality Checks, Costs, Risks, Corporate Agenda Requirements

Refined hypotheses for the potential Unique Value strategies provided a framework for discussions with management. Management input provided the corporate perspective and a reality check before strategies could be finalized. For example, management input showed that the two remaining strategies were not mutually exclusive. In the Triple A case, combining the Local Leisure Market Strategy with the Change the Rules Strategy potentially provided for superior Business/Financial and Consumer/Customer value (figure 10.9).

Unique Value Strategy Recommendation

After meetings with corporate management, further research findings on the systems for cost allocation and rental car pricing were incorporated into the recommended strategy. The strategy recommendation should included a statement of the business goal and a Unique Value strategy articulated in terms of the five fundamentals.

Goal: "Make the Triple A business profitable on a stand-alone basis within one year."

Recommended Unique Value strategy: "Change the Rules Lei-

Figure 10.9   Unique Value = ROI® Model

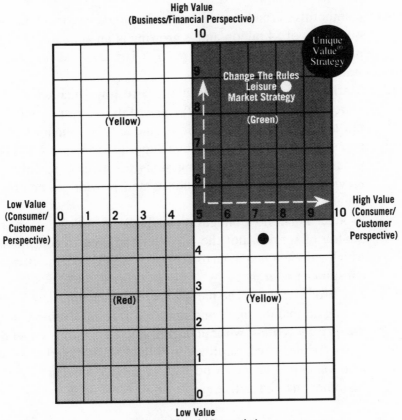

GREEN LIGHT: High Value Consumer/Customer *and* Business/Financial Perspective

CAUTION: High Value Consumer/Customer *or* High Value Business/Financial Perspective

RED LIGHT: Low Value Consumer/Customer *and* Business/Financial Perspective

© Dunham & Marcus International, Inc., 1992.

sure Market Strategy." Focus on the leisure market segment at the expense of local and national competition. Change the rules by costing and pricing at precisely defined levels under competition to increase capacity utilization while maximizing returns.

Fundamentals of the Recommended Unique Value strategy:

(1) Competitive Framework: The leisure market segment has annual sales of $4 billion and is growing at an annual rate of 10 percent. Approximately 20 percent is accounted for by unstable small operators.

(2) Market Target: The California leisure travel market is estimated to be $900 million. Travel agents are responsible for most leisure car rental decisions, and are the primary target.

(3) Basis for Perceived Competitive Superiority: Triple A has the potential to leverage existing skills to increase its level of service to exceed industry norms and provide lower prices (figure 10.10).

(4) Product Portfolio Configuration: Triple A will focus on the quality of service, not the cars being offered to consumers, which will be a much narrower range based on demonstrated consumer preferences.

(5) Key Profit Drivers: The narrow model range will allow Triple A to gain market share and marginal revenue even on very-low-priced rentals without significant advertising expenditures. Triple A will improve profit by focusing marketing efforts on travel agents, who have a greater influence on the customer than advertising.

The fundamentals of the Unique Value strategy were reviewed with management. An understanding was reached as to precisely how and why the fundamentals were interrelated.

Final Recommendation

With management agreement in place, the strategy team planned the implementation phase through a set of substrategies that will became the business plan. The Unique Value = ROI Model provided a structured knowledge base that translates into budgets and operations substrategies such as marketing, MIS and contingency plans for competitor responses.

Fig. 10.10

BASIS FOR PERCEIVED COMPETITIVE SUPERIORITY

- Two options existed to provide perceived value to Triple A leisure traveler consumers:
  1) Enhance quality and service
  2) Enhance affordability

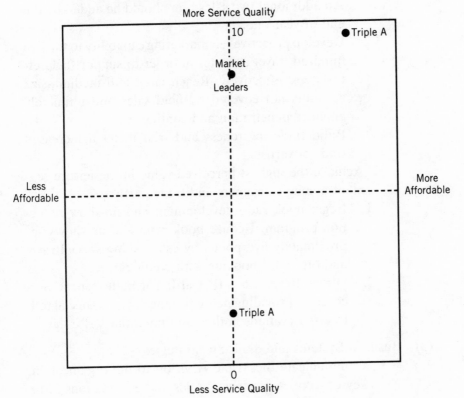

Source: Dunham & Marcus International Database
(Ratings based on market target perspective)

(1) Consumer/Customer Substrategies
  • Build relationships with preferred leisure-oriented trade customers and strengthen loyalty. Three strategic initiatives are developed to support this strategy.
    1. Field ten company-owned sales reps by first quarter year one in primary/high development origin markets to focus against the top two hundred travel agents. An additional two sales reps should be added by the end of year one.
    2. Develop proactive telemarketing capability to top five hundred travel agencies in order to support field efforts cost-effectively. Reach large and medium-size accounts not covered by field sales and ultimately enhance penetration and continuity.
    3. Build trade awareness and trial through increased trade advertising.
  • Achieve the highest perceived value in the leisure segment among consumers and trade partners.
    1. Begin book ratio development and no-show reduction program. Reduce book ratio and no-shows approximately five points by establishing special rates and offers for booking with credit cards.
    2. Direct Response VIP Card. Facilitate repeat purchase by providing new consumers with a special toll-free reservations hotline and potential VIP rates.

(2) Business Systems and Skills Substrategies
  • Communicate the Triple A vision to the organization: key objectives, strategies, roles and expectations of individual departments and management.
  • Develop formal planning, control and reporting system to enhance communication and operating integration.
  • Decentralize decisionmaking authority and accountability to field, in areas that can be influenced and controlled. Key "controllables" at the field level should include:
    — Walk-in (pricing and revenue)
    — Direct costs (fleet, manpower, special projects)

— Utilization (by mix)
— Productivity (people, incremental revenue—LDW, PAC, upgrades)
— Customer satisfaction (complaints/resolution)

- Hire additional training managers to hasten badly needed training and development. This includes accelerating front line training from nine or twelve months to six, retraining customer service and special accounts department to be more responsive, and broadening the training curriculum to include additional service factors.

- Improve the responsiveness of the current complaint handling and special accounts service system. This includes empowering the field to resolve customer issues on sight, rewarding or penalizing city managers on the basis of aggregate complaints received and adding another special accounts manager to handle anticipated future demand.

- Institute a semiannual satisfaction tracking study (prewave first quarter year one) against Triple A top two hundred travel agents and past six months' Triple A rental car consumers. The study should measure recent initiatives and impact on attitudes and usage to justify future program investments. (Triple A has no reliable satisfaction data, and repeat purchase rates are informally estimated at 6 percent versus 70 percent for direct competitors).

- Recruit experienced pricing/yield manager first quarter year one to enhance utilization and optimize revenue. The importance of low price combined with the complexity and importance of integrating fleet, reservations and pricing warrant a dedicated resource to manage and forecast reservation build, utilization, and competitive pricing daily.

(3) Product and Technology Substrategies
- Develop integrated RAC system to enhance operations

and aid achievement of Triple A strategic priorities. Key requirements of the system include:

— Expanded rate structure
— On-line update of pricing, reservation build and vehicle availability by location
— Quicker user-friendly rental counter checkout system
— Integrated (field/corporate) management reporting system
— Fleet costing/depreciation schedules by location
— Capability to reserve future rentals at locations
— Direct connect linkage to enhance communications speed and reliability
— Implementation as soon as possible
• Upgrade facilities in key strategic markets.

(4) Competitive Substrategies
• Develop formal pricing policy and operating guidelines and manage pricing on a day-to-day basis (versus the current twice per week) to ensure competitive position. This includes defining key competitive targets by market including their relative price differential versus Triple A and determining how Triple A pricing should be influenced by point changes in utilization levels.

With a Unique Value strategy, including detailed substrategies, in place, Triple A was prepared to execute against the stated goal of achieving profitability on a stand-alone basis within one year. The functional areas within the company had clear direction, and the organization as a whole had alignment from corporate senior management to the individual business unit. By working with the four sets of building blocks in the Unique Value = ROI Model— Consumer/Customer, Business Systems and Skills, Product and Technology and Competition—the strategy formulation team had given Triple A management a road map to accomplish its short-term goal of turning around the business and also positioned the business to achieve specific long-term goals such as profitability growth or market leadership in the leisure segment.

CHAPTER 11

PROFITABILITY, PRODUCTIVITY AND THE STRATEGIC ORGANIZATION

———— • ————

A Unique Value strategy can achieve short-term goals, as in the case of Triple A, or long-term goals, as in the case of IBM's mainframe business or Alfred Sloan's General Motors. For those two corporations, the long-term goal was share domination of their respective industries in America—then as now, the world's biggest market. To reach their goals each had a Unique Value strategy, but while the structure of the fundamentals was the same, the specifics were quite different. In each case, however, they were fully interrelated.

For IBM, the specific fundamentals were:

(1) Competitive Framework: All other suppliers of mainframes for general business purposes.
(2) Market Target: Large national accounts and, specifically, the technical managers who controlled the budgets for systems hardware and maintenance.
(3) Basis for Perceived Superiority: "IBM means service."
(4) Product Portfolio: Continually updated mainframe systems, which set the standard for general business (notably, IBM did not have a supercomputer and was late with both the mini and personal computer).
(5) Profit Drivers: A large installed base and a customer franchise whose loyalty IBM secured through elaborate technical assistance programs, service maintenance contracts and a managed pace of innovation.

For Sloan's General Motors, the fundamentals applied to the entire corporation, and every division played a designated role.

(1) Competitive Framework: Other U.S. automobile makers.
(2) Market Target: All Americans who could afford a car, segmented by level of affluence.
(3) Basis for Perceived Superiority: Horsepower, styling and price, carefully tailored to meet the needs of General Motors' designated customer segments.
(4) Product Portfolio: A hierarchy of price points, so that for increasingly affluent Americans, the next price level was both aspirational and within reach.
(5) Profit Drivers: Investment in economies of scale—increasing standardization of chassis, with model and style differences often largely cosmetic.

For IBM, General Motors and other successful corporations with a Unique Value strategy, changing times required a major reassessment. of the specifics that was beyond the experience of the management. Thus the realization came slowly and painfully and was resisted until it was too late. The institutionalization of their respective Unique Value strategies created the illusion of permanence and an addiction to prosperity that made the world of constantly changing variables something to be shut out as long as possible.

In classic Western economic theory, the profit motive propels a company to deliver the most value to customers, improve the efficiency of the business system, fuel enhancements to products, services and technologies and generate funds for reinvestment to drive sustained growth. In 1922, Austrian economist Ludwig von Mises wrote in his book *Socialism:*

> It is only the prospect of profit which directs production into those channels in which the demands of the consumer are best satisfied at least cost. If the prospect of profit disappears, the mechanism of the market loses its mainspring, because it is only this prospect which sets it in motion and maintains it in operation.

But in a business enterprise that has allowed itself to become an institution, contact with the real-world drivers of profitability is lost. The system appears to create the profitability, not the actions of individuals. To offset this tendency of longer, successful business enterprises to become bureaucratic institutions, profitability and its drivers should be an everyday reality to the organization.

All constituencies are best served by specific measures of investments and returns that can be correlated with the most productive use of resources at the disposal of a business. A comprehensive set of measurements does, in the near and long term, reward all constituencies, from shareholders to talented managers, with the fruits of real productivity increases.

Because a Unique Value strategy is comprehensive and is the focus of all aspects of resource management, the contribution of the strategy to corporate profitability, return on investment, shareholder value or any other financial measure can be assessed with some accuracy. And since a Unique Value strategy also focuses all levels of management on the drivers of success and profitability, it leads to much more productive reinvestment decisions.

In a business environment increasingly driven by information systems, the precise measurement of many factors of productivity will increasingly be possible, including something as apparently intangible as a strategy. Thus, a Unique Value strategy, which is built on the total business and all its productive activities, provides a competitive advantage over a less integrated approach. By structuring a strategy into measurable components, a business can, over time, test the viability and quality of its strategic thinking with a comprehensive set of measurable results.

The five fundamentals of a Unique Value strategy are measurable at every stage of the strategy implementation process. The process of developing preliminary or refined measures also enhances strategic understanding. For example, in identifying and scaling the competitive framework, an enterprise must answer the classic question: What business am I in? In arriving at an answer, management must agree on a dynamic set of issues that are central to the viability of the business proposition:

- How is the business defined?
- What is the market?
- How big is the market?
- How big are the market segments?
- Who are the key competitors?
- Where and why can we grow at the expense of these competitors?
- What is the size of the opportunity?

The answers to these questions are all measurable and can be translated into quantifiable investment options.

The priorities of customer or consumer segments to be targeted and their satisfied and unsatisfied needs can be measured. The basis for perceived competitive superiority can be objectively analyzed through test markets and other mechanisms. The relative perceived value of the proposed portfolio of products or services can be evaluated against competitive offerings and established benchmarks. And analyses of the strategy's profit drivers and their links to corporate financial requirements improve the management of risk at both the business-unit and corporate levels.

Through the process of identifying, measuring and implementing the five fundamentals of a Unique Value strategy, the organization not only frames an array of viable investment alternatives for the future, but also builds a deeper understanding of the business, which leads to better management.

The need for extensive analysis and precise measurements in the development, monitoring and tracking of a Unique Value strategy appears to be at odds with the trend away from the corporation strategic planning department in the interests of decentralizing the strategy process, but it is not. The search for a Unique Value strategy is a creative process, but it must be supported by strategically relevant qualitative and diagnostic information as well as financial and other quantitative data. Within a corporate framework, it is pursued at the business-unit level. Initially, the process creates an informed dialogue within a business team and with management. Corporate management becomes a productive resource to business-unit managers.

Increasing emphasis on managing relationships, both internally (across regions and functions) and externally (with suppliers, customers, joint venture partners and other external constituencies), means that managers will require more sophisticated communications skills. They have to cope, in a more ambiguous world, with blurred boundaries within and between organizations. In this context, more precise knowledge builds a more secure foundation for relationship management.

Increasing emphasis on "bottom-up," project-based, "emergent" strategy generated by people close to markets and technologies implies that tomorrow's corporation will need to become much better at formulating viable strategic possibilities and refining or discarding them. Although large companies often set as an objective becoming more entrepreneurial, most firms have not altered their processes for investment project appraisal, which influences whether and what projects are generated and proposed in the first place, and how much people are willing to take personal risks.

Management increasingly encourages "making things happen through people" because, at a detailed technical and market level, most of the knowledge in the firm resides at an operating middle management level. That is, it is the operating managers who "know best." Investment opportunities have to be created by the imagination and desire of people at this level. For this reason, everyone in the organization—not just top managers—must be able to think strategically.

World-class corporations—those on the cutting edge of management theory and practice—recognize the critical importance of strategic thinking, which is distinctly different from strategic planning. Central corporate strategic planning has often been a bureaucratic drag on an organization. Strategic thinking about the longer-term growth of the business has, therefore, become the responsibility of the line manager, precisely because it is line managers who have the day-to-day responsibility for the performance of the business.

Because the line manager's function is concerned with the day-to-day, however, strategy development must often be put on the back burner. As Henry Hawley, vice-president and director of marketing at Seagram Beverage Company, so aptly puts it, the managers involved in Seagram's strategy development process also have "day jobs" that command all of their time and attention. The problem in an established business environment is that if the concept of strategy and the goal of strategic understanding are not institutionalized, the essential skills required to put knowledge and ideas to work with the "prospect of profit" are much less likely to be developed.

Precisely because they recognize the difficulty of making strategic thinking part of the company's day-to-day operations, world-class companies are experimenting with formal and informal ways to institutionalize a strategy process. But while strategy development task forces, multidisciplinary teams, cross-cultural communications, cross-pollinization of ideas, and creative brain-storming move in the right direction, they do not impose the strategic rigor necessary for an objective evaluation of viable alternatives.

At Unilever, a driver of strategic thinking at all levels in the organization is communication. Former chairman Sir Michael Angus says, "We believe that you have to have an organization where the passage of ideas both up and down and laterally is encouraged and made easy. The term we use is networking, which means that in a comparatively structured way, most people working at Unilever know how to communicate across boundaries."

In developing new operating units and management structures, Sir Michael says, Unilever builds and links them to encourage communication and multidisciplinary interaction:

> As these new organizations develop, the most important thing will not be who is in the center, or who is in the local company. What will matter is the way people work together. It is never strictly true to say that structures are flexible. Structures permit or encourage flexibility. But flexibility is about the way people behave within—or occasionally outside—the structures. It is about the way managers interpret their own roles, and their working relationships with other people in the system.

We will be asking more managers to fulfill more roles which overlap center and company, national and international, line and staff. And more will be in roles which cross traditional functional boundaries—for instance in logistics and in information technology.

The intent is to encourage thinking. The question remains, How rigorous will the thinking be?

SmithKline Beecham is reshaping its culture to encourage continuous improvement. According to CEO Bob Bauman, the company has overhauled its approach to human resource management to aid this process.

Our underlying theme for success is continuous improvement. Part of this process is constantly striving to break new ground. For instance, everyone in the company has a customer. People need to figure out ways to satisfy their needs. Innovation on products is also critical. Everyone needs to look for ways of doing things better and to bring innovation consistently to the process.

To create this environment, we need to break down walls and help people work together more effectively. We want to promote performance as a team and as a corporation. We need to start moving people between sectors, and help sectors know each other better, work better together and share resources. It will take intervention from the top to make this happen.

Ultimately, the key is having the right people—people who are tough-minded, who will ask the right questions. You want people who are going to push to the next level of thinking and bring that touch of creativity that gives you a new dimension.

Among American companies, General Electric has long been a benchmark for institutionalizing strategic thinking at all levels of the organization. GE's Management Development Institute in Crotonville (Ossining), New York—which pioneered such concepts as strategic planning and decentralization—is considered a premier "business school" in corporate America. And under the leadership of Chairman Jack Welch, the curriculum at Crotonville is being reoriented toward so-called soft skills that emphasize management-employee communication and interaction.

To help cross-pollinate ideas, General Electric's program Work-Out brings groups of employees together to discuss issues, generate ideas and solve problems. The Work-Outs are unusual in that "the boss," who may be a plant manager, a division vice-president or any other supervisor, is barred from the session (usually held at a local hotel) until the employees have developed a list of actions and ideas they want management to consider.

With the same intention of stimulating independent, creative thinking as well as a learning environment, Ikujiro Nonaka, director of the Institute of Business Research at Hitotsubashi University, proposed the concept of "middle-up-down management." The first phase of this "involves visions or dreams proposed by top management to generate *creative chaos* in the firm. Middle management is stimulated to create and activate practical concepts to bridge the gap between the status quo and the visions or dreams. In other words, the middle managers deploy grand theories presented by the top into more empirically testable, middle-ranged theories and take leadership initiative in executing them by involving top management, as well as employees at the bottom." According to Nonaka, "This is the most effective management style for the continuous creation of new concepts or information in a firm, a step which is indispensable to the firm's self-renewal."[1]

John Seely Brown, a Xerox vice-president and director of the company's Palo Alto Research Center (PARC), says:

> Management must recognize that in the 1990s and beyond, the companies that learn the fastest will have a sustained competitive edge. The goal, then, is to create a truly reflective organization that accepts ideas and innovations from all places in the corporation and uses these innovations to constantly reinvent and improve itself.

The limitation of these approaches is that they fail to provide a consistent framework for strategic thinking. On the other hand, planners and formal planning systems that do provide frameworks and disciplines for strategy tend to set up barriers to continuous strategic learning. One possible exception is Royal-Dutch Shell Oil, which pioneered a radical approach. Arie de Geus, for many years chief planner at Shell, grappled with the subject of strategic learning in the context of his role as a long-range planner. He defines strategic learning as "the process whereby management teams change their shared mental models of their company, their markets and their competitors."[2]

This definition encompasses a number of key elements:

(1) It is a *process*—it is not just about analysis.
(2) The only strategic learning that matters is learning by people with the authority to take action—that is, line *managers* (not planners or other staff people).
(3) Significant organizational change requires learning by *teams,* not just by individuals.
(4) Obviously, learning involves *change*—if nothing is changed nothing has been achieved.
(5) What changes are managers' *mental models,* and ideally these mental models are *shared* by different managers within the same teams. In practice managers find it difficult to share such models: Each individual will tend to structure any strategic problem in his own way, and what one gets from a group of managers is a decision rather than the theories on which that decision is based.
(6) The substance of such models is the *company* itself (including its technologies and other capabilities) and its *markets and competitors*—in other words, the various elements of strategy.

De Geus agrees that the way that change is induced involves managers (and maybe others) working together on a problem that engages energy. The most energizing problem is a crisis. The challenge, then, is to accelerate organizational learning without—or at least before—such a crisis. Planning systems are not good at this.

A graphic example of Shell's approach to planning was provided when the planners, at a time when the dollar price of oil was in the upper twenties, asked management to play the game of thinking through what they would do if the price fell to fifteen dollars. No one thought this likely, but the game encouraged management to make a number of immediate changes, which served it well a few months later when, to everyone's surprise, oil fell to fifteen dollars a barrel.[3]

In most organizations, a combination of factors prevents the transformation of mental models from taking place. The barriers to strategic learning are both structural (forums and mechanisms for communication, teamwork, sharing and building are not in place) and attitudinal (skepticism, the NIH [not invented here] syndrome, ignorance, arrogance and a political concern about defending previous positions).

Overcoming Structural and Attitudinal Barriers to Learning

It is relatively new for most corporations to entertain, let alone embrace, the idea of a learning environment. But the concept was seeded over sixty years ago, by an English theorist, Mary Parker Follett, who studied and lectured on organization theory in the 1920s and 1930s, and whose work is referred to in Pauline Graham's published work *Integrative Management: Creating Unity from Diversity.*

What Mary Parker Follett identified in the early part of this century was the need for balance: "the need to mix concern for group dynamics and individuality with a balance between competition and cooperation, where trust is an important element of control." Pauline Graham's expression of this thesis is that "the key organizational challenge today is to combine the disciplined structures necessary to administer history with a much more flexible, holistic approach when there is a need to manage change."[4]

For example, in an attempt to overcome structural barriers to learning, IDS, the financial advisory service which is a subsidiary of American Express, instituted a comprehensive program of "change" relationships under Harvey Golub when he became CEO. Since 1984, when American Express bought the company, IDS has posted average annual earning jumps of 22 percent, and assets under management have nearly tripled, to more than $65 billion. The typical IDS planner handles client assets of $3.8 million, up 75 percent from 1984. In 1992, IDS became American Express's most profitable division, eclipsing flagship American Express Travel Related Services Co., the limping charge card and travelers check business, which posted a $342 million restructuring charge that same year.[5]

The working philosophy in this case is a type of intellectual egalitarianism, in which the significance is placed on the quality of the idea itself, rather than the level of organization from which the idea was born. Says Golub:

> Our system is relatively nonhierarchical. It is hierarchical in some sense—clearly structure is there. But there is an intellectual egalitarianism that at least applies. It doesn't matter who has an idea, it's the quality of the idea, irrespective of the level of the organization. People are free to build around their own ideas within reasonable limits.
>
> In one instance, we had organized teams in the mutual fund product line, each serving a particular region of the country on all aspects of our business, from accepting a new piece of business to handling death claims. During the past two years, these teams have gained experiences managing their day-to-day business with personal involvement on many service decisions. The teams came alive when Hurricane Hugo struck South Carolina in 1990. Working with IDS financial planners and district managers, they put in place service ideas which would benefit IDS clients in South Carolina, such as free Federal Express delivery, taking instructions for wiring funds to a client's account via fax, expanding the hours of telephone service and expanding the services offered over the phone. Team members felt very empowered to manage their day-to-day business and take charge for implementing these ideas with support rather than direction.
>
> People in our annuity products business decided that it would be very useful if they developed their own process for

conserving funds if their clients looked like they were drawing money out. So they designed their own system for calling people to find out why they were cashing in policies so they could talk to them if they were doing it for reasons that were wrong. As a result, they ended up with one of the highest preservation rates in the industry.

This freedom to make critical decisions is precisely what is lacking in most corporations, according to John Kotter, professor of organizational behavior at Harvard Business School, who says that "organizations have difficulty adjusting to market or technological change" precisely because "people in those firms feel relatively powerless. They have learned from experience, that even if they correctly perceive important external changes and then initiate appropriate actions, they are vulnerable to someone higher in the hierarchy who does not like what they have done."[6]

Historically, few organizations have been structured to institutionalize the sharing of ideas and knowledge that is essential for learning. In 1983, Professor Rosabeth Moss Kanter of the Harvard Business School wrote that "innovative managers agreed that the most common roadblock they had to overcome" was "poor communication with other departments on whom they depended for information." She concluded that "a communication system, depending on the kind adopted by a given corporation, can either constrain or empower the effort to innovate," and that in companies where she observed open communication, "information and ideas flowed freely and were accessible; technical data and alternative points of view could be gathered with greater ease."[7] Kanter wrote:

> The frequent use of integrative team mechanisms at middle and upper levels . . . both encourage the immediate exchange of support and information and create contacts to be drawn on in the future. The organizational chart with its hierarchy of reporting relationships and accountabilities reflects only one reality; the *other structure,* not generally shown on the charts, is an overlay of flexible, ad hoc problem-solving teams, task forces, joint planning groups, and information-spreading councils.

Note that it is not just any team that aids innovation but a tradition of drawing members from a diversity of sources, a variety of areas. Innovating companies deliberately seem to create a "marketplace of ideas," recognizing that a multiplicity of points of view need to be brought to bear on a problem. It is not the "caution of committees" that is sought—reducing risk by spreading responsibility—but the better idea that comes from a clash and an integration of perspectives.[8]

World-class corporations today are organizing their workforces into teams composed of people with diverse but relevant backgrounds and areas of expertise. But the problem of overcoming structural and attitudinal barriers is compounded in multinational corporations, where teams must share knowledge across nations and cultures. Bob Phillips, former CEO of Chesebrough-Pond and currently president and CEO of Elizabeth Arden, observes that Unilever's culture has always encouraged global travel and conferences for this reason:

> The way Unilever works is through personal interaction. Most business is conducted on a personal basis, so we all travel all the time. It is one thing to set plans or to send information back and forth, but that's not the same as discussing ideas with people face to face. So after Unilever acquired Chesebrough-Pond, everybody just started criss-crossing the Atlantic. I would see to it that people from various areas within C-P (Chesebrough-Pond) were immediately over in the U.K. working in the development labs, familiarizing themselves with the Unilever marketing staff. The same was true here. The U.K. groups spent a lot of time visiting U.S. facilities. The whole purpose for this was that as we spent time together and became more comfortable with each other, we began to achieve a real dialogue whereby you really get down underneath it all and begin sharing and cooperating.
>
> Because many of our corporate skill areas can be applied globally, we try to share functions such as advertising, customer service, and R&D. Unilever has a series of conferences for different disciplines—marketing, operations, research—which allows divisions from all over the world to share ideas.

Although there are exquisite manuals and documents on how these functions should be approached, the generations of experience and knowledge of our management is mostly transmitted through lots of meetings and personal interaction.

Information technology can also drive organizational learning by routinely providing continuous feedback from the external environment to support decisionmaking. In the case of Frito-Lay's system of hand-held computers for field personnel to record daily inventory changes, there was wide acclaim for the efficiency gains it produced. In two years, sales increased 30 percent without an expansion of the sales force. But the long-term benefits reach even further.

Because the sales and inventory data is relayed to a central computer at Frito-Lay headquarters, which processes and summarizes the information management at all levels of the corporation can identify and analyze trends that will drive future marketing, purchasing, manufacturing and product development decisions. The system is a tool for multilevel performance tracking in realtime that is shared by the entire organization. This information has also proven to be a source or leverage with retail customers. "If you can show [retailers] that Frito-Lay snacks move faster or produce a higher margin than the snacks of another brand that is getting bigger displays," says former president and CEO Michael Jordan, "you have a powerful argument for winning more space."[9]

At General Foods in 1984, the Marketing Information Systems (MIS) Department gave product managers direct access to current marketing data as part of a state-of-the-art decision support system. George Williams, now a senior consultant at Dunham & Marcus International, Inc., who received two Chairman's Awards for his work at General Foods, describes the advantages of the system he developed to implement this vision:

The first benefit to General Foods was that the system made data available to product managers and their assistants so that they could perform their own analyses to see what was happening to their brands and to the competition. Second, the MIS group was able to model the data to isolate the factors that were driving each brand's volume and share.

We also pioneered the use of artificial intelligence software to direct product managers to the key indicators of market performance and trends. At a time when scanner data was just emerging as a marketing tool, and the number of measures tracked was skyrocketing, information technology enabled product managers to cope with this overload of data, build an enhanced understanding of the market, and make key decisions to strengthen the competitive positioning of their brands.

A related productivity and learning tool is "Total Quality," as pioneered by W. Edwards Deming and Joseph M. Juran in Japan. As Deming has written:

> Why is it that productivity increases as quality improves? Less rework. There is no better answer. These people know how important quality is to their jobs. They know quality is achieved by improvement of the process. Improvement of the process increases uniformity of output of product, reduces rework and mistakes, reduces waste of manpower, machine-time, and materials and thus increases output with less effort.[10]

Deming has demonstrated that traditional "measures of productivity do not lead to improvement in productivity. . . . Measures of productivity are like statistics on accidents: they tell you all about the number of accidents in the home, on the road, and at the work place, but they do not tell you how to reduce the frequency of accidents."[11]

Deming pioneered statistical quality control, which differentiates between avoidable and unavoidable errors by mapping output deviations at each stage of the production process. By extending Deming's principles to all aspects of the business, including customer service, manufacturing and distribution, Juran developed the total quality concept that Japanese companies adopted and perfected.

Since the 1980s, American and European corporations have been implementing total quality programs of their own, learning from the success of the Japanese (figure 11.1).

Why have the Japanese been so successful? Because they insti-

Figure 11.1 Average Productivity and Quality of Volume Automobile Manufacturers, 1989

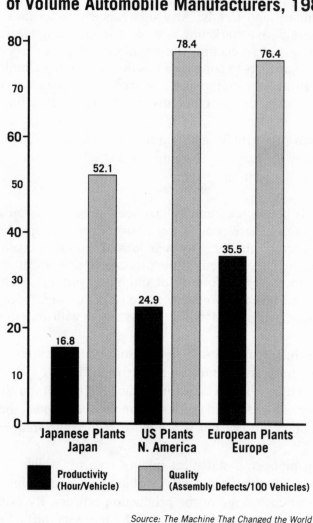

Source: *The Machine That Changed the World*

© Dunham & Marcus International, Inc., 1991.

tutionalized total quality control throughout their organizations. Japanese companies "learned" total quality, applied it to all aspects of their businesses and constantly worked to improve it through *kaizen*, the Japanese concept of "continuous improvement."

Of the American companies that have succeeded in institutionalizing total quality management, one of the best known is Motorola. In an article by B. G. Yovovich, entitled "Motorola's Quest for Quality," John E. Major, senior vice-president and general manager of Motorola's Worldwide Systems Group, describes his company's approach:

> If it does not work the way that the user needs it to work, the defect is as big to the user as if it doesn't work the way the designer planned it. Our definition of a defect is, "If the customer doesn't like it, it's a defect." This has put more pressure on our teams to understand the customer better.
>
> The initial reaction to the idea that we would count the customer's view of a defect to be our view of a defect created horror with our engineers. They said, "Wait. I am designing to our specs, and if I've met our spec and he doesn't like it that means that I am wrong?!" and we told them, "Yep, that means you are wrong."[12]

Eventually, the engineers began to seek ways of linking their design procedures to fulfill customer requirements, which led to Motorola's current emphasis on design-for-quality. Major continues:

> Design-for-quality has been bubbling up through the ranks in the last couple of years, and it is changing the way that people design products. My [product development and design] people are "nutso" about it, and it is sweeping through this place.
>
> [The result] is that the products have been developed faster because we had an explicit way to figure out what the customer wanted, what we could provide, and how to work our way through the trade-offs.[13]

Motorola won the 1988 Malcolm Baldrige Award (figure 11.2), in recognition of its achievements in total quality and in 1989 preempted Japanese rivals with its MicroTac portable cellular phone, to win two of Japan's top product quality awards. More importantly, its commitment had significant commercial results,

---

FIGURE 11.2   MALCOLM BALDRIGE NATIONAL QUALITY AWARD

•Baldrige Award winners are selected by the secretary of commerce and the National Institute of Standards and Technology.
•Up to two awards may be given in each of three categories:
  Manufacturing companies or subsidiaries
  Service companies or subsidiaries
  Small businesses
•Fewer than two awards may be given in a category if the standards of the program are not met. Recipients may publicize and advertise their awards provided they agree to share information about their quality strategies with other American organizations.
•Quantitative data furnished by applicants should demonstrate quality achievement and improvement in seven areas:
  Leadership
  Information and analysis
  Strategic quality planning
  Human resource development and management
  Management of process quality
  Quality and operational results
  Customer focus and satisfaction

Source: 1992 Malcolm Baldrige National Quality Award Criteria.

---

such as a much-strengthened position in the world semiconductor market.

By becoming strategically committed, Motorola extended its total quality efforts into measurably improved standards of customer satisfaction, which translated into measurable productivity, profit and share gains.

Objective, measurable standards and evaluative criteria go a long way toward overcoming the attitudinal barriers to learning. Resistance to change, skepticism, the "not-invented-here" syndrome and the arrogance that comes, all too often, with success can be overcome if the new measures of success are properly institutionalized and are seen to make sense. For insulated corporate executives, tempted to focus on the internal environment, the ever-present reality check must be the feedback of customer satisfaction and other measures that predict the "prospect of profit."

Human resource policies in successful organizations are reward systems for those who are executing a winning strategy, and reinforce the actions, values and priorities that drive success. Just as organizational structure expresses strategy, so do personnel's performance criteria. If times change and strategies must change, then the organization's structure and performance criteria must also change.

But often the drivers of a Unique Value strategy are not fully understood. They drive the established culture, its values and its reward systems, and they drove the long-term profitability that resulted in a rich and powerful enterprise. But often success is institutionalized and not consciously understood. In most cases, the most successful enterprises are the most vulnerable to external factors that change the strategic requirements for success. Values then become counterproductive because they are focused on history. For example, the emerging PC markets represented a unique opportunity for IBM ten years ago, but the organization that was rewarded for delivering IBM service ("IBM means service" was the credo) could not imagine a business where service was not the driver.

Eventually, every corporation must be ready to learn a new set of rules when the alternative is significant lost opportunity.

In the case of Seagram, there were many new rules. But what made Seagram's cooler business successful at the outset was a strategic way of looking at a new set of realities.

WHAT SEAGRAM LEARNED
ABOUT CONSUMERS AND CUSTOMERS

- In 1985, the wine cooler category appeared to be the only bright spot in alcoholic beverages—it was the only significant alcohol-based beverage category that was growing.
- Among the population at large, nearly 80 percent of U.S. consumers who drink alcohol had tried a wine cooler.
- From Seagram's perspective, wine cooler triers were not part of Seagram's franchise—very few of them drank Seagram's traditional whiskey products, or were ever likely to. On the other hand, they were all familiar with the Seagram name and associated it with sophisticated, adult drinking occasions. Sea-

gram, overwhelmingly, was perceived to be a premium quality adult drink, no matter what the specific product.

WHAT SEAGRAM LEARNED ABOUT BUSINESS SYSTEMS AND SKILLS

• The business model for wine coolers was much more like that of carbonated soft drinks or beer than it was like that of spirits. The distribution network was driven by relationships with independent bottlers, who were the local producers (they owned the bottling plants) and distributors (they owned the trucks and sales force). Because of the carbonated soft drink and beer industries, which had depended on regional bottler operations, there was a strong tradition of partnership between bottlers and suppliers. Bottlers expected suppliers to provide marketing strategies, business skills, product formulas and marketing budgets to support brands. In most cases, Seagram was well-equipped to be the marketing and business partner that bottler networks were looking for. The requirement was marketing funds, not plant investments.

WHAT SEAGRAM LEARNED ABOUT PRODUCTS AND TECHNOLOGIES

• In 1986, the category leader in wine coolers was Gallo, because Gallo's strategy was to dominate every segment of the U.S. wine industry. Gallo had all the requisite technologies for wine coolers—it was the low-cost processor of grapes, and theoretically of all grape-based products, including wine coolers. Consumers, however, saw wine coolers quite differently—they were not an introduction to the pleasure of fine wine; they were an alternative to everyday wine and to beer. They were carbonated, like beer and soft drinks. They could be fruity, unlike beer or wine. Making them more fruity made them better—as long as it was a relatively sophisticated, premium-quality fruit flavor.

WHAT SEAGRAM LEARNED ABOUT THE COMPETITION

- California Coolers had created the category but appeared to have little understanding of why consumers had responded. Its advertising downgraded the product experience, making it impossible to command a premium price. Gallo had accurately assessed the situation and had introduced the first "premium wine cooler" with a slightly higher price and with a much more appealing image. Gallo's premium pricing and strong national distribution made a national advertising campaign affordable, putting Gallo in a leadership position. But Gallo's strategy was single-mindedly focused on the wine industry, where its competitive advantage was share domination (driven by aggressive low pricing whenever required) and its low-cost producer status (driven by vertical integration), and its buying power.

The opportunity for Seagram was to take the initiative in redefining the category—by developing flavor alternatives such as peach, wild berries and tropical blends to stimulate category trial.

Once Seagram had established the success of its strategy in the marketplace, it formalized the principles which would drive sustainable profitability:

- Minimize capital outlay.
- Keep costs out of the business.
- Optimize inventory levels.

The result of the Seagram Beverage Company's preoccupation with all the measures that kept track of these three profit drivers was a 50 percent ROA (return on assets) for the corporation for the years following the establishment of Seagram wine coolers in the marketplace (figure 11.3).

FIGURE 11.3　THE FIVE FUNDAMENTALS OF SEAGRAM'S UNIQUE VALUE STRATEGY—THE MEASURABLE FACTORS THAT PRODUCED A 50 PERCENT ROA (RETURN ON ASSETS).

FUNDAMENTAL	BASIS FOR UNIQUE VALUE STRATEGY
(1) Competitive Framework	In 1985, the wine cooler market was large (over $500 million at retail) and growing—but much of the volume was in the hands of weak competitors.
(2) Market Target	Nearly 80 percent of the adult population who consumed beverages with some alcohol content had tried a wine cooler. People who disliked beer saw it as an appropriate replacement.
(3) Basis for Perceived Superiority	The Seagram's name was recognized by 83 percent of the population interested in coolers and was regarded as a superior credential for an alcoholic beverage.
(4) Product Portfolio	Taste testing provided guidance for a superior line of premium fruit flavors.
(5) Key Profit Drivers	While Gallo was the low-cost producer because of vertical integration, Seagram invested in advertising to build brand equity, thus enhancing the trademark as a corporate asset. No significant capital investment was made in plant.

CHAPTER 12

UNIQUE VALUE
STRATEGIES OF THE FUTURE

———— • ————

The rules change, or are changed, all the time. Leaders change the rules; followers play by the rules of the leaders. In the words of Tim Breene, worldwide marketing director of United Distillers, the upside of change is that it "creates tremendous challenge and opportunity for management." The downside is that it is also disruptive. "It undermines continuity and inhibits teamwork. Valuable experience is all too easily lost and there is rarely time to codify knowledge and experience. Success in the past is no longer a guarantee of success in the future."

In his keynote address to United Distillers' 1992 Worldwide Marketing Conference, the challenge of change was taken up in terms of the characteristics necessary for today's world-class corporations, and specifically world-class marketing companies, which he defined in terms of "five quite distinct characteristics."

The first characteristic is a deep-rooted belief in brands, a recognition that brand building is a constant process of revitalization. The great marketing companies of the world do not believe in brand life cycles. The second characteristic is a world-class corporation's commitment to stretching goals. Often the goals are formed in terms of beating a competitor. They express what we might describe as strategic intent. The third characteristic is commitment to superior capabilities. The fourth characteristic is that they shape their environment. They define the ground rules on which others must compete. And the fifth characteristic of world-class marketing companies is an ability to do more with less through continuous quality improvement and value analysis.

He then goes on to cite specific examples of each characteristic. In terms of the fifth characteristic, for example:

Mars (in Europe) is driven by a management concept called "ROTA"—return on total assets. ROTA is the key measure of management performance. The two other measures are asset turn and profit margin, which between them produce ROTA. The whole Mars philosophy is driven by the concept of modest profit margins, but high turn so that its products represent outstanding value for money yet still produce an above average return on assets. The ROTA philosophy infuses every aspect of the Mars business. It means that the whole marketing philosophy is designed to ensure intensive asset utilization. It means that the business avoids investment in assets unless it can obtain competitive advantage through involvement in that specific activity. It means that they avoid line proliferation that could reduce asset utilization, that all new products are designed to be production-friendly, that working practices permit seven-day, twenty-four-hour working of the production assets. It means that they have avoided acquisitions, that they focus their investment behind a few core brands and that they will do whatever they can to stretch those brands.

In the United States wine cooler market, Seagram redefined "the ground rules on which others must compete" and gained a competitive advantage over Gallo, the previously unbeatable leader in the United States wine industry. In coolers, Gallo had to play by Seagram's rules—following the Seagram Beverage Company into malt-based instead of wine-based formulations for the more favorable brewing industry tax rates. Gallo has also followed Seagram in flavor variety, where fruit blends have replaced wine blends as the consumer's frame of reference.[1] Gallo's attempt to maintain the category as an offshoot of wine, thereby maintaining economic control, failed because Seagram's understanding of the market dynamics was superior; Seagram had the trademark with the greatest potential value to consumers; and Seagram was innovative in its approach to the overall business.

Ten years ago, IBM changed the rules in the computer industry inadvertently, by legitimizing personal computers for business use. Apple made computers personal, but IBM made PCs into business machines and empowered individuals in the workplace—a far more influential economic event in the history of the world (see Appendix A).

Don Estridge, who led the Boca Raton team that brought the IBM PC to market, was a loyal IBMer who believed in both the IBM way and the power of the marketplace. When his second product, which he called the IBM PC Jr., failed, he learned from the debacle and introduced the IBM AT, a more powerful second-generation PC that put IBM back on a strategic track with the business market. When he was moved from the leadership of the PC unit in Boca Raton, so that Armonk could bring the fledgling business under tighter control, he accepted the transfer obediently, confident that IBM knew best.

In the 1990s Japan, Inc. is also experiencing the impact of a new set of rules. Fujitsu, second only to IBM among global information technology companies, warned it would incur pretax losses of about 10 billion yen ($78.7 million) in the first half of 1992.[2] The problem for both IBM and Fujitsu is the decline of the world mainframe market. IBM has had access to many new technologies that might have changed the rules in IBM's favor. A recent example is high-temperature superconductors, which IBM discovered in 1986, and which could bring business machines that are ten to one hundred times faster than what's available today.[3]

In automobiles, General Motors Cadillac Division has taken the lessons of total quality to heart, winning the Malcolm Baldrige Award for Quality in 1990.

And GM's Saturn Division has changed the rules of automobile manufacturing in America.[4] The implications for the Japanese automobile industry are sobering—a new approach to strategy will be required, according to Dick Recchia, executive vice-president and chief operating officer of Mitsubishi Motor Sales of America:

The economic situation in Japan changed. I don't think it's possible for any foreign company, not only the Japanese, to operate anymore on a home-based strategic planning system, if they're going to be successful in a worldwide market. You have to be sensitive to the demands of the marketplace. If you're going to be successful in America, you have to have an Americanized company.

The concept has to be that these are not Japanese companies doing business in the United States. These are American companies doing business in the United States that are owned by the Japanese. Concept one means the Japanese work to support the home-based strategic planning of Japanese parents. Concept number two means that you've developed a strategy for the market. It is a market-driven, not a manufacturing-driven, strategy, and then you see how you can integrate that strategy into the overall worldwide strategy.

I think that there is going to be a generation of businessmen who are going to be truly international traders who are adaptable, who have developed the ability to adapt their thinking to the conditions of the market. Because everything, every product that's sold or serviced in a worldwide market has to be market-driven. The tendency in the past with a lot of export countries—it was the case with Germany when they were strong there with Volkswagen, it was the case with Mercedes before they got the competition from Lexus and Infinity, and it was the case with the Japanese, and in some cases still is— was to be manufacturing-driven. We are a manufacturer, this is our philosophy, and what we build you will sell. We will decide what to build, we'll tell you what to sell. Now the competition in the marketplace has changed and the market is saying we'll tell you what we're going to buy. If you build this, we'll buy it. If you don't build it, you're going to have to pay a heavy price.

You've got to learn to hear rather than listen. There has to be a willingness to accept the local management as an equal in terms of strategic planning.

That's historically not the case. You have to learn to accept the fact that the demand for a product in eastern Europe may dictate a change in some of the requirements that you're going to put on your own production here. So you have to accept it as the voice of the market rather than the voice of an importer.

How should business strategists think about the future? Very creatively, and very carefully.

John Seely Brown of Xerox believes the business challenge of the future is to understand "in effect, what is innovation in the company: How do people innovate? There are a lot of things out there in the workplace that have been ignored by everybody because it goes against the current wisdom of what work really is."

One of Yotaro Kobayashi's visions for Fuji-Xerox is a "new direction, called a new work way, which has two meanings, one externally and one internally. Internally, the new work way is to bring a sense of fun and a sense of humanity to the office environment. Externally, we are saying our products will make your office environment more fun for your people to work, more pleasant, as well as more efficient. We are driving, we are working to reward more creative people, to make places different for people, because a good company is strong, but strength is not everything a good company strives for." Strategy is about the future, and when you deal with the future, linear thinking is a trap. The future demands the development of new information and hypotheses, the detection of emerging patterns and trends, and multiple options. This is the essence of creative business thinking.

Traditional market and industry research seeks to answer questions such as: What is the structure of the market? Who are the key competitors? What do they offer and to whom? Who is our customer? How does he or she perceive us and our products?

All these questions are susceptible to traditional information-gathering methods because they all deal with "what is." They can be answered with fact finding and statistical analysis.

But the future requires asking questions like: What might the structure of the market be? Who might the key competitors be? Who might our customer be?

In business the need is not for undisciplined creativity. When millions of investment dollars ride on decisions, the process of good decisionmaking is a matter of balance—a balance of divergent and convergent thinking.

Linear thinking is detrimental to business growth because it shuts out new information. It consists of a straight line from the data to the conclusion (figure 12.1). "Blue-sky" thinking (figure 12.2), which only emphasizes divergence or the generation of options, is not constructive because there is no closure—you can't make meaningful decisions.

By contrast an iterative approach consists of a divergent stage that pushes out to ask new questions and develop new information, followed by a convergent phase that organizes the information into pat-

Fig. 12.1   Linear Thinking

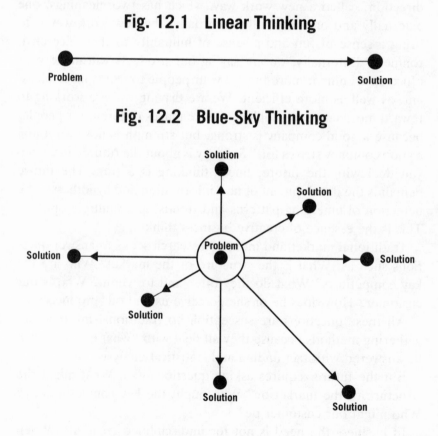

Fig. 12.2   Blue-Sky Thinking

Source: Dunham & Marcus International, Inc.

terns that are consistent with existing knowledge and data but go beyond them to build a larger conceptual framework that can be the foundation for new thinking, hypotheses and options (figure 12.3).

The development of Unique Value strategy requires a process of creative rigor, because true management productivity reflects a

Fig. 12.3 Creative Problem Solving

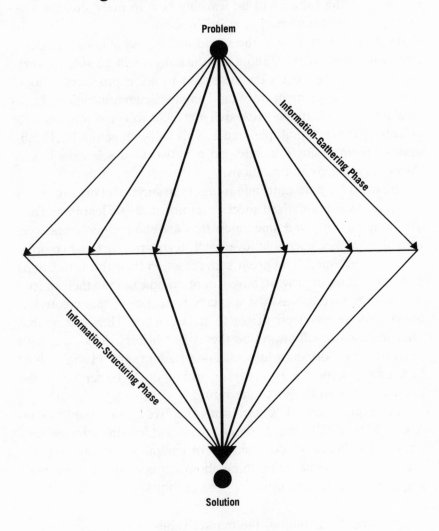

Source: Dunham & Marcus International, Inc.

balance of insight and analysis, of creativity and discipline, of human imagination and "the prospect of profit." Attention to strategic fundamentals and the attendant processes, structures and questions, provides world-class corporations with the tools they need today to be the creative, problem-solving strategic organizations of the future.

One of the most challenging requirements of the strategic corporation of the future will be learning how to make creative use of the wealth of information at its disposal.

As data travels around the world and across national borders, corporate employees, vendors and customers will be able to work together, on-line, to create ideas and to solve problems. Video conferences supplement travel and enhance communication. Technical designs and complex research materials will be communicated efficiently through multiple media. This will change the R&D laboratory from a single location to a network of scientists linked through global communications.

The need for a new attitude is urgent in successful organizations that have institutionalized success but not strategic learning. They are living on borrowed time unless they are eliminating layers, long formal meetings, corporate overhead, territorial turf and complacency. Highly successful profit generators, in their third, fourth or fifth generation of growth, have forgotten how unique their special formula for success was, the special circumstances that created it, the visionaries who were driven to make it work. They assume that their institution will always be there. But history does away with organisms and organizations that don't adapt, and in the case of businesses, someone is always working on a better way—the Unique Value strategies of the future.

In an article entitled "Capitalism's Creative Destruction" (*Economist,* May 1992), the *Economist* quotes Joseph Schumpeter's phrase, the "creative destruction" of capitalism, in pointing out that "the most remarkable thing about big companies is not their longevity, but their transience." For example:

At about $22 billion, the market value of Microsoft, a 17-year-old customer-software firm, is now as great as that of

General Motors, the world's biggest manufacturer. GM is still big, but no longer mighty. Its future looks bleak. Big companies assume the trapping of solidity and permanence. Corporate headquarters, glorious or appalling, are always the most ostentatious buildings in any city. Big firms spend lavishly on anniversaries, preach tradition to employees, proudly publish their own histories and generally behave as if they have been around since time began.

As illustration, the *Economist* supports its point with the *Fortune* magazine list cited at the beginning of this book—the top 100 corporations of America's *Fortune* 500, a list published for the first time in 1956. The 100 firms heading *Fortune*'s first list of America's 500 biggest companies, published in 1956, only 29 can still be found in the top 100 of the latest list. Of the 100 biggest non-American firms listed in 1956, only 27 were still there in 1989, the last time the magazine published such a list. Within the span of one working life, well over two-thirds of the world's biggest companies were overtaken or taken over by faster-growing firms. The *Economist* also suggests a clue to the future: In *Fortune*'s latest list, three of the top four places ranked by sales are taken by GM, Ford and IBM. Ranked by profits, their places are numbers 474, 472 and 473, respectively.

The unpredictability of the future is a constant challenge to do better, however good, or bad, a business's current performance. Says Rosetta M. Riley, Cadillac's director of customer satisfaction:

> As a result of the up-front planning and simultaneous engineering teamwork, we have seen a significant improvement in our ability to get to market on time with products that are on target. The first dramatic demonstration of that was the 1988 Eldorado program, which we restyled in just 55 weeks—an industry record. The restyling was driven by our dealers, who rejected our design proposal. They made some changes which we implemented. Because of the processes we'd put in place, we were able to redesign the car in 55 weeks. The result of all that was a 43 percent increase in Eldorado sales.[5]

Before launching an estimated $25 million advertising campaign for two upmarket versions of its Seville and Eldorado models introduced in September of 1991, Cadillac heavily researched the attitudes and issues influencing purchases in their target market, young affluent baby boomers. Cadillac had initially predicted 30 percent of 1992 sales would go to the two upmarket versions, but actual sales ran as high as 60 percent in some regions.

In many respects, Japanese companies are just starting the process of corporate introspection. For Matsushita Electric Industrial Company, the world's largest supplier of consumer electronics and a giant player in factory automation with sales in 1991 of $49.6 billion, profits have been slashed in half since the Japanese stock market crash. "Matsushita is at a turning point and so is Japan," says Masahiro Kosaka, a Matsushita laboratory director. "I don't think things will ever go back to the way they were."[6] For example, Japanese companies that dominate today's memory chip business and thought they would always be at the front of the chip-making race are finding that the more recent market for "flash" memory chips is being led by Intel, the American semiconductor firm. Flash memories will replace the hard disk drives used in laptop computers and could eventually take over many of the uses of DRAM (dynamic random-access memory) chips, which are the stronghold of the Japanese computer chip industry.

Japan's Nomura Research Institute estimates annual sales of flash chips will exceed $7 billion by the year 2000, up from $100 million in 1991. Intel now has 85 percent of the worldwide market for flash chips, whereas Toshiba has just about 3 percent.[7]

U.S. competitor Motorola has been successful in penetrating every aspect of Asia's telecom and semiconductor markets. By building thirteen factories in nine Asian countries and employing Asian managers to run them, Motorola increased its chip sales in non-Japanese Asia by 20 percent in 1990, reaching $528 million.

The continuous process of self-examination and scrutiny that is part of Motorola's working philosophy has been central to its success.

Apple, the computer company that started the PC revolution, is also in the process of transformation. The Apple Computer, Inc., of the future will not be just a personal-computer maker, according to Apple chairman John Sculley. "Apple plans to become a global electronics holding company overseeing multiple businesses."[8] So Apple will begin to sell consumer electronics, software and telecommunication devices in addition to personal computers.

Ten years ago Don Estridge was afraid the IBM PC might put Apple Computers out of business and revive the federal government's antitrust suit. Today, Apple and IBM do business with each other as equals. Don Estridge's antitrust concerns were an important consideration for IBM in 1983, but in the 1990s few corporations have the resources to operate alone. The need to share markets, distribution systems, skills and technologies is making many of yesterday's competitors into today's strategic partners.

If the market opportunity is the driver, then an alliance of partners with complementary skills and strengths, and with a shared strategic focus, can exploit it more effectively than a traditional competitor with relevant strengths but an obsolete structure.

In 1986, Beecham and SmithKline Beckman saw a need and a market opportunity and consciously forged a partnership to take advantage of it. The merger between Beecham PLC and SmithKline Beckman, conceived in strategic terms from its inception, focused on a single industry with many global markets. From the beginning of the new corporate entity, SmithKline Beecham, the relationships between the market needs, the operations requirements, the product lines and the competitive challenges, would be different in each market. Each market strategy would be designed to leverage the resources of the new corporate entity but focus on specific local market opportunities. The new corporate culture would shed old, partisan values and embrace the vision of the new SmithKline Beecham—a change that had to be worked into the structure of the enterprise through comprehensive changes in personnel policy, reward systems and training programs at every level.

Fred Kyle, now a senior vice president with the American Red Cross and currently charged with a $140 million reorganization of the Red Cross network of blood banks (a $800 million annual program, which supplies 52 percent of America's blood needs), was at the center of SmithKline Beckman's reorganization in the United States before the merger.

In June of '88 we had begun a restructuring of SmithKline Beckman; started the spin-off of a couple of divisions, restructured the surviving businesses with a no-kidding restructuring. It was a massive change of structure and staffing and during that period the initial contacts between Henry [Wendt] and Bob [Bauman] took place and negotiations essentially started. From an organizational standpoint there was an amazingly congruent fit [between Beecham and SmithKline Beckman], surprisingly so. If we hadn't picked the right partner all the other action we took wouldn't have made a difference on its own. We said we are going to get responsible people at each level of the organization to develop what was, in their view, the most logical way to put these two companies together.

We had a corporation with 55,000 employees. We didn't want to change the basic ways they behaved, but more to reinforce the way they behaved in certain directions.

Two years after the merger, *The Wall Street Journal* reported:

SmithKline Beecham PLC has gotten off to a surprisingly smooth start. An initial work force of 55,000 has been cut nearly ten percent and annual costs pruned more than five percent. Combined marketing clout has hoisted sales in markets around the world. Marketing, research and development outlays have climbed sharply. At the same time, pretax profit surged 19 percent in 1990 and 17 percent last year. Profit margins shot up more than five percentage points, to 22.6 percent of sales.

But what of the future? Says Kyle:

It is all very nice to say that we have a good organization in the U.S. and U.K., for example. But what about Japan, which is the second largest market in the world for pharmaceuticals? What do we have there? In fact Japan is probably a much tougher market and much more a determinator of future competitive superiority than Germany or Italy or France would be. Not only as a place to do business, but as a source of new technology and as an example of good management practices. A respect for quality, a respect for doing a job well, a respect for education, loyalty to the institution, I would say those are some explanations for Japanese success.

Let me give you a specific example of Japanese performance in the manufacture of a SmithKline Beecham product that is produced worldwide, including Japan. All of our manufacturing plants adhere to the same product standards, the same chemical standards, the same physical standards, the same specifications for every significant, performance-related characteristic of the product. The Japanese always met these standards within a very narrow band in the middle of the range. But beyond that, if you compared a Japanese tablet with a non-Japanese tablet under a microscope, the non-Japanese would have tiny chips in the edge while the Japanese product was perfectly smooth. This had no effect on the product performance and would never be noticed by a normal consumer, but it was important to them—it represented doing things right.

If you have that sort of devotion and diligence and sense of caring about results worldwide and were able to instill it in your management, you can imagine the results.

Corporations without an integrated strategic focus will always be on treacherous ground, vulnerable to aspiring competitors. But even businesses with today's Unique Value strategies, in which the fundamentals are fully integrated and the resources are all strategically aligned, are vulnerable if they institutionalize success instead of institutionalizing strategic learning.

When Fred Wang, son of the founder of Wang Laboratories, first faced a cash crunch in 1989, he reportedly told shareholders, "We're a three-billion-dollar company. We're not going to just blow away."[9] By 1992, the company had just blown away.

The key to the Unique Value strategies of the future is not empowerment or decentralization or even being market-driven, even though these concepts are important at the business unit and the corporate level. The key for the initiators of Unique Value strategies is that they unlock creativity in a way that is action-oriented. The process of developing a unique value strategy encourages creativity in everyone involved. They observe, they relate their observations to the concerns that are uppermost in their minds, they integrate new information with information they had before and they form new hypotheses or come to new conclusions.

But for an environment to encourage this applied creativity, there must be a base of useful knowledge already in place, and a way of incorporating new knowledge, without destabilizing the environment.

Creatively driven industries, such as entertainment, fashion, communications, and computer software, have always prized and rewarded ideas. But an idea-driven culture is not necessarily strategic—by definition, ideas just happen, they are not planned for. On the other hand, industries that depend on innovation, such as software or drug companies, must plan—by focusing on areas of inquiry, where, for example, there will be a long-term market for the right product, because there is a well-documented business opportunity or intractable health problems.

Dick Recchia of Mitsubishi observes:

> There's nothing automatic any more. Even if you're a success for a year or two. Now Honda Accord is starting to suffer after eight or nine years of dominance. I mean there's an example, still a great product.
>
> The main thing that is going to affect how the worldwide economy develops as well as the U.S. economy is continued development of worldwide competition. I think that any company now that looks at itself as a major player in only one country is destined for failure. You have to look at your market as worldwide. And have a strategy.

A strategically focused organization continually asks the right questions and continually makes new integrations. Strategic learning leads directly to creative insights and tomorrow's Unique Value strategies.

See Appendix C: Excerpts from "Understanding Consumer Acceptance of Videotex" (address by Andrea Dunham, managing director, Dunham & Marcus International, Inc., delivered to the American Banking Association, November 16, 1984); and Appendix D: Excerpts from "Creativity and Research" (address by Andrea Dunham delivered to the American Marketing Association, October 2, 1982).

Tomorrow's strategic organization will also require a strategic leader, in tune with the times—a leader capable of making the paradigm shifts that constant and dramatic change necessitates. In the words of George Fisher of Motorola:

> The most dangerous thing that takes place is that success breeds arrogance, and arrogance seems to make people stop listening to customers and to their employees. And that is the beginning of the end. The challenge is not to be a great company, the challenge is to *remain* a great company. There have been many great companies in the history of the world. The challenge is how do you continue to revitalize yourself so you are always a great company. Our feeling about that is you have to re-create yourself.
>
> The initiatives that drive the corporation are out of here [the CEO's office]. In software, in training, in education, those things apply across all of our businesses and, in fact, provide the fabric that makes us a corporation with its own culture. There is added value there. The whole is greater than the sum of the parts.

Corporations that successfully reinvent themselves, that create tomorrow's Unique Value strategies, cannot be led by figureheads. They will be led by builders who can tap into personal knowledge, technical expertise and the wisdom of experience. The CEO of the future will be on the line, along with the operating managers.

When Seagram developed a Unique Value strategy to reenter the wine cooler category, the mission czar was Edgar Bronfman, Jr., who applied this successful experience to the development of a long-term global vision. The vision was to become a premier beverage company. The transformation of Seagram from a traditional spirits company to a much broader-based global business cannot be delegated—the pain of transformation is only tolerated by an organization that believes in the personal commitment of its leader.

AT&T was recreated in 1984 with the mandate to make a viable corporate entity out of a portfolio of businesses that were part of the old Bell Telephone monopoly. After a difficult, unfocused and unprofitable start, AT&T is projected to earn over $4 billion in 1993. In the last ten years, its current focus, and apparent winning strategy, has been achieved in the midst of the same global and technological traumas that have driven other industry leaders to the wall. Robert Allen, CEO since the sudden death of James Olson in 1988, has a similar management philosophy and style to that of George Fisher at Motorola—a sensitive balance of hands-on and hands-off, which does not include the delegation of the overall strategy under which individual businesses operate.

When he took the reins in 1988, Robert Allen reorganized the company into individual business units to get accountability, and brought in outside management to broaden his perspective and experience base—Allen himself is a career veteran of the old Bell system. "Allen has no chief operating officer working under him. Rather, he has what might be called a synergy committee to help run the business." It consists of five executives. "When these five get together for four days a month, it is to come up with ways to capitalize on the convergence of telephony and computing. The rest of the time, they are running their own almost independent businesses."[10]

What George Fisher thinks is most important in a CEO is

making sure that people who run our businesses have the freedom to run their businesses. Making sure we have the best people running our business. Beyond that, it is necessary, in a corporation as global and as complex as this one, to make sure there is coherence, a binding force. A lot of my job is to assure that those cohesive foces represent our corporate culture, a result over time of the practice of our principles and values. So, part of my role is strengthening our culture. Our culture is very, very much focused on our people and our customers. The fabric needs to be woven to define our culture. For instance, the only centralized function we have in the whole company is personnel. It reports to me. The reason it does is so that all the businesses practice the same people-related principles and standards.

This provides the environment in which synergy, "the added value that ensures the whole is greater than the sum of the parts," can happen.

A recent dramatic example of that is the Iridium satellite system we have developed. It was an idea that came out of our government electronics group. It is being developed as combined effort of the entire corporation. Our electronics government people, our modem people, our semiconductor people, our communications people, all got together, and in that case were driven by a customer. Likewise, all of our equipment businesses are dependent on a foundation. There is a natural built-in need for synergy between our semiconductor expertise and our equipment businesses. It (semiconductor technology) gives us a distinctive competitive advantage in the marketplace.

But you can go through other examples of types of businesses we are working on: something called an intelligent vehicle highway system, which is really pulling together our radio frequency communication experts, and combining them with our automotive electronics experts, our semiconductor expertise and our global communications satellite expertise, and putting them all together. It is an intelligent vehicle highway system that really allows you, when you are driving into a city, to find a location, map traffic and make better use of the highway system.

Many of us here are engineers or scientists and hopefully we stimulate each other. Our people are all intelligent. Ideally, I would like there to be added value. We roll up our sleeves and work together. We (senior management) try to stimulate creative thought.

Jack Welch, CEO of General Electric, takes the same approach: "We've got to take out the boss element. Twenty-first-century managers must forgo their old powers—to plan, organize, implement and measure—for new duties: counseling groups, providing resources for them, helping them think for themselves. We're going to win on our ideas, not by whips and chains."

Jack Welch's investment in the development of ideas, and his personal involvement with the organization, is undeniable. For example, "I've almost never missed a class at Crotonville" (home of GE's Management Development Institute), he says. (He has a Ph.D. in chemical engineering, University of Illinois.) His monthly visits to Crotonville are "a great way to take the pulse of the organization" in question-and-answer sessions with GE managers. The informal academic setting lets him hear from people he wouldn't encounter in the ordinary course of business."[11]

For the first-class corporations of the 1990s and beyond, who will make a difference to the quality of life in the next century, creativity, personal accountability, technical proficiency and openness will all be prerequisites at the top.

Where style was often a consideration for the traditional CEO profile, content will be the central issue in CEO candidates for tomorrow's global competitive arena. If the competitive and technological environment did not require it, the demand for greater shareholder value would.

APPENDIX A

EXCERPTS FROM "COMPUTERS AND THE HOME OF THE FUTURE"

Address by Andrea Dunham, managing director, Dunham & Marcus International, Inc., to the Harvard Business School Club of New York, November 12, 1983.

———— • ————

Remember Citizen's Band radios? Believe it or not, there are some influential people in the computer industry who are worrying about whether PCs (personal computers) in the home will go the way of CBs in cars.

The people worrying about the future of computers for personal and family use are strategic planners. They're concerned because they've learned over the past few years, in an era of fundamental cultural and industrial transition, future markets cannot be linearly projected from the statistical trends of current markets. In the '70s, strategic planners were still assuming today's sales trend was tomorrow's market. If product shipments were increasing steadily, whether the numbers reflected retailer inventory or consumer purchases, the trend was projected into the future. In the case of CBs (citizen's band radio), legal and technical problems began to dampen sales as manufacturers were increasing capacity to satisfy what appeared to be insatiable consumer demand.

The worry among computer makers today is that the appeal of computing in the home market may not be fully understood. Who wants a computer at home, and why? Have they already been oversold? How many boxes got home, but were never unpacked? If there are as many unopened or unused personal computers at home as there were CBs on the shelves, the computer industry is heading for hard times.

Over the long term, there is no question: This technology has the power to change human life for the better. There's an inevitability about its incorporation into all our lives. But the near-term outlook is dependent on whether or not engineers and salesmen can become marketers, whether they can work *back* from the needs of key customers and consumer segments to products which optimize the technology in terms of relevance to our lives today, instead of working *forward* from the technology to products which reflect the values of the engineers.

The responsibility of a marketer is to uncover and address the fundamental needs that a technology can satisfy:

This is how you structure industries for market-driven strategies. Three sets of considerations must be understood and interrelated:

(1) Business Considerations: What's the state of the industry? Who are the key competitors now? Who will they be in the future? Where are the trade-offs between market value and manufacturer profitability?

(2) Product Considerations: What is the state of the art in technology? What are the key *benefits* it can deliver now, and in the foreseeable future? Can it reduce the trade-offs people expect to have to make? For example, can it help make life fuller, and also easier?

(3) Customer/Consumer Considerations: How does the market segment demographically, behaviorally, attitudinally? A loyal franchise is the key to long-term profitability. Loyalty is established by satisfying your key customers' most important functional *and* emotional needs better than the competition. To do that, you have to understand those needs in depth, and guide R&D efforts toward delivering the benefits that meet them.

What can computers do for your mind? A lot, but how soon depends on the people who are marketing them. I have no doubt that the next generation will realize their potential. But why should we be the lost generation? The computer illiterates? In the future, being computer literate won't be a matter of choice—nor will it be any harder than learning to read was for previous generations. But what if you were already grown up when the Gutenberg Bible was put into your hands? If you didn't understand the historic significance of it, why go back to school?

The technology is already here. What has happened over just the last five years has made that clear. Two major barriers to its use, price and ease of use, are steadily being eroded, and will continue to be. The microchip is making computer power cheaper, but it also means the computer can be programmed to do more of the mechanics. So the "human element," as computer programmers call the computer operator, is free to be human and think. A few years ago, you had to be able to think like a robot to love a computer.

Of course, when human beings get involved, the future is, by definition, unpredictable. That's what's both exciting and scary about it. It's unpredictable because human creativity causes too many variables to compute. We simply don't know who is going to invent what next year.

The next generation will probably be more sophisticated in terms of accessing and organizing extensive libraries of information; professional about managing money and cash flow; knowledgeable in managing household energy, security and supplies; and experienced in interacting electronically for social and business purposes—an extension of today's telephone-linked society.

I believe, and so do many potential computer customers, that the future is two things: a risk to be minimized and an opportunity to be grasped. Computers, intelligently used, will fulfill their promise of magic and wonder for us and our children. They might even help adults become children again.

UNIQUE VALUE = ROI® MODEL
ANALYSES TO BE PERFORMED

——— • ———

Consumer/Customer Analysis

Consumer/Customer
- Growth rates/trends (industry, category)
- Size of consumer or customer segments
- Hierarchies of needs
- Key functional and emotional benefits category delivers generically, and by brand
- Price/value perceptions
- Demographic, behavioral and attitudinal profiles
- Relative market share position
- Customer distribution
  - Channel size
  - Channel growth rates
  - Channel penetration
  - Channel potential
- Customer bargaining power
  - Customer profiles (purchase size, frequency, etc.)
  - Importance of product to customer's business
- Price sensitivity
- Importance of quality to purchase decision
- Current marketing-support programs including advertising, promotion, merchandising and spending strategies (e.g., push vs. pull)

Business System/Skills Analysis

Business System
- Production inputs
  — Access to raw materials
  — Volatility of raw material costs
  — Labor climate
  — Input substitutes
  — Importance of input to business
  — Concentration and number suppliers
  — Possibility of forward integration among suppliers
- Plant
  — Economics of scale
  — Experience curve
  — Capital requirements
  — Technological sophistication
  — Flexibility of facilities and equipment
  — Fixed costs
  — Plant capacity
  — Unique cost advantage
  — Skills in quality control
- Distribution
  — Access to distribution channels
  — Structure of distribution
    · Direct sales force expense
    · Distributor mark-up
    · Retail mark-up
    · Number and location of warehouses
    · Warehouse expense
    · Shipping costs
  — Order size
  — Lead time

Business Skills
- Organizational structure and human resources
  — Age, training, functional orientation of management
  — Flexibility and adaptability of management
  — Turnover

— Goals of parent
— Importance of business unit relative to those goals
— Economic relationship among business units
  · Intercompany sales
  · Cross-merchandising
  · Shared sales force, etc.
• Balance sheet management and borrowing capacity
— Current and historical balance sheets
— Accounts receivable, accounts payable terms
• Systems integration and analysis
— Strategy and implementation
— Comparative systems analysis
— System integration in total operations

Product/Technology Analysis

Product
• Elasticity and cross-elasticity of demand
— Degree of differentiation
— Number and quality of substitutes
— Complements
• Current and past pricing strategy
• Breadth of product line
• Number and type of SKUs
• Stage of lifecycle
• Skills in new product development

Technology
• Proprietary/patents, copyrights, licenses
• Pace of technological change
• R&D spending
• Internal R&D capability
• Access to outside R&D

Competitor Analysis
• Trends in industry (e.g., acquisitions, consolidation)
• Number of competitors
• Diversity of competitors
• Performance of competitors

- — Sales
- — Market share
- — Profitability
- — Advertising/marketing
- — R&D
- — Fixed costs
- — Investment
- — Borrowing capacity
- — Balance sheet management
- • Strategies of competitors
  - — Distribution channels
  - — Product portfolio
    - · Growth priorities
    - · Prices
    - · Quality perception
    - · Lifecycle
    - · New product introductions
    - · Degree of differentiation
  - — Relative cost position
  - — Technology status
- • Adaptability to escalation in marketing, operations, economic decision making, price competition
- • Entry barriers
- • Potential competition
- • Exit barriers

APPENDIX C

EXCERPTS FROM "UNDERSTANDING CONSUMER ACCEPTANCE OF VIDEOTEX"

Address by Andrea Dunham, managing director, Dunham & Marcus International, Inc., to the American Banking Association, November 16, 1984.

— • —

A forecaster recently predicted:

• In 1990, 24 million U.S. households will be equipped with integrated video information services.

And that:

• Total revenues from videotex could reach $30 billion by 1995 . . . [with] a full-service videotex penetration of 30 million households by 1995.

Forecasters have never been as consistently wrong as industry analysts and observers have been on the subject of videotex. The reason is that there is no realistic market plan, and therefore, they're not tracking predictive, marketing variables.

The establishment of marketplace fundamentals such as mass-market distribution systems, the development of a market-driven structure, and the demonstration of marketing expertise on the part of industry leaders is what they should be looking for.

IBM strategies and decisions will fundamentally affect the development of any PC-dependent industry, which videotex probably will be. The lack of a distribution infrastructure has been a major barrier to growth.[1] In the final analysis the results of organizational action rest not on a single technology but upon a technological matrix. A complicated technology incorporates the products or results of many other technologies.

Principles of Marketing-Driven Development

Experienced development organizations know how misleading simplistic concept testing is in established markets, let alone in industries in transition. There are two reasons:

(1) In unfamiliar situations (such as confrontation with a new technology), customers must interact with new product offerings to develop an experience base. Researchers must evaluate actual customer behavior, which may not be predictable from responses to early concept tests. (In the case of automatic teller machines, for example, today's heavy users are not the same segment that responded positively to early concepts.)

(2) Product refinement must be guided by both consumer requirements and a business knowledge base.

To change human behavior, the incentive should be very great, and the hurdles very small.

Marketers who have changed human behavior profitably provide critical lessons. Solutions to the complex problems of market development evolve from the education of both the marketplace and the marketer.

The investment of industry developers must be in self-education about market needs and benefits as much as in technology and product configurations.

When industries are in transition, development research must solve complex product and positioning problems in an environment that is itself changing. Solutions that appear simple and powerful are in fact complex integrations of all the variables key to a successful business proposition. Chances of marketplace success will be significantly enhanced by thoroughness, planning and patience.

For example, allow at least two stages of pretest market development:

(1) An Early Development Phase, which creates and evaluates an array of product concepts and preliminary prototypes, in the context of the identifiable needs of key market targets.
(2) A Late Development Phase, which tests, through several phases of iteration, the ability of prototypical product offerings to deliver key benefits to key market segments, better than existing alternatives.

Each stage should have an exploratory phase, which creates options, and an evaluative phase, which prioritizes options from the customer's (or consumer's) perspective.

APPENDIX D

EXCERPTS FROM "CREATIVITY AND RESEARCH"

Address by Andrea Dunham, managing director,
Dunham & Marcus International, Inc.,
to the American Marketing Association, October 2, 1982.

— ● —

As shown in figure D.1, strategy development using the Unique Value = ROI Model has three phases, no matter how simple or complex the issue being researched. The problem might be whether to diversify into a new industry, invest in a new technology, develop a new product or change advertising strategies. In all cases, an inescapable sequence of information gathering and integration must be followed because each phase lays the foundation for the next phase of creative thinking. This is the discipline you need to ask the right questions at the right time, whether you are developing a strategy for the next month or the next decade.

The goal of the first phase is to identify existing knowledge and ask questions that lay the foundation for a broader base of information needed to develop preliminary hypotheses about new opportunities. With this information, the market can be structured both as it is now and, more importantly, as it might be in the future as a result of consumer, regulatory, economic, technological or competitive changes to the business environment.

The results of the structuring phase lead to preliminary hypotheses, which suggest the direction of a further, more refined set of hypotheses. The third phase addresses questions relating to the implementation of the strategies. Again, strategists must diverge before converging to develop the broadest array of possible answers, and the most relevant information to gather, before structuring its application to the development of new information.

Fig. D.1 Define Measurable
Business Goals/Objectives

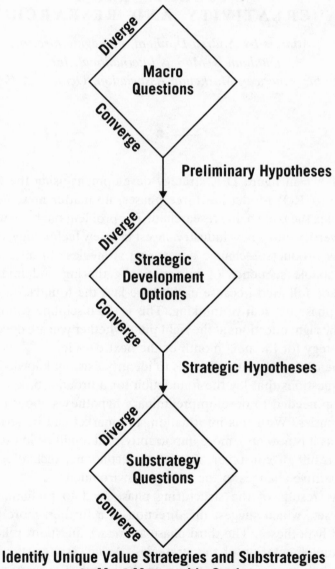

Source: Dunham & Marcus International, Inc.

NOTES

— • —

Chapter 1

1. Kanner, Bernice, "Hot Coolers," *New York* magazine (September 23, 1985), 18.

Chapter 2

1. *Wall Street Journal* (January 22, 1993).
2. Gross, Neil, with Otis Port, "Making Deals—Without Giving Away the Store," *Business Week* (June 17, 1991).
3. *Automotive News Market Data Book* (1980 and 1990).
4. Treece, James B., and Karen Lowry Miller, "The Partners," *Business Week* (February 10, 1992), 103.
5. Von Braun, Christopher, "The Acceleration Trap," *Sloan Management Review* (Fall 1990).
6. Saito, H., "4M DRAM Production Augurs Further Advances," *Japan Economic Journal,* English edition (February 3, 1990), 19.
7. Spencer, William J., and Deborah D. Triant, "Strengthening the Link between R&D and Corporate Strategy," *The Journal of Business Strategy* (January–February 1989).
8. Quinn, James Brian, Henry Mintzberg and Robert M. James, "Case III-2: Federal Express Corporation," *The Strategy Process* (1988).
9. Brown, John Seely, "Research that Reinvents the Corporation," *Harvard Business Review* (January–February 1991).
10. Hounshell, David, and John Kenley Smith, *Science and Corporate Strategy* (1988).

Chapter 3

1. Chandler, Alfred D., Jr., *Strategy and Structure: Chapters in the History of the American Industrial Enterprise* (1962), 11–12.
2. Aaker, David A., "How to Select a Business Strategy," *California Management Review,* vol. 24, no. 3 (Spring 1984), 167.
3. Quinn, James Brian, *Strategies for Change: Logical Incrementalism* (1980), 15.
4. Mintzberg, Henry, *Mintzberg on Management* (1989), 27–31.
5. Pascale, Richard T., "Perspectives on Strategy: The Real Story Be-

hind Honda's Success," *California Management Review,* vol. 24, no. 3 (Spring 1984), 47–64.

Chapter 4

1. Cline, Catherine Long, "Holiday Inn Worldwide—Current Market Position and Potential for Future International Growth," *Bass: A Corporate Profile* (July 1991), 60.
2. Ibid., p. 62.
3. Ibid., p. 64.

Chapter 5

1. Castro, Janice, "Kicking Junior Out of the Family," *Time* (January 1, 1985).
2. "100 Leading Advertisers with U.S. Sales," *Advertising Age* (September 26, 1985), 28.
3. "How Apple Is Bullying IBM's PCjr," *Business Week* (April 16, 1984).
4. Watson, Tom, Jr., and Peter Petre, *Father, Son & Co.* (1990), 228.
5. Lewis, Geoffrey C., "Junior Was Too Expensive, Even For IBM," *Business Week* (April 1, 1985).
6. "How Apple Is Bullying IBM's PCjr," *ibid.*
7. Dunham, Andrea, "Computers and the Home of the Future" (November 12, 1983). (See Appendix A.)
8. "Television Digest VCR Market Share Survey," Warren Publishing.
9. Nulty, Peter, "Matsushita Takes the Lead in Videorecorders," *Fortune* (July 16, 1979).
10. Schuyten, Peter J., "A $1,300 Christmas Toy Made in Japan," *Fortune* (September 1977).
11. Quinn, James Brian, Henry Mintzberg and Robert M. James, "Case III-1: Sony Corporation," *The Strategy Process* (1988).
12. Schendler, Brenton R., "How Sony Keeps the Magic Going," *Fortune* (February 24, 1992), 82.
13. Marcial, Gene G., "Video Wars: Sony Could Get Another Bloody Nose," *Business Week* (May 12, 1986).
14. Tanzer, Andrew, "Sharing," *Forbes* (January 20, 1992).
15. Quinn, James Brian, Henry Mintzberg and Robert M. James, "Case III-1: Sony Corporation," *The Strategy Process* (1988).
16. Schendler, Brenton R., "How Sony Keeps the Magic Going," *Fortune* (February 24, 1992), 82.

Chapter 6

1. Dunham, Andrea. "Segmentation and ROI: How Precise Segmentation Impacts Profit Performance." Address given at the Conference Board's 1990 Annual Marketing Conference.
2. Tooker, Gary. "As I See It: Cycles of Time Reduction and Learning." *Opportunities* vol. 9, no. 7 (November/December 1992), 4.

Chapter 7

1. Davis, David E., Jr., "Driving Impression: Cadillac Cimarron," *Car & Driver* (October 1982), 57.
2. Ceppos, Rich, "Short Take: Cadillac Cimarron," *Car & Driver* (March 1985), 133.
3. Protzman, Ferdinand, "Siemens Buying 51 percent of Nixdorf," *New York Times* (January 11, 1990), D1.
4. Whitestone, Debra, and Leonard Schlesinger, Harvard Business School Case Services, 14.
5. Prokesch, Steven, "Behind People Express' Fall: An Offbeat Managerial Style," *New York Times* (September 23, 1986).
6. Byrne, John, "Donald Bury May Be Ready to Take to the Skies Again," *Business Week* (January 16, 1989), 74.
7. Ibid.
8. "Nixed," *The Economist* (January 13, 1990), 66.
9. Abegglen, James C., and George Stalk, Jr., *Kaisha: The Japanese Corporation* (1985), 47.
10. Burrough, Bryan, and John Helyar, *Barbarians at the Gates* (1990).
11. Abegglen, James C., and George Stalk, Jr., *Kaisha: The Japanese Corporation* (1985), 49.

Chapter 9

1. Spiro, Leah Nathans, "Behind the Bombshell From Amex," *Business Week* (October 2, 1991).
2. Womack, James P., Daniel T. Jones and Daniel Roos, *The Machine that Changed the World,* 1990.
3. Ravenscraft, David, and F. M. Scherer, "The Lag Structure of Returns to Research and Development," *Applied Economics* (1982).
4. Buzzell, Robert D., and Bradley T. Gale, *The PIMS Principles: Linking Strategy to Performance* (1987), 223.
5. Kanter, Rosabeth Moss, *The Change Masters* (1983), 19.
6. Spencer, William J., and Deborah D. Triant, "Strengthening the Link between R&D and Corporate Strategy," *The Journal of Business Strategy* (January–February 1989), 38–42.
7. Kuwahara, Yutaka, Osami Okada and Hisashi Horikoshi, "Plan-

ning, Research and Development at Hitachi," *Long Range Planning,* vol. 22, no. 3 (1989), 54–63.

8. Ford, David, "Develop Your Technology Strategy," *Long Range Planning,* vol. 21, no. 5 (1988), 85–95.

9. Czinkota, Michael, and Masaaki Kotabe, "Product Development the Japanese Way," *The Journal of Business Strategy* (November–December 1990), 31–36.

10. Dertouzos, Michael, Richard K. Lester and Robert M. Solow, *Made in America: Regaining the Productive Edge* (1989), 75.

11. Humble, John, and Gareth Jones, "Creating a Climate for Innovation," *Long Range Planning,* vol. 22, no. 4 (1989), 46–51.

12. Takeuchi, Hirotaka, and Ikujiro Nonaka, "The New New Product Development Game," *Harvard Business Review* (January–February 1986), 137–46.

13. Holusha, John, "Japan Is Tough But Xerox Prevails," *The New York Times* (September 3, 1992).

14. Quinn, James Brian, Henry Mintzberg and Robert M. James, "Case I-7: IBM (A): The System/360 Decision," *The Strategy Process* (1988).

Chapter 11

1. "Self-Renewal and Human Resources Strategy," *Human Resource Management* (Spring 1988).

2. De Geus, Arie, "Planning as Learning," *Harvard Business Review* (March–April 1988), 70.

3. Ibid., 72–73.

4. Lloyd, Bruce, *RSA Journal* (October 1991), 683.

5. American Express Annual Report, 1992.

6. Kotter, John P., *A Force for Change* (1990), 59.

7. Kanter, Rosabeth Moss, *The Change Masters* (1983), 160–62.

8. Ibid., 166–67.

9. Main, Jeremy, "Computers of the World Unite," *Fortune* (September 24, 1990).

10. Deming, W. Edwards, *Quality, Productivity, and Competitive Position* (1982), 1.

11. Ibid., 12.

12. Yovovich, B. G., "Motorola's Quest for Quality," *Business Marketing* (September 1991), 14–15.

13. Ibid.

Chapter 12

1. Levin, Gary, "Why Coolers Are Hopping to Malt Base," *Advertising Age* (August 3, 1992), 26.
2. Thomson, Robert and Alan Cave, "Fujitsu Now Faces Up to Harsh Economic Realities," *London Financial Times* (August 11, 1992).
3. Verity, John, "Twilight of the Mainframes," *Business Week* (August 17, 1992), 33.
4. Woodruff, David, "Saturn," *Business Week* (August 17, 1992), 86.
5. Dunham & Marcus International, Inc., Cadillac Case Study, 1992.
6. Neff, Robert, "Japan: Will It Lose Its Competitive Edge," *Business Week* (April 27, 1992), 51.
7. "Japanned by Intel," *The Economist* (April 18, 1992), 70.
8. Rebello, Kathy, "Apple's Daring Leap into the All-Digital Future," *Business Week* (May 25, 1992), 20.
9. Buckley, William, and John Wilke, "Filing in Chapter 11, Wang Sends Warning to High-Tech Circles," *Wall Street Journal* (August 19, 1992).
10. Slutsker, Gary, "The Tortoise and the Hare," *Forbes* (February 1, 1993), 66.
11. Stewart, Thomas, "GE Keeps Those Ideas Coming," *Fortune* (August 12, 1991), 41.

Appendix C

1. Thompson, James D., *Organizations in Action* (1967), 26.

BIBLIOGRAPHY

———— ● ————

Aaker, David. "How to Select a Business Strategy." *California Management Review* (1984).

Abegglen, James C., and George Stalk, Jr. *Kaisha: The Japanese Corporation*. New York: Basic Books (1985).

American Express Annual Reports (1991 and 1992).

Barwise, Patrick, with Paul R. Marsh and Robin Wensley. "Must Finance and Strategy Clash." *Harvard Business Review* (September–October 1989).

Benderly, Beryl Lieff. "Everyday Institution." *Psychology Today* (September 1989).

Benjamin, Robert I., John F. Rockart, Michael S. Scott Morton, and John Wyman. "Information Technology: A Strategic Opportunity." *Sloan Management Review* (Spring 1984).

Bohn, Joseph. "Luxury Market Growing, Changing." *Automotive News* (September 10, 1984).

Brown, John Seely. "Research that Reinvents the Corporation." *Harvard Business Review* (January–February, 1991).

Buckeley, William, and John Wilke. "Filing in Chapter 11, Wang Sends Warning to High-Tech Circles." *The Wall Street Journal* (August 19, 1992).

Burrough, Bryan, and John Helyar. *Barbarians at the Gate*. New York: Harper & Row (1990).

Burstein, Daniel. "Computer Marketing: No Longer Fun and Games." *Advertising Age* (March 5, 1984).

Buzzell, Robert D., and Bradley T. Gale. *The PIMS Principles: Linking Strategy to Performance* (1987).

Byrne, John. "Donald Bury May Be Ready to Take to the Skies Again." *Business Week* (January 16, 1989).

Cadillac Cimarron Case, Dunham & Marcus International, Inc. Case history.

Castro, Janice. "Kicking Junior Out of the Family." *Time* (April 1, 1985).

Ceppos, Rich. "Short Take: Cadillac Cimarron V-6." *Car & Driver* (March 1985).

Chandler, Alfred D., Jr. *Strategy and Structure: Chapters in the History of the American Industrial Enterprise.* Cambridge, Massachusetts: M.I.T. Press (1962).

Clemons, Eric K., and Michael Row. "A Strategic Information System: McKesson Drug Company's Economist." *Planning Review* (September–October 1988).

Cline, Catherine Long. "Holiday-Inn Worldwide—Current Market Position and Potential Future International Growth." Bass: A Corporate Profile (July 1991).

Czinkota, Michael, and Masaaki Kotabe. "Product Development the Japanese Way." *The Journal of Business Strategy* (November–December 1990).

Davis, David E., Jr. "Driving Impression: Cadillac Cimarron." *Car & Driver* (October 1982).

De Geus, Arie P. "Planning as Learning." *Harvard Business Review* (March–April 1988).

Deming, W. Edwards. *Quality, Productivity and Competitive Position.* Cambridge, Massachusetts: M.I.T. Press (1982).

Dertouzos, Michael, Richard K. Lester, and Robert M. Solow. *Made in America: Regaining the Productive Edge* (1989).

Drucker, Peter F. "The Coming of the New Organization." *Harvard Business Review* (January–February 1988).

Dunham, Andrea. "Understanding Consumer Acceptance of Videotex." Address to the American Banking Association (November 16, 1984).

Dunham, Andrea. "Computers and the Home of the Future." Address delivered to Harvard Business School Club of New York (November 12, 1983).

Dunham, Andrea. "Segmentation & ROI: How Precise Segmentation Impacts Profit Performance." Address delivered to the Conference Board Marketing Conference (1990).

Du Pont Stainmaster Carpet Case, Darden Graduate School of Business Administration, University of Virginia.

Fisher, Anne B. "Winners (and Losers) from IBM's PCjr." *Fortune* (November 28, 1983).

Foltz, Kim. "The PCjr's Sudden Death." *Newsweek* (April 1, 1985).

Ford, David. "Develop Your Technology Strategy." *Long Range Planning,* 21. no. 5 (1988).

Greenspan, Alan. "Small Is Beautiful." Address delivered to the Annual Dinner at the Japan Society, New York (May 26, 1989).

Gross, Neil, with Otis Port. "Making Deals—Without Giving Away the Store." *Business Week* (June 17, 1991).

Heany, Donald F. "Degrees of Product Innovation." *The Journal of Business Strategy* (Spring 1983).

Holusha, John. "Japan Is Tough But Xerox Prevails." *New York Times* (September 3, 1992).

Hounshell, David A., and John Kenly Smith. *Science and Corporate Strategy.* New York: Cambridge University Press (1988).

"How Apple Is Bullying IBM's PCJr." *Business Week* (April 16, 1984).

Humble, John, and Gareth Jones. "Creating a Climate for Innovation." *Long Range Planning,* vol. 22, no. 4 (1989).

Imai, Masaaki. *Kaizen.* New York: Random House (1986).

"Japanned by Intel." *The Economist* (April 18, 1992).

Kanner, Bernice. "Hot Coolers." *New York Magazine* (September 23, 1985).

Kanter, Rosabeth Moss. *The Change Masters.* New York: Simon & Schuster (1983).

Kotter, John. *A Force for Change.* New York: The Free Press (1990).

Kuwahara, Yitaka, Osami Okada, and Hisashi Horikoshi. "Planning Research and Development at Hitachi." *Long Range Planning,* vol. 22. no. 3 (1989).

Levin, Gary. "Why Coolers Are Hopping to Malt Base." *Advertising Age* (August 3, 1992).

Lewis, Geoffrey C. "Junior Was Too Expensive, Even for IBM." *Business Week* (April 1, 1985).

Main, Jeremy. "Computers of the World, Unite." *Fortune* (September 24, 1990).

Marcial, Gene G. "Video Wars: Sony Could Get Another Bloody Nose." *Business Week* (May 12, 1986).

McCann, John M.: *The Marketing Workbench*. Chicago: Dow Jones-Irwin (1986).

Mintzberg, Henry. "Mintzberg on Management." New York: The Free Press (1989).

Moore, Stephen D. "SmithKline Beecham Settles Smoothly into Marriage." *The Wall Street Journal* (August 13, 1992).

Neff, Robert. "Japan: Will It Lose Its Competitive Edge." *Business Week* (April 27, 1992).

"1992 Award Criteria: Malcolm Baldrige National Quality Award." *Automotive News Market Data Book* (1980 and 1990).

"Nixed." *The Economist* (January 13, 1990).

Nulty, Peter. "Matsushita Takes the Lead in Videorecorders." *Fortune* (July 16, 1979).

Pascale, Richard. "Perspectives on Strategy: The Real Story Behind Honda's Success." *California Management Review* (1984).

Prokesch, Steven. "Behind People Express Fall: An Offbeat Managerial Style." *The New York Times* (September 23, 1986).

Protzman, Ferdinand. "Siemen's Buying 51 Percent of Nixdorf." *The New York Times* (January 11, 1990).

Quinn, James Brian, et al. *The Strategy Process*. Englewood Cliffs, New Jersey: Prentice-Hall (1988).

Ravenscraft, D., and F. M. Sherer. "The Lag Structure of Returns to Research and Development." *Applied Economics* (1982).

Rebello, Kathy. "Apple's Daring Leap Into the All-Digital Future." *Business Week* (May 25, 1992).

Riley, Rosetta M. "Cadillac Motor Car Division. *The Conference Board Report*, Number 990: Baldrige Winners on World-Class Quality."

Saito, H. "4M DRAM Production Augurs Further Advances." *Japan Economic Journal* (February 3, 1990).

Schendler, Brenton. "How Sony Keeps the Magic Going." *Fortune* (February 24, 1992).

Schumpeter, Joseph. "Capitalism's Creative Destruction." *The Economist* (May 1992).

Schuyten, Peter J. "A $1,300 Christmas Toy Made in Japan." *Fortune* (September 1977).

Seagram's Case, Dunham & Marcus International, Inc. Case history.

"Self Renewal and HR Strategy." *Human Resource Management* (Spring 1988).

Slutsker, Gary. "The Tortoise and the Hare." Forbes (February 1, 1993).

Spencer, William J., and Deborah D. Triant. "Strengthening the Link Between R&D and Corporate Strategy." *The Journal of Business Strategy* (January–February 1989).

Spiro, Leah Nathans. "Behind the Bombshell from Amex." *Business Week* (October 2, 1991).

Stewart, Thomas. "GE Keeps These Ideas Coming." *Fortune* (August 12, 1991).

Tanzer, Andrew. "Sharing." *Forbes* (January 20, 1992).

Thompson, James. *Organizations in Action.* New York: McGraw-Hill (1967).

Tooker, Gary. "As I See It: Cycles of Time Reduction and Learning." *Opportunities,* vol. 9, no. 7 (November-December 1992).

Treece, James, and Karen Lowry Miller. "The Partners." *Business Week* (February 10, 1992).

Verity, John. "Twilight of the Mainframes." *Business Week* (August 17, 1992).

Von Mises, Ludwig. *Socialism.* New Haven: Yale University Press (1951).

Watson, Thomas J., and Peter Petre: *Father, Son & Co.* New York: Bantam Books (1990).

Wayne, Leslie. "Shareholders Exercise New Power." *The New York Times* (February 1, 1993).

Womack, James, Daniel Jones, and Daniel Roose. *The Machine that Changed the World.* New York: Rawson Associates (1990).

Woodruff, David. "Saturn." *Business Week* (August 17, 1992).

Yovovich, B. G. "Motorola's Quest for Quality." *Business Marketing* (1982).

INDEX

——— ● ———

Aaker, David, 30
Accommodation, strategic, 31–32
Acquisitions. *See* Joint ventures
Adaptive persistence, 31–32
Agents of change, management as, 8
Airline industry. *See* People Express
Allen, Robert, 252
Almost Home, 141
American Airlines, 142, 172
American Express, *xix,* 169–71, 224
American Red Cross, 247–48
Ampex, 178
Angus, Sir Michael, 32, 102
Apple Computer, 12, 66–68, 70–71,
   74, 76, 239
   future of, 246–47
   joint venture with Sony, 20
Arakawa, Minoru, 43–44
Aspartame (NutraSweet), 22–23
Atari
   personal computers, 68, 70
   video games, 39, 42
AT&T, 179, 251–52
Audi, 140
Automobile industry, 19–20. *See also*
   specific topics
   contemporary luxury cars, 125–26,
      128
   intelligent vehicle and, 253
   joint ventures and, 19–20
Automatic teller machines (ATMs),
   112–15
Aviation industry, 20

Baldrige, Malcolm. *See* Malcolm
   Baldrige Award
Banking industry

automatic teller machines (ATMs),
   112–15
Deutsche Bank, 103–4
   business systems and skills sub-
      strategies at, 173–75
Bartles & Jaymes, *xxi,* 2, 4–5, 49,
   144–45, 157–58
Basis for perceived competitive supe-
   riority, 36, 38
   in case study, 197–98, 205, 207, 210
   at GM, 216
   at Holiday Inn, 62–63
   at IBM, 215
   IBM PC Jr. and, 70–73
   at Nintendo, 43–45
   at Seagram, 51–53
   Sony Betamax and, 79–80
Bass PLC, 57–58
   acquisition of Holiday Inn by,
      56–65
Bauman, Bob, 221
Beatrice Foods, 161–62
Beecham Group, 101
Beecham PLC, 34, 247
Bell Labs, 179
Betamax. *See* Sony, Betamax
Beverage industry. *See also* Wine
   coolers
   globalization and, 176
Bewley, Stuart, 1–2
Bierich, Marcus, 33, 98
Blades of Steel, 45
Blue-sky thinking, 242
BMW, 126, 140
Boeing 777, 184
Braun, Christoph von, 21
Breene, Tim, 237–38

DATE DUE	
GAYLORD	PRINTED IN U.S.A.